▲▲ FATHER | *The Family Protector*

▲▲ FATHER | *The Family Protector*

JAMES B. STENSON

 Scepter

Other books by James B. Stenson, published by Scepter Publishers

Lifeline: The Religious Upbringing of Your Children

Preparing for Adolescence: A Planning Guide for Parents

Preparing for Peer Pressure: A Guide for Parents of Young Children

Successful Fathers: The Subtle but Powerful Ways Fathers Mold Their Children's Characters

Upbringing: A Discussion Handbook for Parents of Young Children

Anchor: God's Promises of Hope to Parents

Compass: A Handbook on Parent Leadership

Father, the Family Protector
Copyright © 2004 James B. Stenson.
All rights reserved
Second Printing, June 2005

Published by Scepter Publishers, Inc., New York
(800) 322–8773 / www.scepterpublishers.org

ISBN 1–59417–033–9

Text composition in Monotype Plantin fonts
PRINTED IN THE UNITED STATES OF AMERICA

Contents

Acknowledgements

More than most other books, this book is the work of many people. It's a composite of many parents' generous contributions to my understanding of how family life works.

I wish to thank, therefore, the many great men and women I've been honored to befriend in my years of teaching and lecturing, parents who shared their family-life experiences with me and whose experienced insights form the substance of this work.

I owe special thanks to the dedicated fathers of The Heights School in Potomac, Maryland, and Northridge Preparatory School in suburban Chicago, who taught me so much and whose families I was honored to serve. Much as I would like to thank each of these friends personally, they are far too many to list here.

Finally, I extend my warmest gratitude to the directors of the R. Templeton Smith Foundation of Cleveland Heights, Ohio, whose generous assistance over several years made this work possible. Without their encouragement and support, I could not have undertaken this project or brought it to completion.

Prologue | WHAT THIS BOOK IS ALL ABOUT

If you are a man with hefty responsibilities in your job and family life, you probably don't have much spare time for reading. You have precious little time to waste on "motivational" pep talks telling you why you should be a good dad or lengthy, sentimental story-telling that belabors the obvious. That's why I've written this book to be straight to the point and smartly practical. This book is based on other men's experience as fathers, and it presents you with real insights into family life as well as thought-provoking ideas that you can put to use right now.

My aim is ambitious: It is to help you become a great father, a great husband, and a great man.

There is a lot at stake here. Your children's later success in life will depend enormously on how well you do your job as their dad.

But first you, like other men today, need a job description. As the great Yogi Berra once supposedly said: "If you don't know where you're going, you'll wind up someplace else."

As you will see, a man's main job in his family is to *protect from harm*. A man protects his wife and children from whatever threatens their welfare and happiness, both now and later in life. If he fails at this great responsibility, his family suffers.

If you succeed in learning from this book and then turn what you learn into manly action, with God's help you will live to see great achievements in your life as a father:

—Your masculine strengths will forge lifelong strengths in your children.

—Your sons will be manly and your daughters feminine.

—Your moral judgment will form the compass of your children's conscience.

—Your life at work and at home will blend into an integrated whole.

—Your family life will become a sporting adventure.

—Your wife and children will esteem you a great man.

—Your youngsters will grow up as competent, responsible men and women who love and honor you all their lives.

This high ideal, living as a great father, is achievable. It can be done. I know this because I have seen it done in the lives of many fathers. Everything in these pages—the strategy and tactics of fatherly leadership—derives from what I've learned in my years of professional experience with many normal, conscientious men like you. I want to teach you what I've learned from them. I want to pass on to you their collective experience, the *wisdom of fatherhood.*

Let me back up a bit and explain this, and how I came to write this book.*

For twenty-one years, I worked to help establish two independent secondary schools for boys, one in Washington, D.C., and the other in Chicago—The Heights School and Northridge Preparatory School, respectively. I was director of Northridge for almost a dozen years. By any measure, I'm pleased and proud to say, both of these schools have been hugely successful.

During that time, I made it my business to know hundreds of families intimately. I studied their family lives. I watched children grow into maturity, very often successfully but sometimes not. Over many years I talked with hundreds of fathers and mothers, visited their homes, asked questions, learned a lot.

I did this for two reasons.

First, I believe that a school should serve the whole family, parents as well as children, and so it should see parents, not kids, as the main clients for its services. After all, parents are the principal teachers of children, and youngsters rise or fall in life mostly because of their upbringing at home. A school's business is to support parents, not replace them, in this hugely important mission.

Second, I wanted to learn how parents succeed or fail with their children.

Let me be clear here. When I say, "succeed or fail," I do not mean parents' methods of discipline, or how they keep kids under control, or how they handle hassles in family life. These are short-term achievements but only part of the picture.

Parents really win success only in the long term. *Parents succeed with their children when the kids grow up to become competent, responsible, considerate, and generous men and women who are*

---

* *Father, the Family Protector* is a companion work to my book *Compass: A Handbook on Parent Leadership* and necessarily has some text material in common with it. *Compass* explains how both parents work as a team in unified dual leadership. This book explores how fathers exercise their powerful, and particularly masculine, contributions to family life. For updated and expanded material on these and other books of mine, please check my Web site: www.parentleadership.com.

committed to live by principles of integrity—adults who bring honor to their parents all their lives through their conduct, conscience, and character. Raising children to become adults like this is what parenthood is all about.

I watched many parents succeed in this, while others failed. Some parents saw their kids mature into excellent men and women. Others, especially as their kids struggled through adolescence and young adulthood, met with disappointment, regret, and even tragedy. Their children suffered from lack of self-confidence and self-control, substance abuse, protracted immaturity, irresponsible and self-destructive behavior, aimlessness in life, troubles with careers or marriages or the law.

Through my countless conversations with fathers and mothers, I tried to account for the differences. I looked for patterns of family life among those parents who triumphed with their children. What did these successful men and women have in common? What did they manage to do right? Most important: What could other parents learn from their experience?

Over the years I paid more and more attention to the powerful role of the father in children's lives—and that's the reason for this book.

Repeatedly, in one family after another, I witnessed how the father has a crucial influence on his children's success in life. A man's success or failure as a protector and leader directs the course of his children's lives for good or for ill. Our national epidemic of "missing fathers" is not simply a problem of single mothers struggling without a husband. It's also that of intact two-parent homes in which the father is morally absent from his children's lives.

Many men, though physically present in the family, simply fail to perform their job as a father. Indeed, it seems they don't even know what that job is. And unfortunately, even tragically, their ongoing neglect damages both their marriage and their children.

Let me tell you one instance of this failure from my professional experience.

One morning, I received a call from a distraught mother of a twelve-year-old boy. Her son was having terrible problems in another school. She wanted him transferred to ours, for she was worried about his worsening depression, lack of self-confidence, and low motivation. The boy's emotional problems were clobbering his academic performance. She asked to set up an appointment for herself and her husband to visit and talk over the situation, and for her son to come in for testing and an interview.

Though Northridge's entrance requirements were tightly competitive and our school had a policy of declining students with motivational problems, I felt sorry for this mother, and so I agreed to meet with her and her husband. I thought I might at least offer her some advice and refer her to professionals who could help the boy.

But we couldn't meet right away. Unfortunately, her husband was out of town. Over the next couple of weeks, she and I set up and then had to cancel three appointments because one thing or another kept cropping up with her husband's busy schedule. I began to suspect that this boy's problems went beyond poor grades. So many times before, I had seen this same situation. What father, I wondered, faced with a son in serious trouble, couldn't manage to squeeze in a couple of hours to get a handle on this worsening situation? What were this man's attitudes and priorities?

The mother and I finally gave up trying to meet with the father in attendance, and so we arranged for the boy to come in first for an interview. My meeting with Mike confirmed my impressions.

Mike entered my office looking nervous and scared. His eyes scarcely met mine; they flitted around the room as if desperate for escape. I offered an introductory handshake; his hand felt limp and sweaty. As we talked, he stared out my window. Our conversation was mostly one-sided and limped along like this:

"What does your father do for a living, Mike?" I asked him.

Mike murmured, "He's an engineer."

"Where does he work?" He told me the name of the company.

"What sort of engineer is he—mechanical, electrical, civil?"

He murmured, "I don't know."

"Where did he study, and when did he graduate?" He told me the name of the university. He didn't know the year of graduation.

"Where did he meet your mother—in college?"

"I think so, but I'm not sure."

"How long were they engaged before they married?"

"I don't know."

"When your Dad was your age, what hobbies and sports did he enjoy?"

He shrugged. "I'm not sure."

"Does he like his work?"

"I guess so. He doesn't talk about it much."

"What do you and he do together?"

He reflected. "Sometimes we play ball or do video games. Usually he's too tired and just watches TV or reads."

"Does he ever check over your homework?"

He paused again. "Not much . . . Sometimes he gets mad at me."

Another gambit: "When he was your age, how well did he do in school?"

"I don't know."

On and on this went: "I don't know . . . I'm not sure. . . ." Even as Mike relaxed a bit and opened up more with me, he revealed a glaring fact. Mike knew almost nothing about his father's past and present life, nothing about his dad's thinking and interests. He knew little about his father that would win his respect. Fear, maybe, but not respect. Just as clearly, this bothered Mike deeply. At the age of life when boys start to search for a masculine figure as a pattern for their lives, this boy looked to his father and saw—what? An enigma . . . a mysterious near stranger. . . .a "virtual father."

I wish I could say that this story had a happy ending. Truth to tell, I don't know how it turned out—that is, how Mike turned out. I referred his mother to professional help, for under the circumstances this was all I could do. As you might suspect, I never did get to meet the father. He was too busy.

Mike's eventual fate was probably like that of so many other boys from "virtual father" families. Lacking approval from his dad, he would likely seek it among his peers and so become a pushover for the rock-drugs-sex culture. With no confident leadership and encouragement from his father, he would lack confidence in himself and seek escape from his free-floating dread through the pleasures of pills and alcohol. Dominated by shapeless fears, he would follow his dad later as a workaholic or simply drift rudderless through a pointless succession of jobs. With no memory of fatherly advice and wisdom to lead him, he would spend years seeking guidance from father substitutes: doctors, mental health specialists, clergy, and marriage counselors. His marriage, if any, would be built on sand, and his wife and children (if he had any) would suffer.

Was Mike's peculiar situation unusual? Unfortunately, no. This distance between fathers and children—whereby kids hardly know their fathers and thus fail to respect them—is commonplace in our society.

In many American families, the gap between fathers and children is papered over by pick-up games of sports and other "buddy" activities. In many children's eyes, their father appears as a kind of amiable older sibling or part-time second mother. This is not enough. Sports and games are not the same as fatherly leadership. On a broad basis in our society, something is *not* happening between fathers and children—and it is damaging our kids.

▲ ▲

Mike's story is one of fatherly failure. His experience with his "virtual dad" stood out in my mind because it contrasted so sharply with the successes I witnessed among so many fathers of children in my school.

Through a kind of natural selection, Northridge attracted a great many parents with their heads on straight. I saw that these fathers and mothers were doing a fine job, often an outstanding job, in raising their children.

Parents and visitors complimented us on our students' confident cheerfulness and good manners, their powers of producing high-quality work, their developing sense of professionalism, their personal integrity. Of drug problems, we had none—that's none, as in "zero." Certainly our kids had sporadic bouts of wackiness and glandular ups and downs, as most normal teens do. But our young people were, in the main, fine adolescents who grew quickly into excellent young adults. Eventually they entered good careers and married well. We teachers and parents were proud of them, and still are.

I tried to find out how their parents managed to pull this off. Frankly, I was often struck by their widely different temperaments and ways of raising kids. I carefully took notes on odd scraps of paper and filed them away until I had several mulch-pile folders. Gradually, some patterns—some common *approaches* to children's upbringing—came into focus, and these lessons I passed on to other parents by way of advice and encouragement.

Certainly, one common element was this: the best among these well brought-up young people respected their dads and learned from them. At home, both parents, father and mother, were doing a great job, but the father's role seemed to be critical. He was *doing* something smart in family life, something important that won his children's respect, and I focused on finding out what that was.

I began talking with the teenage children of these men. I

asked them to relate an incident that would pinpoint or illustrate why they respected their dad. Sometime later, I also asked this of the most effective fathers I knew—to relate something from the memory of their own dads. These are some of the things they told me: *

"When we were kids, we knew Dad was strong. Whenever we all tried and failed to open the top of a jar that was stuck, we'd take it to Dad. He was the only one who could open it—every time!"

"When I was about three or four years old, I was out walking in a park with my dad. I lagged behind him a bit and stopped to look at something on the ground. Suddenly a huge Irish setter dog ran toward me and leaped on me, knocking me to the ground. The dog stood over me, panting and sniffing at my face. Of course he was simply being playful, but I didn't know this. I was absolutely terrified, screaming in horror as I thought the dog would eat me. My dad ran back fast, shooed the dog away, and swept me up in his arms. He held me tight, dried my tears with his hanky, and smiled while telling me everything was okay. I held on tight to his neck and felt safe with him."

"After we were a certain age, our dad wouldn't do things for us much. He'd show us how to do it ourselves and then tell us to do it on our own. He always said we had to learn to handle our own affairs."

"Dad had a temper and sometimes he'd lose it with us. But he always came back later to apologize. He was sometimes tough with us, but he was always fair."

"Our family had to live with the fact that Dad was super-busy in his job. Sometimes he had to work late or on Saturdays. But all of us knew somehow that he was always available. If any of us really needed him badly, we knew he'd drop whatever he was doing and be there."

"Dad and Mom always stuck up for each other. Always. When we'd ask Mom for permission to spend a night over someone's house, she'd say to wait until she checked with Dad. And if we went to him, he'd say the same thing: to wait and let him first check with Mom. They made decisions together."

"Dad always said that Mom was number one in his life—and we kids had better treat her right, or else . . . We knew he meant it, too."

* Nearly all the quotations in this book are approximate because they are reconstructed from memory, often from many years ago. The quotation marks used are only a literary device. Moreover, I have usually changed names and personal circumstances of persons quoted in order to preserve their privacy.

"One summer evening when I was thirteen, my friend and I, merely as a joke, took all the air valves off tires from cars parked at a local VFW hall, and rode our bikes to my house. Dad overheard the two of us laughing about it and went into a cold rage. He drove us back there and made us replace all the valves, then took us inside to apologize to the cars' owners. I almost died of shame but really learned a lesson."

"I'll never forget Dad's taking me to his office when I was small. Everyone was nice to me, and I watched him writing and working with people all day. I was sort of proud of him."

"When we were planning vacations, Dad and Mom would ask us for suggestions. They let us have our say: what we'd like to do, where we'd like to go. And they did this for other things, too—listen to our input. But then they made the final decisions."

"When my sister was in high school, she was going to go out to a dance dressed in a new skirt that she'd just bought. It was a short— I mean really short—miniskirt. Dad saw her and hit the roof. He was very upset. He said no daughter of his was going to leave the house looking like that. Even though she was pleading and crying, he made her go upstairs and change. Next weekend, he made her return the skirt for a refund."

"Our dad was pretty easygoing about things. He'd respect our freedom of opinion and let us disagree with him on most things. But in some matters—like staying out late, or the way we'd dress—he'd put his foot down. We knew that when he took a stand like this, he considered the matter really important for us, for our welfare as he put it—and so the matter was closed, period."

So, what were the words and terms that kept bobbing up to describe these effective fathers? You see them here: *strong, directive, just, available, lovingly united with his wife, competent, protective, respectful of his children's freedom, a good listener, a leader who teaches right from wrong.* Not a bad thumbnail sketch of fatherhood, a good beginning.

Over the years, I kept questioning fathers in particular, rummaging through their stories, pulling thoughts together, and arranging them into patterns. I frequently passed on what I had learned in public lectures I gave, first to our school's parents, then to other groups in the Midwest, and eventually throughout the country. I wrote some small works that were privately published and, much to my surprise, widely read and appreciated. Occasionally I was interviewed on radio and television.

I began to suspect that I was on to something important when some incidents took place—events that eventually prompted me to step down from my school and devote myself full-time to teaching and encouraging young parents.

People started calling from around the country asking me to come speak to their parenting groups. Then I began receiving invitations from England, the Philippines, Ireland, Singapore, and Australia.

I had handouts for my talks run off at a print shop, and when I dropped by to pick them up, the owner asked if she could keep a few copies to give to her married siblings and friends.

Sometimes older men, grandfathers, attended my talks. Several of them approached me afterwards and said, "I wish I'd heard all this twenty-five years ago! It would have saved me a lot of trouble. . . ."

Lectures of mine were videotaped for later showing on television. On three separate occasions—in Milwaukee, Washington, and Sydney—camera operators came up afterwards to shake my hand and thank me. One technician told me, "I learned a lot here, and I'm sure glad *someone* is saying these things!"

One man approached me during an intermission and said he'd heard me speak three years before. He warmly thanked me and said, "There's definitely a before and an after in my life. Your advice was the turning point. You showed me what I need to do as a father, and gave me the push I needed."

In all my years as headmaster and later as lecturer, I faced a problem. Many men would ask, "Can you recommend some books I could read about fatherhood?" Here I found myself stumped.

For many years, I searched hard for books to recommend, works specifically written for men and from a masculine point of view. It was a disappointing and frustrating chore. While there was no shortage of so-called "parenting" books on the market, I found that nearly all of these works were written for women. Most focused on the crucially important role of wives and mothers, but they ignored or minimized the father's special role at home—a dimension of family life that my experience showed me was extremely important.

Starting in the mid-1980s, my hopes perked up when some books on fatherhood as such finally showed up in bookstores.

But these, too, were mostly a letdown. Some were sociological and abstract in their approach: long on discussion lamenting the "missing father" but short on practical solutions. Most belabored the woes of dysfunctional families but had little to say about common problems among normal families. (After all, normal families have problems, too.)

Other books offered "quick fixes" and unhelpful bromides ("Play more often with your kids") or stressed fatherly behavior in nitty-gritty detail but without a larger philosophical framework—not merely what a father *does*, but what a father *is*.

These books all had the same flaw: They paid practically no attention to a father's masculinity, his inherent male strengths, and how these powers direct children's growth in judgment, competence, and character. So many of these works seemed to view the ideal father as little more than a large-scale pal or playmate to his children or as a kind of second mother. None of these views squared with my experience.

The book I wanted would have an entirely different approach. It would sum up, as it were, the *collective wisdom of fatherhood* as men learned it from their own dads up until, say, the end of World War II—when societal and family forces began to erode and even cut off this manly intergenerational teaching.

The book I wanted would explain the importance of a father's long-term strategic foresight and commitment. It would tell how a father's own powerful and passionate vision can serve as an empowering ideal for his children's later lives as men and women. It would describe how a father's special, most critical responsibility is to teach and form *character* in his growing children. It would explain the main obstacles in today's society that undercut a father's teaching role, and tell men what they could do to overcome them. Then, within this framework, the book would spell out experienced, practical advice on how successful fathers deal with their children in the most crucial areas: family rules, discipline, schooling, sports, recreation, the media, and ongoing teamwork with one's wife.

To put it another way, the book I was looking for would provide what any man needs to carry out a serious responsibility, whether at home or in the workplace—that is, a clear job description, a long-term realistic goal, a warning about potential obstacles, and the experienced know-how of others who have tackled the job and succeeded.

Because I couldn't find this book anywhere, I wrote it myself. It's the one you are now holding.

So, let's move on to the job description of fatherhood.

I | *The Smart Father: A Job Description*

I have good news for you: *practically anyone can be a good father.* Any normal man with a measure of common sense and a capacity for sacrifice can raise his children right. I know this because I've seen it done again and again.

As I talked things over with the effective fathers I knew, in their homes or at ball games or in my office while cradling a mug of coffee, one thought kept striking me: What an incredibly diverse group of men these are! Effective fathers, men respected and beloved by their families, come in all temperaments and from all sorts of backgrounds.

All of these men frankly admitted that they had made mistakes and big blunders from time to time. All had known occasions when they were unsure exactly what to do with their kids; but they merely shrugged and pressed on ahead, doing the best they could. All had suffered some frustrations and disappointments with their children's misbehavior, especially in the preschool years and later in their children's early adolescence.

These men reflected about their fatherhood; when I asked them what they'd do differently now, they would smartly spell out details (which I include in this book). All seemed to have a kind of cautious but confident optimism that pressed them to ignore their setbacks and bounce back from disappointments, while learning from their experience. They strongly sensed that they had an important job to do with their children, something they could not afford to neglect, and this empowered them to press on through the rough parts. They were determined to raise their kids right, and they had a fairly clear idea what this meant.

Some were in good to excellent physical shape. Others were slightly built. Still others were, shall we say, a bit roundish in the middle; they would shrug, smile, and admit they could stand to lose a few pounds. A couple of them frankly explained that they were recovering alcoholics.

Some were clearly charismatic leaders on the job and at home, the sort of people who would be noticed in any small gathering. But others were quiet, self-effacing, and even a bit shy. A few were extremely easygoing—in fact, I thought if they were any more laid back, they would be embalmed.

To one extent or another, all seemed to have a good sense of humor, that sort of light touch noticeable in quietly self-confident people. We shared many a good laugh.

A high percentage were sports enthusiasts. Many liked to golf or play tennis or risk injury playing basketball. Others were, at most, fairly indifferent athletes—though, oddly enough, they often had sons and daughters who excelled at sports. A couple were bird-watchers. All seemed to enjoy some sort of hobby, usually collecting or making things or fishing. Nearly all liked to read whenever they had time, especially in history and biography.

A handful heartily enjoyed talking politics. But most, though reasonably well informed about national and foreign affairs, couldn't care less for political matters. (One of them quoted Will Rogers to me: "Ninety percent of all politicians give the others a bad name.")

Many of these men grew up in healthy families themselves, and so they could remember how their fathers thought and acted as family leaders. Others came from deeply troubled or even dysfunctional homes, but they were determined not to repeat their parents' mistakes. Some grew up without a father in the home, but they had learned from their heroic mothers and adult males whom they respected.

Some were fairly strict with their children; others quite easygoing in minor matters—though they put their foot down on matters of principle, and in this way taught their kids what their principles were.

All of them loved their wives. And all seemed to look upon their spouses with a kind of quiet awe: "I honestly don't know where she gets the stamina . . . she's incredible—never lets up, never stops giving, can handle several tasks at a time . . . .She does 95 percent of the kids' upbringing; I'm simply there to back her up . . . I don't know how she does it!" Over and over again, in open or subtle ways, these men would express their pride and love for the number-one person in their lives.

Conclusion? If history has taught us anything, it is the astonishing resilience of human nature and the power of family love. People of passionate love and principled convictions can endure any hardship and surmount any obstacle. Nobody needs to be a victim of his past. Love endows power and direction to life and makes anything possible. Any normal man holding his child in his arms can find the strength to become a great father and a great man.

Though all these men differed in personalities and what might be called leadership styles, they seemed to have a few traits in common, some ways of thinking and acting in a smart, effective way. I must stress that they were *smart*. Whether they relied on rational, reflective thought about their fatherly role or were moved more by intuition, they seemed to *understand* what a father is and does. This kind of life knowledge—wisdom really—showed up most in three important areas.

First, a basic, broad understanding of a parent's main mission, to build strong character in their children, and how savvy parents make this happen in family life.

Second, an understanding how a father's main role is to protect his wife and children from harm, not only now but also later in life. That's what he's there for.

Third, an understanding of how a man of integrity strives to unify his life—to be the same person, a responsible and respected leader—both at work and at home.

In the chapters of this book, I will explain all three of these critical areas with many examples. But here at the outset, I'd like you to clearly understand the big picture, the grand strategy of leading as an effective father. To do that we must look at these key dimensions of fatherly leadership: character formation, protection, and unity of life.

A Father's Mission: To Form Character and to Protect

Every smart father I've known seems to understand, one way or another, some timeless and universal truths about a man's mission in the family:

• An ancient maxim about child-raising says, "As the twig is bent, so grows the tree." This reference to twigs and trees underscores an important fact of life: Raising kids right is not an engineering problem, or a task with rational steps, clearly connected components, and theoretically under perfect control. Rather, it's more like an agricultural problem. That is, certain tried and true approaches work most of the time, but at some point the process of raising kids blurs into mystery—and, like the mysterious growth of crops from seeds, is essentially out of control. To look at it another way, a father, like a farmer, does the very best he knows how, and then leaves the rest in the hands of God.

• A smart father senses that parents who fail with their kids seem to fall into two extremes. They are either irresponsibly permissive or tyrannically domineering—either wimps or control freaks. Both extremes are basically self-centered and do serious, lasting damage to children. Kids with such parents tend to grow up either as immature narcissists or as rebels and sneaks. A loving, self-sacrificing father does not fall into extremes—he will not neglect his fatherly duty to lead, nor will he impose more control than his children need. He respects his kids' freedom without being permissive, and he works to strengthen his kids but not to dominate them. He puts his children's welfare ahead of his comfort and his ego.

• He sees his number-one job as that of building inner strengths in his children—powers of judgment, conscience, will, and action—that will last them a lifetime. This takes years of loving leadership, ongoing teamwork with his wife, and persevering effort. He knows that kids cannot start acquiring character overnight at age thirteen, the onset of adolescence. What kids learn in childhood will powerfully sway how well or how badly they behave as teens and young adults.

• He has to teach them that responsible grown-up life is not self-centered play (the attitude of children), but mostly *service to others*. He knows his kids will grow up not when they can take care of themselves, but only when they can take care of others—and want to.

• He cannot teach anything of importance to his kids unless they respect *him* and his rightful authority. It's not enough that they like him; they must also respect him, and nobody respects a play-oriented "buddy" or a shadowy, passive figure around the house—an apparent weakling.

• Respect in life, at any age, arises from some perception of strength: physical, moral (judging right from wrong), and intellectual (telling truth from falsehood). So a man's children need to know him well and witness his strong character in action. The more they witness and experience his strengths of judgment, will, and action at home—as his colleagues do at work—the more they will respect him.

• As they grow up, kids need heroes to emulate, and they eagerly seek these out. For the most part, children grow in character by unconsciously imitating people they admire, starting with their parents.

• If Mom and Dad are both strong, confident leaders, the children will pattern their own lives after them. The more highly kids admire Dad and Mom, the more deeply will they adopt their parents' attitudes, values, and character.

• But if their parents are weak nonleaders—living as passive "consumers" without a mission to carry out in family life—then the kids will pattern themselves after other attractive figures instead: the clownish rock performers and "celebrities" of the entertainment industry. They will be suckers for sales pitches, whether for gadgets or loony ideas or lifestyles. And when pressured by peers, they'll be pushovers.

• Time passes ever more quickly. Every decade of life passes twice as fast as the one before, and kids grow older with startling swiftness. A father has only a short time, a tiny window of opportunity, to shape his kids' conscience and character for life. So his job is not only important; it's also absolutely urgent. Every smart father knows he has one chance—and only one—to raise his children right.

In other words, a smart father senses that he must work real change in the lives of his children. Kids do not come into the world with strong character. So if a man and his wife neglect this task and effect no change, the kids grow older without growing up. They emerge into adult life with the faults and weaknesses of childhood. They remain spoiled, weak-willed, impulsive, self-centered, irresponsible—and headed for calamitous careers and marriages.

A smart father will never permit this to happen. He loves his children too much to let them grow up with their faults uncorrected. So he takes action now to strengthen his children's minds and wills and thus save them from future harm.

This leads us to look at how a man protects his family.

First, let's examine a man's masculinity, the distinctive character of any normal adult male.

Men are different from women. They are wired differently, and they think differently. They have instincts and attitudes and physical strengths that empower them for tough-minded, sacrificial service to those people who count most in their lives, starting with their families.

All the special features of an adult male's personality, developed from boyhood—his muscles, willpower, stamina, competitive drive, aggressiveness and assertiveness, mathematical and abstractive powers of mind, love for strategic planning and manipulating physical objects, strong sense of fairness and ethical conduct—all coordinate toward a single purpose in life: *protection.*

Nature, it seems, endows men with the physical and mental powers they need to protect their loved ones. The instinct *to protect from harm* lies at the core of a man's masculinity, and it is an immensely powerful force.

I once witnessed dramatically this protective instinct in action. One warm Sunday afternoon a few years ago, I was strolling with a friend near the Boston Public Garden in Boston's elegant Back Bay neighborhood. My friend and I stopped at a pedestrian light and waited with a few other people to cross Commonwealth Avenue. Cars whizzed by, true to the pattern of that city's notoriously frantic traffic.

Across the street, an elderly lady was walking slowly alongside two young girls, about six or seven years old. I would guess they were her granddaughters or grandnieces. She was blind. In one hand she carried a red and white cane while her other held the leash of a German shepherd seeing-eye dog. One of the little girls was stroking and patting the back of the huge, friendly animal.

Suddenly—chaos. From down the block hurtled a large mongrel street dog, barking and snarling loudly, spoiling for a fight. Swiftly he lunged at the German shepherd, who sprang back at him in snarling, furious rage. The two dogs pounced and snapped with bared teeth at each other, growling and barking ferociously in an all-out serious fight. The noise was loud and shocking.

What happened next was even worse. The blind woman wildly thrashed her cane back and forth trying to scare away the attacker, while the two children screamed hysterically. The little girls stood transfixed, absolutely horrified, loudly shrieking and sobbing in terror. The street echoed with the children's terrified screams mixed with wild, furious barks and growls.

Something in that sudden, frightening sound—kids screaming and dogs wildly barking—electrified everyone within earshot. My friend and I dashed across the street to help the lady and the little girls. As we did, we saw other men running at full speed from every direction.

A taxi screeched to a halt, and the driver and his passenger leaped out. Other cars slammed their brakes, and men, leaving their car doors open, dashed out to help. Doors flew open in the townhouses nearby, and men ran down stairs into the street.

One professorial-looking man had evidently been reading the newspaper. He held his glasses in one hand and his paper in the other, quickly pocketing the glasses and rolling up his newspaper to use it as a kind of club as he ran toward the dogs. In seconds a group of twelve or fifteen men, including a couple of college students, pulled the screaming kids and the woman back to safety, while the others belted the dogs with jackets and rolled-up papers, anything at hand, to separate them and chase off the attacker. (A brave thing to do, for it's dangerous to meddle in a dogfight.) The mongrel quickly broke off and ran away. All the men then turned to calm down the children and assure them everything was okay. A woman, the professor's wife I assume, beckoned from a townhouse doorway and gently led the blind lady with her dog and the kids inside to rest up. People stepped back into cars and drove off, while pedestrians drifted away.

What happened in this rescue was something primitive and powerful, a force thousands of years old. Each adult male within earshot heard a sound that reached deep inside his male instincts and jolted him into enraged defensive action—"Children being attacked by beasts! Save the children! Repel the beasts!" Men dropped what they were doing and, heedless of their own safety, flung themselves forward to protect the kids.

That's my point here. Men are hard-wired—in their minds, muscles, and tough aggressiveness—to protect women and children from harm. This incident, though dramatic and violent, underscores what a man does in countless subtle ways in family life. He is there to ward off harm.

This fatherly protection works in several different and important ways.

A family man devotes his powers, first of all, to protect his wife from anyone who would threaten her. It seems to be a natural instinct among males to protect the women in their lives—wife, mother, sisters, daughters—from outsiders' aggression. For instance, if a man were standing next to his wife in line and a male stranger turned to speak loudly and angrily toward her, the man would rise in rage to her defense. Adrenaline would rush through his blood, his muscles would tighten, and his first impulse would be to rearrange the aggressor's face.

Peace, it is said, is the condition we enjoy when other people leave us alone. Throughout history, the father of a family would protectively stand in the doorway of his home and say to the world, as it were: "Leave us alone. . . ."

And here's another aspect of a man's protectiveness, one that men today often fail to understand. A man permits no one to threaten or upset his wife—and *this includes their own children*. A hugely important part of a father's job is to defend his wife against their children's rudeness, insolent disobedience, and impulsive aggression. This protection counts most to his wife when the kids are small (under seven) and later when they enter adolescence. A man will allow no one to disrespect his wife, including—and even especially—at home.

A man also defends his family through what he earns in his work. That is, he doesn't merely provide for his family; he protects them from poverty. He shelters them, takes care of their needs for a roof, food, and clothing. While Dad has a job, the family feels secure. Even in a two-income home, it seems, children sense that Dad is the main provider and, therefore, the family's main protector.

Moreover, he protects his children from forces that threaten them here and now: drugs, bullies, criminals, unjust aggressors of all types, and potential disasters arising from their inexperience and impulsive mistakes (like dashing out into traffic or playing with matches).

For instance, if a father glanced out his living-room window and spotted a male stranger chatting with his small daughter, coyly beckoning to her, he would swiftly lunge into defensive action. He'd race out the door, stride aggressively toward the stranger, then confront the man and demand to know what he wanted. With muscles taut, he would stand between his daughter and this potential aggressor, physically shielding her from harm.

Another example: When his teenage daughter is being picked up for a date, a father goes out of his way to size up the young man she's going out with. He wants to meet him—insists on meeting him—to look him in the eye and intuitively size up his intentions and his worth. A father senses a duty to assess any young male who approaches his daughter. An unspoken message seems to pass between them: "She's my daughter. Treat her nicely, kid, or else . . ."

But most of all—and this is crucially important—a father protects his children by *strengthening them so they can later protect themselves*. In the lives of his children, he asserts *loving leadership toward responsible adulthood*.

It is a father's mission, the challenge that brings out the best in him, to form in his children the powers and attitudes they will need to succeed later in life, so they in turn can protect themselves and their own loved ones. So, in his children's eyes, a great father is a lifelong leader and teacher. His protective, strengthening lessons live on in the inner lives of his children, long after they've left home for good, and indeed long after he has passed to his eternal reward. A great father never stops being a father, for he lives on as a great man in the hearts of his children.

So, how does a man protect his children long term? What sort of lifelong strengths does a smart, effective father teach?

• A father strengthens his children's *competence*. He forms lifelong healthy attitudes toward work, along with serious habits of work. Without a father's leadership in this arena, his kids can have trouble grasping the connection between effort and results, between standards and achievement. If he fails here, his children may never outgrow the dominant attitude of childhood— that life is play—and remain stuck in a permanent adolescence. This can later destroy them, their careers, and their families.

• He teaches *respect for rightful authority*. He insists that his children respect and obey him and their mother. His wife sets most of the moral tone for the household—what's right and wrong in family life—and he enforces it. Being smart and farseeing, he knows that when children fail to respect their parents, they can later clash with all other forms of authority—teachers, employers, the law, God's law, and their own conscience.

• A father teaches his children *ethics* and gives final form to their lifelong *conscience*. That is, *he shows his sons and daughters how to comport themselves justly and honorably in the world outside the home*. In his children's eyes, he is an expert on fair dealings and personal integrity in the workplace and community. He shows his kids how their mother's moral teachings carry over later to life outside the home: telling the truth, keeping one's word, putting duty first, deferring to others' rights and feelings. By his example and correction at home, he shows how responsible adults respect each other's rights and assert their own.

• A father builds healthy *self-confidence* in children. His presence around the home as a physically strong man leads his children (daughters especially) to feel safe, securely protected, and therefore realistically self-confident. As a father, he corrects and encourages, and helps his children to learn from their mistakes. In this way, he leads his children to form a realistic sense of their strengths and limitations. Youngsters who receive this protective parental love, along with self-knowledge and experience with problem-solving at home, eventually form a lifelong self-confidence.

• A father leads his children to adult-level *sound judgment and shrewdness.* He helps them to use their brains like responsible adults: to frame questions and answers logically, to think ahead and foresee consequences, to assess people's character and values, and to know malarkey when they see it.

• A father provides an *attractive example of responsible masculinity.* He acts as a model for his sons' growth into manhood. And he conveys to his daughters (most often unconsciously) the traits they should look for in judging the worth of men their age, especially suitors for marriage. In countless subtle ways, Dad forms a pattern for manly character in each of his sons and, indirectly, for the kind of man each daughter will someday marry. (This may explain why great fathers so often get along well with their sons-in-law.)

▲ ▲

Let me sketch for you here some examples of how a smart father thinks—how his powerful instinct to protect his children in the long term leads him to sense danger now and then presses him to head it off with corrective action. This is what some men told me about their own *protective foresight*:

From Glenn: *One Saturday morning, I stepped into our TV room and saw my two sons, aged nine and six, watching cartoons on our set. They'd been lying there for at least two hours already. I stood in the doorway for a couple of minutes and noticed something I'd never paid attention to before.*

They were hypnotized. Both of them were sprawled out in the chairs, practically poured in, with their shoulders hunched and their bodies limp, unmoving. Their eyes were glazed over and unblinking. Their jaws and lips hung down, their mouths slightly parted. Loud noises jolted out of the set—crashes, bangs, blips of raucous music—but my boys gave absolutely no response. They didn't twitch a muscle, showed no reaction whatever on their faces, nothing but a fixed mindless stare.

"What's going on here?" I thought. "The human mind and body aren't built for this kind of slouching inactivity, especially at such a young age." Kids are wired to be active, their bodies constantly moving to build muscles and coordination. And kids' eyes are also

in motion, or should be, when they're alert and thinking, taking in and sizing up their environment. For children to sit this way seems somehow —how shall I put it?—unnatural.

I then sat down next to them (they were scarcely aware of my presence) and actually watched the cartoons with them. This went on for about a half hour, until I couldn't stand it any more. That did it. I stood up, turned off the TV, and told them to go outside and play. Naturally, they put up a fuss, but I insisted. Within a few minutes they were setting off on their bikes, happy as could be.

This experience moved me to set a policy in our house: The kids will watch as little TV as possible, and never on Saturday morning. They have only a few years to exercise their developing minds and muscles, and this isn't happening while they're hypnotized.

From David, a father of two girls and a boy, ages four through eleven: I drove my eleven-year old son and two friends of his to a weekend Boy Scout camping trip at a site some distance from our suburban town. Somehow I'd been convinced to join them camping for a couple of days, a feat I hadn't tackled since childhood and had mixed feelings about. I'm a busy man and work hard. So I hadn't spent much time with my son in recent years and thought this would be a chance to be together, even if with a crowd shivering under tents in the woods.

We had to drive for several hours. I was at the wheel and my son Robby was crammed into the back seat with his buddies. The kids chattered all the way, practically ignoring my existence in the front. It's amazing how kids will talk frankly when they're being chauffeured, as if no adult could overhear their conversation. (My wife and her friends have noticed this for years in their carpools.) So I overheard my son's conversation with his friends. That is, I heard my son open up as I'd hardly ever heard him before.

What struck me about their yakking was its center of interest. They talked about video games, movies, television shows, and various entertainers. (Robby had recently taken a more-or-less serious interest in rock music. Nobody ever told me that adolescence starts these days at age eleven.) In detail, and with some obvious ploys at one-upmanship, they described plots of movies and shows they'd recently seen, including passing light references to sexual situations. They went through the antics they'd seen on some music videos. They even talked about girls in their class, with occasional whispering followed by outbursts of sniggering laughter.

Now, mind you, I'm not a prude. And I remember the sort of talk that passes among young males, having once been one myself. But at *age eleven? And for four hours straight, without letup? What's going on here, anyway? Whatever happened to talk about sports and games? Don't these kids play anything besides video games? Where do they get the time to watch so much? Do they do anything other than sit and stare at a tube or movie screen? (Robby's friends, I noted, were ever so slightly on the pudgy side. Not fat exactly, but a bit roundish and soft where muscle should be.)*

All this got me to thinking. In centuries past, boys this age would be apprenticed at something—some serious line of work, such as farming or blacksmithing, a preparation for life's responsibilities. So, what is my son being apprenticed at? What is he practicing to become? A watcher? A consumer? A professional enjoyer?

These comfortable suburban kids, including my own son, have been thoroughly schooled in consumerism. At this age, they seem to see life as play—nothing but play. Their entire existence has been spent receiving pleasant sensations. It's not their fault, of course; it's the way we adults bring them up while we go about the serious business of living.

What can happen to Robby if he grows up this way—if he reaches, say, age eighteen or twenty-one with his mindset unchanged: that life is mostly play? At what point should his everyday life be balanced with work? Where and how should he learn that much of life's enjoyment comes from serious accomplishment, a job well done, using one's powers for the betterment of others? If Robby and his friends remain childlike in attitudes and expectations, will they have the edge and savvy to compete in the future marketplace?

Anyway, this train of thought from that weekend (an all-around disaster, by the way) led me to make some serious changes at home, starting with myself. I got the TV under control and put away most of the video games. I gave Robby jobs around the house and supervised how he did them. The two of us took up chess. I oversaw his schoolwork much more carefully, sometimes making him redo it right. We took up jogging and handball. I brought him into my office occasionally on weekends, which he greatly enjoyed. I forced myself to make the time so we could do things together. Much to my surprise, he seemed to have been waiting for this all along. . . .

From Tom, a father of two boys and two girls, all under age ten: *In my office we had a young fellow named Frank who had joined the company only a few months before. He was a good-looking guy, personable and reasonably hardworking. But he had a couple of problems that people started to notice.*

He had a habit of pausing in front of people's desks, when the workers had stepped away for a couple of minutes, and simply standing there, sometimes with coffee cup in hand, reading people's papers and computer screens. Sometimes the people would return to find him looking over their work and, mildly annoyed, they'd ask him if he wanted something. Believe it or not, he wouldn't take the hint. He'd sort of shrug, smile innocently, and move on to his own workstation.

Not surprisingly, word got out quietly that Frank was a snoop. This problem was compounded by his habit of passing on bits of gossip about people. Most of it was pretty harmless, but it was gossip all the same. Pretty soon, people in the office grew careful about what they said to Frank; no one knew where the information would wind up.

How is it possible, I thought, that this talented young guy had never learned some basic rules of office etiquette? Hadn't anyone ever told him that the top of someone's desk isn't a bulletin board and you should stay out of other people's work? How did he reach the age of twenty-six, or whatever he was, without learning to mind his own business?

This led me to further thinking. Who normally teaches this sort of "professional street-smarts" and office courtesy to young people? Not the schools; certainly not MBA programs. It's not written down on office protocols either. It's one of those things you're expected to know—and if you don't know, your reputation and career can suffer.

Clearly, it seemed to me, this sort of education has to come from the home, and most likely from the father. A father traditionally was the one to clue his children in on how to behave ethically in the world of business, how to get along with people in professional affairs. I remembered how my dad used to talk to me about these things, and long before I started my first job.

Then and there, I determined that my sons and daughters would learn from me everything I know about upright professional dealings. And I wouldn't wait until they'd made mistakes that could sidetrack their careers, even do lethal damage.

From Alan, father of three children under six years old: *A friend of mine, whom I'll call John, was a middle-aged manager in our company and a compulsive workaholic. I knew him socially through our church. He had one son and a daughter, both in their early twenties. We used to carpool together to work.*

One Monday, as we were driving to the office, only the two of us, he looked terribly distraught, worse than I'd ever seen him. I normally don't pry into people's affairs, but I asked him if he was feeling okay. He then poured out his problem. That weekend, his daughter told him that she just became engaged to the young fellow she'd been seeing for over a year. So, what's the problem, I asked?

"The guy's an idiot!" John blurted. "He's a lazy, unbelievably immature drifter. He has no degree, no plans, no ambitions, no drive whatsoever. He's childishly self-centered, thinks of nothing but his own amusements." He paused to control himself, then muttered in a low, despairing voice, "I give the marriage about a year, tops."

Well, what could I say? I tried to give some hope, but we both knew that not much could be done. I glanced over to see his anguish and recognized I was looking at the ultimate horror of a middle-aged man—to see his beloved daughter plunging into a bad marriage, stubbornly deaf to her father's warnings, and there's nothing her dad can do about it.

I've long believed that big problems in a family take a long time to develop. They don't just happen overnight. It seemed to me that John's compulsion to work long hours kept him away from his daughter while she was growing up. She hardly knew him. Because her dad, who should have been the main man in her life, was virtually a stranger, she had a void in her judgment about men's character. To whom could she compare her boyfriends and thus judge their worth as men? She had no frame of reference, and so she emotionally settled on a superficially attractive lightweight. In a way, it wasn't her fault.

John, I suspect, knew deep down that the fault of this problem pointed straight to him. He should have spent time over the years getting to know his daughter and letting her get to know him. His ongoing neglect was the real cause of his distress. Now he would pay for his inverted priorities. It's a fact of life: you can't unpour concrete.

Quietly I made up my mind, and firmly: I will never go through this with my little girl. While she's growing up, I will be there, no matter what.

From Curtis, a father of five children under age thirteen: *My second oldest son, Randy, is eight years old and has a couple of problems. Not big problems, mind you. He is childishly slovenly, leaves his clothes and toys wherever they drop, and needs constant reminding to pick up after himself. He also has a bad temper, the worst in the family. He's often rude to his brothers and sisters, and aggressive to a fault.*

I spend hours getting after him to put things away, and I frequently have to punish him and make him apologize for his impulsive inconsiderateness. Over the last couple of years, I'm happy to say, he's made considerable progress. There are ups and downs, occasional backsliding, but the general drift is upward toward mature self-control.

I've frequently been exasperated with Randy's misbehavior, even exhausted, and so has my wife. But I've refused to give up. I've tried to correct him every single time. What keeps me going? It's this. Someday Randy is going to be somebody's husband. And if, at that time, he's still a self-centered, inconsiderate slob, his marriage could wind up in disaster. Though my wife and I may tolerate his aggressive outbursts now, his future wife may not. She may simply quit altogether—and, by court decision, take our grandchildren with her. The very thought of this horrifies me and moves me to act now to correct my son while I still have the chance. To put it bluntly, Randy needs a serious "attitude adjustment" before he's ready for marriage—and I'll never let up until this happens. That's part of a father's job, isn't it?

See what these men have in common? They use their heads, and then they act. They are smart, conscientious, protective fathers.

They think strategically. They project ahead, twenty or more years into the future, to picture their children as grown men and women with jobs and families of their own. They think of their kids' future happiness and welfare, and they think in terms of their characters, not merely their careers.

Within this frame of reference, they scan their children's present lives—attitudes, manners, habits, give-and-take relations in the family—and they sense *danger*. They see something in their children's present way of life that threatens them in the future. So their fatherly instinct to protect from harm switches on to full alert. It presses them to take corrective action now, while they still have time, to make serious changes in their children's attitudes and comportment. They act now, intelligently and urgently, to save their kids from disaster.

If you want to be an effective father, you need to start with this clear idea: with the way our society is today, your children really are threatened by disastrous problems later in life—and it is your greatest challenge as a man to save them. If you fail at this, you may spend the rest of your life regretting it. But if you succeed with your children, by forming conscience and character in each of them, you will win their lifelong devotion. They will esteem you all their lives as a great father and a great man.

Unity of Life

This brings us to a critically important aspect of fatherhood: unity of life. Let me explain it this way.

You are one person, not two. You are the same man, both on the job with your colleagues and at home with your family and friends. You cannot live two lives; you must be the same person in both spheres of responsible action.

As I suggested earlier in the story of Mike, the boy with the "virtual father," men who are weak and ineffective fathers tend to split their lives between work and family. That is, *they live as producers at work but consumers at home.*

On the job they dedicate their powers to serious, responsible service; but at home they lie around passively in pleasurable ease. In the workplace, their character strengths operate at all-out force—everyone sees and respects their sound judgment, sense of responsibility, tough-minded perseverance, and self-control. But at home, their inner strengths rest on idle, set aside (so to speak) for the day, and thus hidden from their children's eyes. To the kids, Dad appears at home as merely an amiable man of leisure, a passive enjoyer, a virtually inert consumer.

From what I've seen, successful fathers do not split their lives like this. They are smart, effective leaders at home as well as on the job. Their strengths of character impress their children as much as their colleagues at work. Their devotion to their family, in fact, gives meaning and purpose to their strenuous life of professional labor. Their work's main purpose is the welfare of their family, and their children know this.

In short, *a successful father exercises leadership at home as much as on the job—and in roughly the same ways.*

What does this mean? Let's first look at how a man typically exercises effective leadership in the workplace, and then turn to see how these same attitudes and actions apply to his leadership at home.

LEADERSHIP ON THE JOB

What are the traits—behavior, attitudes, habits—most common among successful business and professional leaders? I ask you here to think about the best bosses you've ever known or worked with in your line of business, whatever it may be.

What attitudes and conduct characterize an outstanding leader, maybe the sort of leader you hope someday to become yourself?

Here are some that I think you will recognize. . . .*

• An outstanding professional leader has a clear long-term vision about his company's future success, and he communicates this goal, at least occasionally, to everyone who works with him. He thinks five to twenty years ahead, and this goal-setting drives him and his team forward—for he knows that people's efforts are effective only when they're focused on some future achievement.

• He maintains a strong sense of teamwork. He looks mostly for *strengths* in people and sees his job as coordinating those powers toward the team's collective endeavors. He helps his colleagues, especially subordinates, develop their strengths and skills as they carry out clear-cut responsibilities.

• He is service-oriented. He knows that professional success means constant delivery of high-quality service. A business works best when it's dedicated to making *change for the better* in the lives of clients or customers, and his job is make this happen effectively and consistently.

• Though he thinks of the future, he pays attention to present detail, the nitty-gritty spread out before him. His eye for detail—that is, quality control—derives, in fact, from his long-term vision and commitment to service.

• He constantly sets priorities and sticks to them. When faced with a problem, he asks, "How important will this be a year from now, five years from now, or later?" Within this framework, he shrugs off or ignores insignificant snarls and minor setbacks.

• He knows how to concentrate, to focus entirely on what's before him. He works hard to shunt aside unnecessary distractions.

• When faced with problems, he regards them as challenges, not merely hassles. He has a kind of sporting spirit about his work, and he knows that any sport entails occasional bumps and bruises, mistakes, setbacks, and disappointments. He learns from mistakes, his own and others', and helps his subordinates do the same.

* Of course, countless women executives, including some I've worked for, could also fit the description here. I use the masculine pronoun "he" because I want to stress the connection between business leadership and fatherly leadership.

• If resources are scarce, including time, he works *smart*. He makes the most of what he has available, including slivers of time here and there. He does not procrastinate; papers don't sit cluttered on his desk. He thinks before he acts, then acts intelligently and decisively.

• As a man of integrity, he takes personal responsibility—no excuses, no alibis, no whining, no "victim complex," no shifting of blame. He accepts the consequences of his free decisions and actions, including his errors.

• When he's unsure what to do, he secures the best advice he can and weighs it seriously. Then he acts. In any event, he never lets indecision lead to inaction. His job is to act—that's what he is paid for.

• He's conscious of his authority and comfortable with it. He has rights because he has duties. He knows that his rights come with the job.

• He has self-respect and self-confidence, and these traits inspire respect and confidence from others.

• He rewards good effort, making praise as specific as blame —and just as sincere. He affirms and encourages his people, pressing them to put out their very best, regardless of personal shortcomings. He sees it as part of his job to keep obstacles out of his people's way, eliminating whatever holds them back from their best performance.

• When he must correct others, he corrects the *fault*, not the *person*. He comes down on the foul-up, not the one who did it. He corrects people privately, never in public. If he goes too far, he apologizes. He puts fairness ahead of his ego.

• He's a good listener. When people come to him with problems, he gives them his undivided attention. While listening, he tries to understand them: their motives, their experience (or lack thereof), their needs and uncertainties. He reflects: "Is there a bigger problem underlying this little problem? What is it? How can I help?"

• When he thinks about his people's professional development, his frame of reference (consciously or intuitively) consists of their character strengths: sound judgment, responsibility, perseverance, self-discipline. He wants and expects his people's efforts to grow in these areas. His company depends on it. He knows his business is only as strong as the people who work for it.

• He's a professional. That is, he sets high standards for his performance and does his best work, whether he feels like it or not. In a sense, he's strong enough to ignore fatigue, anxiety, or temptations to slack off. He enjoys his top performance; his delight in life comes as much from work as from leisured recreation. And he enjoys his leisure because he has earned it.

• Consciously or otherwise, he knows that no ideal ever becomes reality without sacrificial effort. His high personal and professional ideals, in fact, transform his hard work into a sporting adventure.

If you've been lucky enough to work with a boss like this, or even close to this ideal (as I have), you know how enjoyable and immensely satisfying the experience is. Considerate, confident, competent bosses are a delight to work with. You sense you work more "with" them than "under" them—for real leaders have "joiners," not followers. Great bosses like this teach their people an enormous amount and often win their warm devotion.

In fact, it is common for workers to see a great boss as a type of father figure. The man's combination of vision and practicality, foresight and action, firmness and understanding, healthy self-respect and spirit of service, competence and desire to keep learning, seriousness of purpose and lightness of touch—all equally describe the marks of a great, dedicated father.

Here is the point: If you are now this kind of professional man (no matter what kind of work you do), or if you aspire to this ideal for leadership someday at your job, you can be a great father. The attitudes, values, and conduct of a great boss— effective leadership on the job—apply as well to life in the family. A great father is a great man, a man of integrity, and men like this do not live divided lives.

LEADERSHIP AT HOME

We've described ideal leadership on the job. Now let's turn to see how these same traits apply to a man's role as family leader. What I outline here is a broad-brush picture of a great father. In the rest of this book, I will focus on details.

Here's my description of a smart father-leader, a great man:

• The man puts his wife first. In his priorities, her happiness and welfare are uppermost, and his children know this. They know it because he leads them by his own example to love, honor, and cooperate with their mother. If they ever fail to do this, they answer to him for it. (This is more than half the "secret" of effective fatherhood: striving to live as a devoted, protective, and supportive husband.)

• He has a spirit of lively collaboration with his wife. He sees her as his *partner* in a collective team enterprise. Together they work as much as possible to present a united front to the children. They check with each other about decisions, large and small, that affect the children's welfare. They draw on each other's strengths and, in different but complementary ways, they support each other.

• Very important: A great father works with his wife to maintain a long-term vision (twenty years ahead) about the children's growth in character, no matter what they later do for a living. Both spouses picture their children as grown-up men and women, adults with virtue: conscience, generosity, competence, responsibility, self-mastery. This distant but clear ideal forms the basis for teaching, practice, and correction *now*.

• He sees all his sacrificial efforts—the rigorous work of fatherhood—as an *investment*, not merely a vexing hassle. He is investing most of all in the stability and happiness of his children's future marriages, not only their careers. He senses that whatever inner strengths will make them great spouses and parents will also lead to success with their jobs. He looks forward to his later reward, the payback for his sacrifices: being proud of his grown children and enjoying life with his grandchildren.

• He corrects his children's faults, not them personally. He "hates the sin, loves the sinner." He combines correction and punishment with affectionate forgiveness, understanding, and encouragement. He is neither weak nor harsh but, rather, *affectionately assertive*. He loves his children too much to let them grow up with their childhood faults still intact.

• When he must correct anyone in the family, he does this personally and privately whenever possible. He does not chew people out in public.

• He is never afraid of being temporarily "unpopular" with his children. Their long-term happiness is more important to him than their present sulking and bruised feelings from his correction. He is confident that their resentment will soon pass, and that someday they will understand and thank him for the love behind his correction.

• He encourages his children, showing and explaining how to do things right and how to do the right thing. He *directs* rather than micromanages, and makes praise as specific as blame.

- He's conscious of his authority, which is as weighty as his responsibility. He does not permit electronic entertainment in the home to undermine that authority or undo his lessons of right and wrong. He keeps the media under discriminating control, allowing only what serves to bring the family together.
- He shares conversation with his children until he and they know each other inside out. He goes out of his way to listen to his kids, and he pays close attention to their growth in character. He monitors and guides their performance in sports, chores, homework, good manners, and relations with siblings and friends. He knows what goes on in his home and inside the growing minds of his children.
- He respects his children's freedom and rights. He teaches them how to use their freedoms responsibly, and he exercises only as much control as they need. He sets limits to his children's behavior, draws lines between right and wrong. Within those limits, the children may do what they think best; beyond the lines, they begin to infringe on the rights of others—and this he will not permit.
- He wants his children to be active, and he knows that all active people make mistakes. He leads his children to learn from their blunders. He teaches them that an active life involves intelligent risk-taking, including the risk of error, and that there's nothing wrong with mistakes if we learn from them.
- He sets aside his fatigue, anxiety, and temptations to slack off—putting his fatherly duties ahead of self-centered pursuits. He sets aside the newspaper to help with homework. He goes without TV to set a good example. He lets his kids work with him around the house even when they mostly get in the way. Like a good boss, he is always available to help and advise; consequently, his children sense he would drop anything if they really needed him. He is willing to put off a life of leisure until his children have grown and gone; now, while they're still at home, their needs come ahead of his comfort.
- Without being a bore about it, he uses certain terms from time to time in family life, phrases rich in moral meaning, those "invisible realities" that make for a great life: *integrity, personal honor, honesty, personal best effort, courage, responsibility, family honor, faithfulness to the will of God.*
- He gives his children a sense of family history and continuity. He tells stories about grandparents and forebears—people of quiet courage and even heroism. He lets his children know that they're descended from heroic people.

- He lets the children know his opinions and convictions about current events and their likely drift, the future world his children must cope with. He explains, as best he can, the past causes and future implications of present-day affairs. Because he reads a lot, he knows a lot—and so leads his kids to become readers.
- He is open to his children's suggestions, their "input" about family decisions. After all, it's their family, too. When matters are of little weight, he accedes to their preferences, lets them have their way. But larger, more important matters are decided by the parents. For instance, he will let his children decide sometimes what dessert to enjoy or what game to play, but he and his wife will decide which school the children attend and what TV programming and Web sites are allowed in the house.
- He takes his wife's judgment seriously, especially in matters about the children. He sets aside his ego and faces an evident fact of life: most of the time, she's right. At the very least, she's probably on to something. This includes his performance as a father. He does not let pride blind him to truth.
- When he has caused offense, he apologizes. He puts justice ahead of his ego.
- Habitually he punctuates his speech, especially toward his wife, with *please, thank you,* and *excuse me.* He makes his children do the same.
- He draws strength from his religious faith and love for his family.
- He knows that time passes quickly and he hasn't much of it. So he makes smart use of scant resources. He *makes* the time, even small slivers of it here and there, to live with his children.
- His life as husband and father is, to him, one of noble, self-sacrificing adventure. As long as his children are in his care, he will not quit or slacken in his efforts to form their character for the rest of their lives. He will protect and provide for his family no matter what the cost, for they are the meaning of his life, the object of his manly powers, the center of his heart.

Children with a father like this, wholly supported by a great wife, have a fighting chance to become great men and women. They grow to honor Dad and Mom, live by lessons learned since childhood, and pass these on to their own children whole and intact.

Have confidence. Take hope. Other normal men have become fathers like this, and so can you.

▲ ▲

So much for the overview, the big picture, of what a smart father is and does. The rest of this book will focus in on specifics and give you plenty of practical know-how and wisdom, nearly all of it drawn from other fathers' experience, much of it hard won.

I have raised many points so far that have probably prompted questions in your mind. In the chapters that follow, I aim to answer them. Moreover I've used terms here without really defining them—character, affectionate assertiveness, integrity, and the like—and I intend to explain them clearly.

Before heading into detail, though, I have a couple of points to make.

First, I ask your patience if some terms or ideas here seem repeated. Some actually do pop up in different contexts. The most important aspects of fatherhood, such as character and giving example, can be studied from varying angles—like different facets in a jewel or a varied melodic theme in a Mozart *rondo*. Principles are basically simple, but they jut out in different and sometimes complex entanglements in family life. If we keep returning to them from different approaches, you will grow to see everything, I hope, in a three-dimensional whole—not a sketch but a sculpture.

Second, as you have probably inferred by now, I have written this book for men living in intact, two-parent families. Most of the examples I use are drawn from families like this. If you are divorced and separated from your children, you may find much in this book helpful—or you may not. Truth to tell, I do not know. As I said, I have depended on people's experience for nearly everything herein, and I've known mostly intact families, hardly any others. There is definitely a need for a book like this for separated fathers, but, unfortunately, I am not the one to write it. I warmly encourage anyone who can.

Third, I am well aware that much of what I say about fathers can also be said of mothers. You could substitute "parent" for "father" in many places here. I do this not to downplay the critical, all-important role of mothers—far from it—but because I need to help men clearly perceive the uniquely masculine role of their fatherhood. Men are parents, too, and if they really pulled their weight and lived their parenthood, their spouses' lives would be hugely improved. (Many, many women have told me this.)

Finally, you may disagree, even strongly, with some of what I say here. No problem. I claim no monopoly on truth. In this mysterious business of raising children right, nobody knows all the answers. I simply ask you to keep an open mind and remember that it is real-life experience I'm discussing here, not something I've yanked out of thin air. If, after a careful reading, you still think I'm off base, then I invite you to do what I have done—write your own book. It's a free country. Nobody is stopping you.

All this being said, let's get down to business. . . .

2 | Be Savvy about Your Mission—to Raise Adults, Not Children

I want to begin here with a broad statement that I think you'll agree with: in business and professional life and in affairs of state, our most respected leaders are those who look farthest toward the future and most clearly foresee oncoming perils and opportunities. Strategic foresight and respected leadership seem to go hand in hand.

If you page through the works of outstanding American leaders—people such as George Washington, John Adams, Thomas Jefferson, Theodore Roosevelt, Martin Luther King—you are struck by their hopeful, future-directed vision. They constantly refer to "posterity" and foresee events in a way that's both realistic and hopeful, an idealism without illusions. Napoleon said it well: "A leader is a dealer in hope."

I have noticed this same dynamic at work in families, too. The most effective fathers and mothers I've known all seem to be moved by a strategic, far-seeing vision: *they see themselves raising adults, not children.*

Not all parents think this way. A modern American family is a busy place, far too busy. Or rather, busy about the wrong things, busy for the wrong reasons. Many parents seem trapped like mice in a tumbling cage, scrambling in place while trying to cope with nitty-gritty problems of day-to-day family existence. They fail to think ahead. Their horizons stretch out only to the edge of the next few days or weeks or, at most, to the following summer. These present-trapped parents are often whiplashed, utterly shocked, when their happily busy kids later collide with painful troubles and even tragedy in life, starting in the early teens and accelerating into young adulthood.

Smart, effective parents are busy, too, and they struggle like anyone else with bills and deadlines, schedules and problems, the twisting ups and downs of family life. But all their sacrificial efforts are focused, not wasted, because of the parents' vision. These fathers and mothers look far into the future, twenty or more years ahead, and picture their children as grown men and women, competent adults with family and career responsibilities of their own. That is, *they see their children as adults-in-the-making.*

Consequently, these smart, far-seeing parents understand that they have a job to do, a duty to carry out with their kids. They have to work serious changes in their children, starting now, to build inner strengths that their kids presently and conspicuously lack. In other words, they foresee that they have to civilize their children, and impart in them a lifelong conscience and character that will lead to their kids' later success in all aspects of life, but especially in marriage. This is what parenthood is all about.

Let me put this another way, using a couple of comparisons.

As I see it, American families seem to fall into two broad categories. One I would call the *consumerist* type; the other is the *sporting adventure* type. Some parents treat family life like a picnic, a site for pleasant consumption, and their kids often meet with later trouble. Others see family life as an adventure, a great sport, and their kids largely turn out well. Why is this?

The consumerist parents treat family life as little more than a succession of pleasant diversions. Life for parents and kids centers mainly—I'd say almost entirely—on passive, leisurely enjoyment, fun-filled entertainment: a seamless succession of sports, abundant food and drink, TV shows, video games, Web-surfing, movies, music, parties, shopping. The family's enemy is boredom, something to be shunned at all costs. So kids are kept relentlessly busy, endlessly entertained. Family rules, if there are any, focus mostly on damage control—keeping hassles to a minimum, keeping the kids out of trouble, keeping the kids from wrecking the place. In such picnic-like homes, children are steadily apprenticed as consumers, not producers; they are trained to become enjoyers and shoppers. As a consequence, the kids grow to see life as play, an entitlement to be happily amused, for this is all they experience in family life.

Sooner or later, of course, any picnic withers into boredom; eventually people get up and move on to other, better things.

And the same thing seems to happen in the consumerist family. Starting in their early teens, very many kids from picnic families move on to other, more powerfully pleasurable sensations: alcohol, drugs, the rock culture, recreational sex. Kids who have been brought up to see life as play will treat the automobile as a toy, and they can kill or cripple themselves and others. They are strongly bent to treat people as objects, merely tools and toys for their use or amusement. They see sex as a toy, a high-powered form of recreation, and they propel themselves toward unwanted pregnancies, abortions, and disastrous marriages.

Contrast all this with life in the sporting adventure family, the family centered on teaching character. These parents see that they have a vitally important mission with their children, a job to carry out. They have a goal to strive toward, as in a vigorous sport—that is, what kind of adults their kids should grow to be. The family has plenty of fun, to be sure, but this enjoyment comes from work as much as leisure, from accomplishing something important, a distant ideal that's worth the present sacrifice.

In the sporting adventure family, the parents live like responsible adults and expect their children to do the same. Family rules are set in place for a clear and important purpose: to form the kids' conscience and character through example and repeated practice in responsible living. Family life is active, dynamic, as in any sport, and parents know all the triumphs and reverses, the temporary setbacks and disappointments, all the up and down struggles along the way until final victory—when their children emerge into adult life as ethical, competent, responsible men and women.

If you want to turn your family life into an adventure, you must be smart enough to recognize this fact of life: *Parents either pay now or they pay later.*

Parents who neglect their children's character upbringing, who take it easy in a static picnic life, can pay an enormous price later when their children collide with trouble.

But by contrast, those fathers and mothers who sacrifice now to empower their children's characters can enjoy life later when their kids grow up to their expectations. When the kids go out dating, the parents have little need to worry. Because their children enjoy strong character, they will choose good friends—and later a good spouse. Before they are out of their teens, the children will think and act like mature adults, earn the respect of all who know them, and bring honor to their family.

Pay now or pay later, that is the way it seems to work. Think of your fatherly mission as an investment—and recognize that any big investment demands careful, intelligent foresight. So you must think ahead, twenty years ahead toward your children's adulthood. That foresight is where your smart, effective fatherhood will begin to take hold.

How to begin? Start by cultivating your powerful fatherly

instinct to protect your family from harm. You cannot afford to be naïve, like so many picnic parents, about the dangers poised at your children. Nothing arouses a man to action more strongly and swiftly than sensing danger to his family. Any intelligent man who loves his children grows uneasy, even alarmed, when he's alert to the destructive forces at loose in today's society, maybe even in his own home.

Let's look at the problems a father today is up against.

Clearly, something is wrong in today's society. For several reasons, large numbers of parents are failing to form character in their children.

We look around in our workplaces and neighborhoods and see young people in their twenties who are immature and irresolute, irresponsible and soft, uneasy about themselves and their futures. They may be technically skilled and hold well-paying jobs, but their personal lives and marriages are a wreck. They seem perpetually stuck in adolescence, that dangerous coupling of adult powers with childlike irresponsibility. Some of them suffer through lives crippled or destroyed by substance abuse. Even if they are drug-free (what a strange term!), many see their work as mere ego-gratification or—an adolescent attitude— nothing but drudgery endured for the sake of "spending money." Great numbers of them live as heartless narcissists, caring little or nothing about parents or children. They retain, sometimes tragically, the flaws and weaknesses of childhood. For some reason, they never quite grew up.

It's clear that many troubled teens and young adults like these were wounded, maybe permanently, by a childhood spent enduring the horrors of dysfunctional families—drug and alcohol dependency, physical and sexual abuse, hopeless poverty.

But what is striking today among psychologists, teachers, and marriage counselors is the large number of seriously wounded and troubled young people who come from *normal* families. Unquestionably, the distinction between normal and dysfunctional in our society has blurred. Or, to look at it another way, some sort of subtle but serious dysfunction is at work in too many typical, middle-class American homes.

Children may grow up in a family where father and mother live together, life is comfortable and physically secure, everyone enjoys the pleasures of a prosperous suburban lifestyle. Yet later on in adolescence and young adulthood, their lives are ravaged by alcohol and other drugs, grievous and ongoing marital discord, professional aimlessness and instability, reckless pleasure pursuit, trouble with the law, shapeless psychological agony, even suicide.

Consider this disturbing fact: The suicide rate among young people in the United States is directly proportional to family income. It is kids from our wealthy and middle-income suburbs, not our destitute inner-city neighborhoods, who most often take their own lives.

What is going on in our supposedly normal middle-class families today that could account for these problems? What is happening at home—or not happening—such that children grow older without growing up, that they arrive at adulthood without enough judgment and will to set their lives straight?

Later on, I will outline what I think are the principal problems in today's normal families, those features of family life that obstruct children's growth in character. But first I'd like to sketch for you a close-up picture, a composite description of the normal picnic-type family in operation.

The Consumerist Family: A Composite Picture

It's worth our while here to look more closely at the consumerist family's typical traits. What follows below is a composite picture of those normal homes where, unfortunately, children are poised for later trouble. That is, if you looked back to the childhood of many troubled adolescents and young adults, as described above, what traits of their family lives would you see over and over again with striking regularity?

Even with plenty of variations in detail, this is the pattern of consumerist families. Let's look at the parents first, then the children.

PARENTS HEADED FOR TROUBLE

Consumerist parents live divided lives. They live as producers at work but consumers at home. In fact, to their children they seem to work only in order to consume. Their home, far removed as it is from the real-life world of responsible adult achievement and ethical dealings with others, is a place arrayed with entertainment gadgets, a site devoted to comfort, relaxation, and amusement. But this universe of comfortable delight is all that their children see—and for children, "seeing

is believing." This cocoon of pleasant escapism wholly enve-
lopes children and shapes their sole experience with life. It
becomes the ambiance within which they fashion their deepest
attitudes and habits, indeed their whole outlook on life: "Life
is all about pleasure."

Being self-absorbed and centered mainly on the present,
consumerist parents seldom think about their children's futures—that is, what sort of men and women their children will
grow up to become. Their time horizon stretches, at most, only
a few months or couple of years ahead. Almost never do they
picture their children as grown men and women in their late
twenties with job and family responsibilities of their own. When
the parents do think of their kids' futures, they think in terms of
career, not character. They think of what their children will *do,*
not what they will *be.*

The parents seem to expect—in fact, utterly take for
granted—that their children will naturally grow up okay as long
as they're kept busily amused and shielded (more or less) from
outside influences. In other words, they think that adult-level
ethics, conscience, and sound judgment will gradually form in
their children in a natural and unaided way, along with the
children's physical stature. When the parents think of character
at all, they think it's something to be *maintained* in children, not
formed from scratch.

The parents come down to the children's level, as indeed all
parents should—but (and here's the point) they *stay* there. By
their own evident devotion to a "hassle-free" existence at home,
off the job, they neglect to raise their children to grown-up
levels of responsible thinking and acting. They do little to
prepare the children for later life and lead them toward responsible service. Indeed, their children seem to have no concept
what "adulthood" means—except for what they see in movies
and TV dramas. The parents seem clueless that they have a job
to do, an action to take, a change to make in their children's
minds, hearts, and wills: to strengthen each child's conscience
and character for life.

Both parents give in readily to children's wishes and "feelings," even when they judge that this might be a mistake. Very
often in family life they permit what they disapprove of; that is,
they let children's pleas and whining override their parental
misgivings. The parents are moved by their children's smiles,
not their welfare; they will give in on many issues to avoid a
confrontational "scene." Unwittingly, through their example of

giving in, these parents teach their children to let strong desires, or even whims, routinely override judgments of conscience. So, the children fail to distinguish between wants and needs; to the children, wants *are* needs. As a result, "feelings," not conscience, become a guide for action. (So, what happens later when the kids are tempted by the powerfully pleasurable sensations of drugs, alcohol, promiscuous sex? What is there to hold them back?)

The father is a weak moral figure in the home. He does not teach right from wrong in a confident, purposeful way, and he does nothing to prepare his older children for their later lives outside the home, especially in moral matters. He defers "children's things" to his wife. To his kids, he appears mostly as an amiable, somewhat dull figure, even a sort of older sibling. In family life, the kids see him wrapped up entirely in his own leisure activities (like watching TV, playing sports) and minor repairs. Because they never see him work, they have no idea how he earns his living, or even what this term means. Moreover, he seldom shows much outward respect and gratitude toward his wife—so she, too, seems a weak figure to the children.

Parents are minimal in the practice of religion. Though the family may attend a house of worship from time to time, even regularly, this is done as thoughtless social routine. Family life includes little or no prayer, not before meals or at any other time. So children never witness their parents living a sense of responsibility toward God or some strong internalized ethic. "God" is only a word (sometimes an expletive), not a person, certainly not a friend. In the children's eyes, parents do not seem answerable to anyone or anything, except a relentlessly busy calendar.

Parents watch television indiscriminately and they allow "adult entertainment" into the home. Though they may restrict, more or less, their children's access to inappropriate material, they are driving home a powerful message: "When you're old enough, anything goes." Consequently, to the children, the right-wrong dichotomy becomes strictly a matter of age: "Whatever's wrong for kids is okay for grown-ups, so just wait till I turn fourteen!"

CHILDREN HEADED FOR TROUBLE

At first glance, most children from homes like this don't seem seriously troubled at all. Typically, they're cheery and well scrubbed, pleasant and smiling, often very active, but only for things they enjoy. They're habituated to pleasant sensations. They like to be liked, and in fact they expect to be liked no matter what they do. Because they're used to treating adults (including their parents) as equals, they appear naïvely lacking in respectful good manners. With some troubled exceptions here and there, they seem entirely carefree. Indeed, most of them really are carefree, for now.

Children have a low tolerance for discomfort or even inconvenience. They are horrified by physical pain, however slight, or even the threat of it. They successfully plead and badger and stall their way out of unpleasant commitments and "hassles"— promises and previous agreements, music lessons, homework, chores, appointments, deadlines.

Children believe that just about anything may be done for a laugh. If a prank or ridiculing remark amuses them and their peers, they blithely indulge in it no matter who gets hurt. They think their entitlement to fun must shove aside other people's rights and feelings. Indeed, the existence of other people's rights and feelings almost never enters their minds. Their outlook on life remains unchanged from infancy: "Me first!"

Children enjoy an abundance of spending money and leisure time. As a fixed habit, they overindulge in soft drinks, sweets, and junk food. They spend countless hours wholly absorbed in electronic sensations (computer games, television, the Internet) and other types of amusement. They are generally free to consume whatever they want whenever they want it, and this they do.

Kids show little or no respect for people outside the family: guests, friends of parents, teachers, salespeople, the elderly. They seldom, if ever, display good manners in public. *Please* and *thank you* are missing from their speech. On birthdays or holidays, children rip through a mound of presents, but they neglect to write or call to say "thank you" to relatives—and see no reason to. In some instances, children may be superficially pleasant to people (as long as this costs them nothing) but have zero concern for others' needs or interests.

Ironically, for all the parents' efforts to provide a pleasant home, the children hold little or no respect for them. The kids view their parents as "nice," and they'll admit they "like" Mom and Dad most of the time. But they simply do not esteem their parents as strong and, therefore, people to emulate. When asked whom they do admire, they rattle off a long list of entertainment figures, especially comedians and rock performers.

Children know next to nothing about their parents' personal histories and nothing at all about grandparents and forebears. So they have no sense of family history and moral continuity, that is, how they are the latest in a long line of mutually loving people who struggled, often heroically, to serve each other and stick together through good times and bad.

The children have no heroes in their lives, no real people or historical or literary figures who surpassed themselves in service to others and, by fulfilling duties, accomplished great deeds. In the absence of heroes, the kids admire and pattern themselves after coarsely freakish media "celebrities" and make-believe cartoonish figures. (As someone said, "If kids have no heroes, they'll follow after clowns.")

Children don't care about causing embarrassment to the family. Often they don't even understand what that might mean, for they have no framework for grasping what's shameful. They are unmoved by any cultivated sense of "family honor." If children's dress and public behavior cause shame to the parents, that's just too bad.

Children complain and whine about situations that can't be helped: bad weather, reasonable delays, physical discomfort, moderately heavy workloads, personality differences, and the like. Their most common word of complaint is "boring." Because their lives at home are micromanaged rather than directed, they're accustomed to having their problems solved by oversolicitous grown-ups. They've found through experience that if they hold out long enough, someone will eventually step in to make their troubles go away. Consequently, they learn to escape problems, not solve them; they learn to shun discomfort, not endure it.

Children have no serious hobbies except television watching, computer games, and listening to music (mostly rhythmic noise). Their lives seem entirely plugged in to electronic devices, and they don't know what to do without them. Their thinking is dominated by the entertainment culture; in some senses, they *believe* in it. They know the words to dozens of songs and commercials, but they know nothing of the Ten Commandments.

Children (even older ones and teens) tend to form opinions by impulse and vague impressions. They are scarcely ever pressed to rely on reasons and factual evidence for their judgments. Thus they're easily swayed by flattery, emotional appeals, and peer-group pressures. They fail to recognize claptrap—as in advertising, pop culture, and politics—when they see it. They follow the crowd wherever it goes. They loosely sense that something is "cool," but they cannot express why.

Children never ask the question "Why?" except to defy directions from rightful authority. They are intellectually dull, even inert, showing little curiosity about life outside their family-school-playground universe. In school, moreover, they're often incorrigibly poor spellers and sloppy writers. That is, they are careless in work and do not take correction seriously. For them, nearly all enjoyment comes from escapist amusement, not from work well done, serious accomplishment, fulfillment of duty, serving others, or personal goals achieved through purposeful effort. If a task isn't "fun," they're not interested.

Children have little sense of time. Because they hardly ever have to wait for something they want, much less earn it, they have unrealistic expectations about the time needed to complete a task. They estimate either too much or too little. Consequently, large tasks are put off too long or small jobs appear mountainous. Even older children approaching high school age have virtually no concept of deadline or of working steadily within a self-imposed time frame. The children seem to drift along in a free-floating, ever-present *now*—and this state of mind continues well into adolescence and even young adulthood.

Throughout high school and college, they view school as one last fling at life, not a preparation for it. Graduation looms as a poignantly sad event, for they see the best part of life as behind them, not ahead. What lies ahead is trouble—the "hassles" (as they put it) of real-life work, responsible commitments, day-to-day routine, budgets and bills, two-week vacations, sharply diminished freedom, and a steep decline in their standard of living. So who looks forward to this? Who can endure it? Why grow up?

As explained already, this picture of a family headed for trouble is only a composite sketch, not a comprehensive description. Certainly there are gradations among families; some families will show some of these characteristics, but not all of them. Nonetheless, over and over again, the features listed here show up in the personal histories of troubled adolescents and young adults who have come—we must stress this again—from apparently normal homes.

3 | *Obstacles to Forming Character*

How has this remarkable situation come about? How is it that normal fathers and mothers—well-meaning people who love their kids—go so far wrong in the upbringing of their children (and then pay for it later)? What is happening, or not happening, in the intact two-parent family such that "normal" and "dysfunctional" are melding together and kids are getting so messed up?

I am not a sociologist and do not pretend to be one. In my efforts to understand what is happening, I have read countless studies about the American family. You could build a sizable bonfire with the number of these published each year. But for what it is worth, I offer you here my own estimates of the problem.

If you are to get a handle on your mission, to see the job you need to carry out, you should be aware of the obstacles you face, the prevailing social trends and attitudes you must grapple with. A smart father, like a smart businessman, needs to understand the pitfalls and obstacles that could impede his job performance and frustrate his ambitions.

As I see it, this is what a conscientious father today is up against:

OBSTACLE: *Many parents and schools see character as something maintained in children, not formed.*

One experienced and extremely level-headed teacher I know, father of four grown children (all excellent young people), told me the following story.

He called in the parents of a twelve-year-old boy who was inattentive and uncooperative in class. The boy's homework, when he did it at all, was sloppy, and he seldom studied for quizzes. Moreover, he often moped around tired and irritable from lack of sleep; he regularly stayed up late watching TV or playing video games. His rather soft body showed him to be, already, a confirmed couch potato, much like his parents.

During the interview, the boy's father sat still in his chair, glancing at his watch, and said almost nothing; his wife did most of the talking. (For experienced teachers, this is a bad sign;

the father is disengaged from his children and probably leaves most of the kids' upbringing to his wife.)

After the teacher explained the problem and pressed the parents to demand more from their son's schoolwork, the mother grew defensive, especially about the excessive TV watching. She said, "I want my son exposed to *everything*. He's basically a happy kid at home, and I want him to stay that way. He's a good kid, and I want him to make his own choices. It's your job to teach him—and it's not his fault if your subject doesn't appeal to him."

The teacher quickly sized up the family situation: the problem is with the parents, not the boy. Silently he noted to himself: So the parents want him exposed to everything, do they? But they've put $3,000 worth of braces in his mouth so he won't be exposed to tooth decay or a poor self-image. How about exposing the boy to some manners? How about some exposure to shouldering responsibility, or managing his affairs, or respecting other people's rights? Why not expose him to the concept of work? What will happen to this boy if he grows up with exclusive exposure to unearned leisure—bathing in a stream of never-ending sense experiences? If he can't say "no" to himself now, then how can he say "no" when he's later exposed to drugs, as all kids are today?

As you may guess, the interview was a failure. So were the parents. So, eventually, was the boy. At age eighteen, two weeks before graduation from high school, his parents presented him with a new car. Six weeks later, after drinking too much beer at a party, he killed himself in a car accident.

For some reason I do not understand, over the past couple of generations our society has formed a romantic, sentimental, and basically flawed concept of childhood. This attitude sees children as near-perfect little creatures, adorable and virtuous, who should be nurtured so as to grow up with all their childhood qualities intact. In other words, children are born virtuous, and it is society that corrupts them. Bad character seeps in from the outside, mostly through idleness in children's lives.

This attitude maintains that to raise children right, parents must keep them relentlessly busy and happy with themselves.

Consequently, so it goes, the children's environment should be one that avoids pain, satisfies all wants as well as needs, is full of pleasant sensations, spontaneous self-expression, and careful arrangement of family life to avoid children's boredom.

Along with all this is the faith—surely that's what it is—that children will naturally grow to become adults who can take care of themselves. As long as the kids are kept active and happily amused, they will manage somehow to grow up fine and eventually enjoy successful careers.

So goes the common belief. There is, of course, some truth to it; if it were completely off base, no one would believe it. After all, small children do have wonderful, charming qualities that they should retain through life: affection for family and friends, simple religious faith (when they're instructed in it), curiosity, love for learning, frankness and simplicity, an inborn tendency toward the truth. And it is certainly true that idleness has to be avoided and harmful outside influences shunted aside.

But the basic problem with this outlook is that it looks *backward*. It looks back to childhood as its frame of reference, not ahead toward children's later lives as adults.

Moreover, and more seriously, it blindly ignores the obvious flaws of childhood—selfishness, poor judgment, unrestrained impulsiveness, irresponsibility, and escapism—which, if uncorrected, will harden into rock-like habits that will burden or crush young people in their later years.

After twenty years in education, I have to say this: parents who are determined to preserve their children just as they are in childhood do indeed manage to succeed at this. That is, the character flaws and self-centeredness of the youngest years remain mostly unchanged, and what was annoying when the kids were in kindergarten becomes monstrous in adolescence. The children's lack of loving parental control in childhood leads to lack of self-control in high school and beyond. Habits of parent-supported indulgence lead to habits of self-indulgence, including instant gratification—all too often embracing drugs, alcohol, and promiscuous sex.

Lack of directive parental authority grows into disregard for other authority, including the law. This can lead to speeding and reckless driving, shoplifting, vandalism, and drug dealing. (Ask any police officer how many apparently normal suburban kids get into trouble with the law.)

Finally, a lifelong passivity—expecting parents to step in and handle all problems—leads to passive anxiety in adulthood, a "victim complex," a free-floating lack of self-confidence or, worse, a self-deceiving overconfidence combined with incompetence.

One sign of this attitude in action today: Children are

micromanaged up to age fourteen or so, and then live virtually without any supervision at all. Many adolescents, having been overmanaged but undirected since childhood, rebel and seek escape from their parents. This flight to escape often takes extremely dangerous turns, and its disastrous results can break parents' hearts.

OBSTACLE: *A related issue—parents fail to think enough about their children's future as grown men and women.*

Let me elaborate here on what I mentioned earlier.

On those occasions when picnic-type parents do think of their children's futures, they think almost exclusively in terms of career: Where will the kids go to college, and how can we afford this? What might they do for a living? How can we get the kids moving on the right educational track leading to a successful career?

Curiously, this future-thinking hardly ever involves assessment of the kids' character. Parents think little, if at all, about their children's later judgment, sense of responsibility, personal courage, and self-control, or how these strengths can influence—far more than a college education—the success or failure of their children's careers.

In other words, these parents think of what their children will *do*, not what they will *be*.

What is really striking to me is how very seldom parents think of their children's future marriages, the state where character counts most. Amazingly, they seem oblivious to the present 50 percent divorce rate and the dangers that future marital breakup could pose to their children's lifelong happiness. Nor do they think about this powerful threat to their own happiness as well: the potential permanent loss of their grandchildren, or their grandchildren growing up in a wounded, fatherless home.

This lack of foresight about children's later character is one of the greatest problems in family life today. Remarkably, we also see it in fathers—men who otherwise take pride in their powers of long-range strategic planning, strengths they routinely exercise in their financial affairs and their jobs.

Let me briefly sketch this problem in historical context.

The shift toward career considerations is a recent development in our society, a result of our prosperity, urbanization, and huge expansion of career options.

Up until a century ago, people's employment in life was

generally quite fixed. A man's daughters would all become homemakers—that is, partners in managing the home, where most farm and craft businesses centered. Most sons would follow their fathers in farming, trading, mining, crafts, and the like. Because children's future lines of work were relatively fixed, parents did not concern themselves overmuch about it. Children learned business careers by watching their parents at work or by joining some craftsmen as young apprentices.

Because career choice, as such, was not a problem, parents thought much more about growth in character and their children's future marriages. They asked some key questions as the kids grew up:

Will our children someday become levelheaded, competent, responsible adults? Will they be ethical and worthy of people's respect?

Will they be known as people who tell the truth and keep their word?

Will they be strong enough to shun allurements that threaten their honor, their chastity, their marriages, and their souls?

Will they have sense enough to marry well and present us with fine grandchildren?

Will their conduct and character bring honor to us, their parents?

Then, with these key questions before them, parents acted to form their children well. Their character-centered vision, projected toward the future, led to direct sacrificial action.

Here is the main point. Successful fathers and mothers today—that is, parents from the sporting adventure homes—still think and act along these lines. They still ask themselves these crucial questions about character. They never allow a busy family life to muddy up their future vision. In fact, their long-term ideal for their children's character gives family life far greater meaning. There's a clear, compelling *purpose* to all their efforts in the children's upbringing.

OBSTACLE: *Children almost never see their father work.*

A friend of mine in Chicago once told me a story from his family lore. This man's brother, a highly successful professional, lived in midtown Manhattan with his wife, also an accomplished business executive, and their five-year-old daughter. Time came for their little girl, Amy, to apply for kindergarten at a tony, highly selective New York school. The child presented herself, all dressed up in her finest, for a personal interview with the school's admissions officer. (Yes, they do such things in Manhattan.)

The school official asked the little girl, "What does your daddy do, Amy?"

After a moment's thought, Amy smiled and replied, "He jogs."

Amused but a bit taken aback, the woman went on to ask, "And what about your mother? What does she do?"

Amy creased her brow, pondered a bit, and then, beaming with delight, said, "She shops!"

Dad jogs and Mom shops—that's all the little girl could see. How many kids today view their parents this way? When and how do children see their parents at the serious business of work?

For centuries, boys and girls witnessed their fathers working at home. Today, this seldom happens. Today's home is not a workplace but rather a site for leisure and relaxation. We can easily forget how recently this change came about and how it has altered children's concept of grown-up life.

The home used to be primarily a place of work, a center of serious, money-making labor, such as farming, or some trade, such as blacksmithing or carpentry or boot-making. In the past, children witnessed Dad and Mom working constantly at home, often together, and all the children had to pitch in their own efforts to make the family enterprise work.

It is said that we don't really know someone until we see him work. When children witnessed their father work, they saw his serious side. They saw him actively exert his character to the fullest. They witnessed him dealing with people in a serious but friendly way. Every day, they saw him contend with obstacles, deadlines, difficult people and circumstances. In countless ways, they viewed his virtues in action: his judgment and ethics, his sense of responsibility, his determination and courage, his self-discipline—in short, all his powers of manhood. The home life powerfully presented a daily, constant lesson about character through example and directed practice and ongoing explanation.

Contrast this past situation with that of family life today. Because nearly every father today works outside the home, and therefore outside his children's vision, kids remain deprived of his powerful example. In fact, unless the father goes out of his way to acquaint his kids with this side of his life, his children view him mostly as a man of leisure.

They see him leave in the morning, disappear from sight, and return at night, often too tired to do much but relax in front of the tube. So his children form only a vague idea of his powers, his strengths of character as practiced on the job, where they work at full-throttle. Children see their dad's character strengths mostly on idle, if they see them at all. If he talks little about his work, and if the children are over-occupied with television-watching themselves, then they have only a muddled notion of what he does for a living, or even what this term means. The kids are left with no real-life framework for understanding adult-level responsibilities.

Moreover—and this is important—the kids have little basis for *respecting* their dad.

Respect nearly always arises, among kids as well as adults, from some perception of strength. If children witness Dad only at rest and play, they have little reason to respect him. Certainly, if he plays sports with them, they may form some respect for his athletic skills, but this is drastically different from respecting his character.

So, if the "play" side of Dad is all the kids witness or, even worse, if he spends gobbets of time staring at the tube with them or by himself, then the kids come to view their father as a sort of large-sized older sibling, a pal around the house. He is, in their perspective, amusing and amiable (up to a point) but not worthy of much respect, certainly not emulation.

But kids must emulate somebody. They are wired this way, especially in late childhood and early adolescence. They search for a life to imitate. If Dad won't do, then they unconsciously turn to father-substitutes, some other adult males who are less dull, more interesting and attractive, more powerful. Someone has to fill the vacuum.

In a great many homes, especially as the children enter adolescence, this vacuum is filled by "celebrities" of all types— entertainers, rock performers, actors, comedians, talk-show hosts. After all, what other interesting, appealing adults do the children see? Of course, these media creatures seldom display great character. Arguably, they display the exact opposite. But they do radiate an attractive aura of power and effortless achievement. Certainly it's all merely theatrical sham, but the kids do not understand this. Seeing is believing.

The point is this: Unless a father is alert to this problem and does something about it, his children may come to regard him as a weak figure. Without his being aware of it, he is competing with rock-culture figures for the hearts and minds of his near-adolescent children, and he can lose this rivalry—with sorrowful or even tragic results—if he never won his children's respect in childhood.

OBSTACLE: *Men underestimate their role in the lives of children entering adolescence, and so they draw back exactly when their children need them most.*

A good friend of mine in New York was driving home one night with his oldest son Matthew, twelve years old, beside him. For some time they stared ahead in silence, when suddenly Matthew blurted out, "Hey, Dad, how about if you and I go to LaGuardia Airport this weekend and watch the planes take off and land?"

The father was so startled (he told me) that he almost swerved off the road. Never before had Matthew shown the slightest interest in planes, or ever proposed anything so offbeat for an outing. He replied, "What on earth would we want to do that for? Where did you ever get such an idea?"

Undeterred, Matthew offered, "Well, we don't have to do that if you don't want to. How about fishing? Could we go fishing somewhere instead? It doesn't matter. We can do whatever you want. . . ." The boy went on to list other things they could do together—a long list, at that.

Gradually it dawned on the father: "My son just wants to be with me, that's all. The activity itself isn't important. He just longs for the two of us to spend time together." This smart father picked up on his son's signals, his boy's eagerness for father-son companionship. From that point on, he went out of his way to spend time with his growing son, and just in time.

There's an important stage of life for children, starting at age nine for girls and about eleven for boys, when their eyes turn to study their father carefully. Unconsciously, they scrutinize how he thinks and acts and reacts to things. They pay much more serious attention to what he thinks, what he says, and the way he lives. Why is this?

Remember that a man carries on his life in two areas, at home and in the world outside. Though both parents may work outside the home, there's nonetheless a strong tendency for children to see their father as "outside-oriented" and their mother as "home-oriented." (One recent study showed that in families where both parents work outside the home, the mother still winds up doing about 80 percent of the domestic work. Countless working mothers could attest to this.)

Up until recently, of course, this dual specialization was true of Western families, and it still holds sway in the rest of the world. In any event, children seem naturally to consider Mom as expert in domestic affairs while Dad specializes in handling matters outside the family's front door. In children's eyes, Dad acts as the bridge between the home and the rest of society.

Also remember that the word "adolescent" used to mean, quite accurately, "young adult." Before the contrivance of our teen-age culture in the mid-twentieth century, the onset of puberty signified the beginning of real adulthood, with nearly all of its serious responsibilities. Consider how many historic figures were undertaking serious work before they were eighteen, and how many adolescent women were either engaged or married by that age.

Today our grammar schools traditionally end at eighth grade because, until early in the twentieth century, young people left school at age thirteen to begin work. Continuing on into high school was relatively rare, and college education was an expensive luxury.

Then as now, puberty brought new powers in life—but at that time in history it also brought new, serious responsibilities. So adolescent powers quickly channeled into productive exercise. Shortly after acquiring power to beget children, young people married. As soon as muscles and minds acquired near-adult powers, young people set out to work on their own. While still in their teens, adolescents were truly grown-up, or nearly so, and thought of themselves that way.

Some historical examples:

—At age seventeen, George Washington worked as chief surveyor for Culpepper County, Virginia, and supervised a staff of assistants; since most wealth in that era derived from land, his was a highly responsible job.

—Thomas Jefferson entered the College of William and Mary when he was fifteen. Alexander Hamilton ran a busy export-import company in the Virgin Islands when he was fourteen.

—When the Marquis de Lafayette offered his services to Washington during the American Revolution, he was nineteen years old; back in France, he left his relatives to care for his beloved wife—whom he had married at sixteen—and his two-year-old daughter.

—Thomas Edison, arguably our greatest inventor, started a business selling goods on board trains, traveling hundreds of miles a week, when he was only thirteen.

—As for girls, most were engaged or married by sixteen, and were busy mothers and home managers by their nineteenth birthday.

In other words, teenagers throughout most of history were grown-ups in everything but experience, and this they gained rapidly.

A parenthesis here: Many adolescent problems today seem to stem from the tensions of extended childhood. Teens have nearly all the physical and intellectual strengths of adults, but they continue to live like large children. They possess powers without balancing responsible outlets. This state of affairs leads to adolescents' boredom—unexercised power—along with its consequent social problems: reckless driving, drug use, petty crime, vandalism, and other thrills. In a real sense, this is hardly the kids' fault. Just as gamma radiation is perilous if unfocused, so too, if powers have no responsible outlet, they lead to mayhem.

To get back to the point: This perfectly natural drive toward independence begins slowly a couple of years before puberty. Intuitively, it seems, children sense they will soon be leaving home. Because Dad is perceived as the expert in affairs outside the family, then his children turn toward him as a guide. He serves as a model and mentor for successful endeavor in the outside world they will soon enter.

This process of watching Dad more closely is gradual and subtle, but it's quite real. Boys and girls ask more questions of their father. They like to spend time with him, be around him more often, pay attention to his judgment about affairs, find out more about his professional and ethical dealings with others.

In this dynamic, the father plays an extremely important role in his children's ethical judgment. In the earlier years, his wife did most of the work in forming the children's conscience, or at least did it more often than her husband. He backed her up, of course, but she imparted most of the teaching about right and wrong. *Now, as the children approach adolescence, the father's role is to show his kids how their mother's lessons also apply to the world outside.*

For instance:

—We put our best efforts at home into our chores and home-work—and we do the same later with our jobs. Sloppiness leads to unemployment.

—We practice good manners in the family—and we must do the same at work and in society.

—We tell the truth and keep our word at home, and we must do this in the workplace. In business, whoever lies or breaks promises loses his job.

—We respect parents' authority—and all other authority as well, including bosses and the law. What is called "obedience" at home is called "teamwork" on the job. In real grown-up life, everybody answers to somebody.

—We respect the rights of siblings—and must respect the rights of everyone in society.

—Parents punish wrongdoing—so does the law.

And so on. In other words, a father gives final, mature form to his children's lifelong conscience: *"Everything we've taught you about right and wrong at home is also the way we adults live as honorable, responsible, considerate people."*

In addition to all this, there's another subtle dynamic at work.

As boys approach adolescence, they look to their father as a model of manly accomplishment: the way one lives as a man. As young teens, they may question or even defy their father's moral judgments on given points, but they are really looking for the adult-level reasoning behind them. They want to know why he draws the line where he does. And sometimes Dad needs to show this line clearly by putting his foot down.

Interestingly, girls also study their father very closely. Intuitively they are sizing him up as a model, a living pattern, for evaluating other men. Adolescent girls who know their father well and deeply respect him tend to use him as a standard for assessing males their own age.

If a father gives respectful affection to his daughters, they are generally careful about the ways they give and receive affection in their dealings with young men. Dad sets the standards. In fact, it seems that a young woman who deeply respects her father is attracted most strongly to suitors who resemble him, especially in his strength of character. She often winds up marrying a man who unconsciously reminds her of Dad.

In many families today, unfortunately, men are oblivious—blind and deaf—to their pre-teen children's overtures for attention and conversation. Typically such men long ago formed, and still retain, a habit of handing off children's matters to their wives. They fail to see how their children are changing, not simply growing. (Children grow, but adolescents change.)

Besides, many men approaching forty often find themselves wrapped up with midlife concerns of their own. Inwardly they grapple with and worry about greater pressures at work, larger bills to pay, some concern about those first gray hairs and hints of declining physical strength. Though they may not suffer a wild and crashing midlife crisis, they're still inclined to spend too much time in self-absorption. Just when their children need them most, during this tiny window of opportunity, they are far less available and attentive than they were in their children's infancy.

Result? In full-blown adolescence, kids turn instead to their peers for leadership and confidence-building support. Boys hunt elsewhere for role models and find them in the entertainment industry. Girls let emotions and peer pressures determine their attitudes toward males and have a weak framework for evaluating boys their age. They may wind up giving their hearts to anyone—and breaking the hearts of their parents.

OBSTACLE: *Parents have to compete with electronic entertainment for their children's serious attention.*

Before the era when electronic media burst upon family life in a big way, fathers and mothers enjoyed their children's undivided attention. Every day, children personally witnessed their parents carry out responsible work and then relax with healthy recreation, and children joined them in both work and play. Because the home was fairly quiet, children overheard parents talking with each other and with siblings, live-in relatives, and neighbors. In this way, through the give-and-take of conversation in family life, the kids learned adult ways of thinking, reacting, and judging.

Free time in the home was filled with chatting, reading, games and puzzles—activities of the mind. Moreover, kids had time and incentive to read and to do homework carefully.

In many Western families today, maybe most, these healthy family interactions have practically disappeared. Children, often led by parents' example, spend hours in isolated, trance-like gaze at a cathode-ray tube. Or they push buttons in a hectic stupor with video games or the Internet, totally self-absorbed in frenetic, often violent fantasies. In some homes children retreat to their rooms, drawn away from the family entirely, to keep company with television and their computer and no one else.

Today fathers themselves often retire to an armchair, sitting silent and motionless for hours before the tube, inert as a potted plant. These men seem totally unaware, completely clueless, about an important fact of life: elsewhere in the house their children are growing older—but they are not growing up.

Children need time to learn from their father's actions and spoken judgments. What children learn in the first sixteen or eighteen years will fix how they live for the fifty years of life that follow. But today this time spent together is severely truncated, extremely brief. In the sixteen hours of wide-awake time each day, kids typically spend only a sliver of time in Dad's company, no more than a couple of hours, if that. And if the TV blares on for hours, kids' time with Dad is reduced to minutes, certainly less than a half-hour a day. This is precious little time to teach so much, and it's an irreplaceable resource. All this is why isolated television watching, by fathers and children, works to corrode the bonds between them. The tube is a rival for children's attention.

What's more, electronic entertainment also acts as a rival for the parents' authority. Television is a powerful authoritative force in young people's lives. The sociological documentation for this force is monumental.

Consider this: When teens and young adults today are asked to list people they admire, they nearly always name entertainers and other public figures appearing on television. Rarely do they mention their parents; almost never do they cite "my dad."

When children in a picnic home see their parents share their addiction for haphazard TV watching, then they tend to see Dad and Mom as *equals*—passive fellow captives, simply part of the audience, more like consumerist enjoyers than powerful producers, followers rather than leaders.

On the other hand, when parents exercise discerning control over TV watching, keeping it to a rationally planned minimum, they seem in the children's eyes as more powerful than their rival. Because TV is powerful, whoever controls it is even more powerful. Both parents clearly show themselves in charge of things. Unquestionably they emerge as leaders in the home.

This rivalry takes yet another form. Conscientious fathers and mothers want their children to grow in the virtues, yet television glamorously portrays the *opposite* of virtues.

Kids need repeated practice in logical, discriminating judgment; but TV presents them with waves of shapeless sensory stimulation, not thought.

Children need living examples of patient, determined, purposeful effort; but television portrays quick fixes, easy escapes, and violent resolution of conflicts.

Youngsters need heroic figures of self-sacrificing courage, generosity, and gracious self-restraint; but television glamorizes coarseness, profanity, emotional excess, and material self-indulgence.

Children need encouragement to read; but television replaces reading and even seems to ignore its existence: When was the last time you saw someone on TV reading a book?

In short, conscientious parents want to weave a tapestry in family life for their children to learn from, a fabric of realistic, upright living. Television works to unravel it.

None of this implies, of course, that electronic entertainment has no legitimate place in the home. On the contrary, television and its related devices can benefit a family under certain conditions: when it is of good quality, when it brings family members together in conversation (as with sports events), and when it's kept under parents' discriminating control.

The media are not enemies as such, but rivals, and especially rivals for children's attention to Dad. A smart father knows this fact and acts on it. He treats the media like powerfully devious rivals in any other important contest—that is, he watches them warily and will not let them win.

OBSTACLE: *Our prolonged prosperity has transformed our children and adolescents into a leisure class.*

Throughout history, most societies harbored a tiny, wealthy aristocracy (or its equivalent) that used its riches and power to live as a leisure class. What were the main features of this prosperous elite? And why do its features look so familiar? Think about it . . .

• The leisure class did no serious productive work. It lived off unearned income—that is, someone else's money.

• Members of this class lived entirely as consumers. Their only positive function in the economy was to spend money.

• They enjoyed extraordinary benefits: good health and medical care, regular meals, relative safety, secondary-level and university education, warm and comfortable surroundings, time and freedom to travel, rich and varied entertainment summoned up at will, plenty of free time to enjoy sports and parties.

• They also suffered from the vices linked with wealth and power: frenetic flight from boredom, alcohol and drug abuse, preoccupation with amusement, sexual promiscuity, marital infidelity, nearly total ignorance about their society's serious social problems—and heartless indifference to others' suffering.

It doesn't take much imagination to see how these features apply today to large numbers of our young people. Not to all, by any means, but to a strikingly big percentage. If you doubt this, take a close look at the weekend scene among teenagers in any suburban shopping mall, or what life is like in a typical college dormitory. Life among many teens and college students today looks remarkably like the French aristocracy's way of life at Versailles sometime in the mid-1700s.

Unlike history's elites, though, our own young leisure class faces a serious problem: most young people will not inherit great wealth. At some point, usually in their early to mid-twenties, they must take on the serious responsibilities of work and family—that is, a decrease in leisure's delights and an increase in the normal challenges of adult life. Having known little or nothing but fun sensations since infancy, they face the prospect of adulthood with wariness and apprehension. (Talk with some anxious college seniors and you'll see what I mean.) From their perspective, sadly, the best years of life are behind them.

This state of affairs produces little incentive for growing up. Many young adults work hard to learn a marketable skill and earn a decent living. But their personal lives, the hours off the job, show a relentless drive to continue the hassle-free irresponsibility of their youth, a refusal or inability to grow up. Young people shuttle between drudgery during the week and debauchery on the weekends. When they marry, they treat their children—if they choose to have any—like playmates or pets around the house. They bribe their kids with gadgets and amusements, striving to keep hassles to a minimum. They expect their spouses to coddle them the way their parents did. By force of habit, they are takers, not givers, and this selfishness eats away like acid on their marriages. They put things ahead of people, and often treat people like things. Underneath their pleasure-seeking, they are anxious and lonely, unsure of themselves or what they really stand for. For them, married life consists of shared amusements punctuated by boredom, freefloating complaints, and strife.

▲ ▲

There is not much you can do, certainly, to change these trends in our society.

But there's a great deal you can do with your children to raise them right. Many young people today are brought up well at home, and they grow to become responsible, competent adults who live for others' welfare. Your own children should be—*must* be—among them.

All of these significant problems have wormed their way into family life for some time now, almost three generations. Together they form a challenge to you as you move ahead in your all-out efforts to raise your children right. As your children grow to adulthood and (you hope) to real maturity, you will have to draw on all your resources of intelligence, dedication, and sacrificial love—the full measure of your powers as a man.

This thought leads us to yet another, more subtle obstacle you may face.

A significant number of men today, maybe including yourself, are unsure of themselves in their role as a father. They want to do the right thing with their children but they are uncertain what this means, or how they are really expected to carry out the job.

No surprise. Many men today grew up in the family landscape sketched above. They hardly ever saw their dad work. They lived in a home with too much entertainment and not enough role modeling. They had few demands made of their powers before age twenty-one. Their parents, for whatever reason, never schooled them purposely in strength of character. Indeed very many men, especially over the last generation, had no father in the home at all. They had no confident, admirable male leader to follow, and so they do not know what to do or how to do it.

In other words, the past few decades—say, since the end of World War II—have seen a break, gradual and deep, in the process by which fathers passed on to their children the collective wisdom of fatherhood built up over centuries: the great life-lessons that men taught their children by example, directed practice, coaching conversation, and encouragement. This has left today's fathers shakily uncertain how to approach their greatest responsibility. Sad to say, far too many men remain unaware they even have a character-forming responsibility. They do not learn until their children move through adolescence and into young adulthood, when it's practically too late.

So, if you're uncertain about what to do, you have plenty of company.

But you also have reason for hope. If history has taught us anything, it's that human beings possess incredible powers of resilience, unsuspected resources of strength in the face of great challenges. Some of history's greatest men of accomplishment—Washington, Jefferson, Hamilton, Lafayette, Robert E. Lee, Isaac Newton, to name only a few—came from single-parent homes.

When we must, when we have no choice, we can survive and triumph even without "necessities." In the final analysis, success in life—as a father or anything else—is a matter of far-seeing vision inspired by some great passionate love.

4 | *Focus on Your Children's Character*

It is time to hone in on what "character" means. I've used this word in previous chapters, and I've hinted at its meaning. Because forming children's character is the mainspring of a father's mission, he needs to know what he is doing. It's time to shape up a clear working concept, a practical understanding.

Character is a spiritual quality that resides in the mind and will and heart. Like other spiritual qualities we admire in people—charisma, courage, willpower, healthy self-confidence, "class"—character is elusive to define but fairly easy to detect. We recognize character when we spot it in people, and we grow distressed, or at least uneasy, when we see it missing among people we must live with or depend upon.

Let's circle around the meaning with some commonsense descriptions; then we can target in with more precision.

• As a wise person once said, character is what we have left over if we ever go broke. Character is what each of us *is*, minus our money and possessions.

• Character is the aggregate of qualities that people esteem in us despite our personal shortcomings. In fact, it's what they admire about us in the way we cope with our shortcomings. (For instance, it's easy to respect a man who admits he's a "recovering alcoholic" and struggles to overcome his problem.)

• Character is what people admire in us besides our talents and acquired skills. People can possess outstanding talents and skills but still lack character. (For examples, read the sports page and look at the glaring, even destructive personal flaws of unquestionably gifted athletes. Or glance around your place of work: our business world suffers no shortage of technically skilled barbarians.)

• Character is what employers hunt for when they read between the lines of prospective employees' résumés and references.

• Character is what makes people proud to have us as friends, not merely as acquaintances. It is what makes friendships last a lifetime.

• Character is what children long to see in their parents. It's what children unconsciously imitate in their parents' lives. It is the measure by which they later judge other adults and even their own peers. A man's character is what moves his sons to yearn to be like him when they grow up—and his daughters to marry a man, someday, exactly like him.

Because character is so slippery an idea, we need a framework of some sort to think about it, a rational breakdown into components. Here I will show you the one I have found most helpful. It comes with a pedigree more than two thousand years old, a scheme originally devised by the Greeks.

The ancient Greeks had a lot to say about character. Removed as they were from our messy, complicated world of computers, nuclear weapons, and complex gadgets, they formed a clear and unsurpassed insight into human nature. Though they lived imperfect lives—they massacred whole peoples and practiced infanticide—the best minds among them still thought deeply about ethics, goodness, beauty, and truth. After two millennia, we still turn to them for wisdom because they make us think.

To the greatest minds of antiquity, especially Aristotle, character appears as an integration of what they termed the virtues, those powers of mind and will and heart built up through repeated practice: *prudence, justice, fortitude,* and *temperance.* Character, to them, is the sum total of these habitual powers joined together in one's personality. It determines what we are at the center of our very self, our soul. And it directly affects how we go about living with others.

Unfortunately, in our own era a couple of these ancient terms have suffered from a bad press. *Prudence* today has taken on a negative meaning: a timidity or excessive calculation, a kind of fearful hesitation in the face of some tough situation. *Temperance,* likewise, has taken on a twisted meaning: abstinence from alcohol, a prudish hostility toward spirited drink.

For the sake of a much clearer understanding, and your confident fatherly action, I suggest you consider the great virtues—that is, character strengths—in more modern-day, commonsensical terms:

— Prudence is *sound judgment and conscience.*
— Justice is *a sense of responsibility.*
— Fortitude is *courage, persistence, "guts."*
— Temperance is *self-mastery, self-discipline, self-control.*

To these four classical concepts of virtue, I will add another inner strength drawn from our Judeo-Christian ethic, that of *heart.* (The ancient Greeks were, in many ways, a heartless people.) This is *generosity, magnanimity, charity, a capacity for compassionate understanding and forgiveness.* In religious terms, it is faith, hope, and charity.

I will explain these virtues in detail throughout the rest of this book. But before we move on, I must lay out a couple of ideas you need to understand at the outset, for they are crucial to your job as a father. They are the foundation stones for what a man builds up in his children.

First, kids do not come into the world with these virtues. For sure, small children shine with many beautiful qualities, features that charm us and move us to love them. But—let's face it frankly—they do not start out in life with sound judgment, responsibility, courageous perseverance, or self-mastery. These powers must be built from scratch as the children grow up—or else the children grow up without them.

To put your challenge another way, children come into the world with the exact opposite of these virtues. Despite youngsters' charms and cuteness, children are driven by fuzzy and emotional thinking, irresponsible self-centeredness, escapism, and a constant compulsion to self-indulgence. They live as *me*-centered hedonists, given over to gratifying their passions and appetites at once, and determined to impose their wills on everyone around them, sometimes by manipulation and occasionally by force.

Anyone who doubts this should talk for a while with any experienced teacher or parent. Or spend a couple of days monitoring a school playground. Or watch and listen as young kids wildly misbehave when out shopping with their parents. (Why is it we notice flaws and vices more readily in other people's kids?)

The second key point, related to the above, is this: Your job as a father is to collaborate with your wife to make sure your children do not grow up this way—as thoughtless, self-centered, impulsive, irresponsible hedonists and manipulators or bullies. *Your job is to teach your children habitual powers of sound judgment, responsibility, courageous perseverance, self-control, and heart. This is the core responsibility of fatherhood.*

The universal experience of the human race is this: to fail at this job, to see your kids grow up with their childhood flaws still intact, all you have to do is . . . nothing.

To do nothing is to court disaster. If you neglect your responsibility as father—if, for instance, you leave the job of upbringing to your wife—you may find one day (as, tragically, so many men do in our country) that your children have grown into teens and young adults with their childish vices still fixed firmly in place. At age fifteen or twenty or twenty-eight, your physically grown-up children could be six-foot high versions of what they were at age two. As young adults, they could still live as self-centered pleasure-seekers, dominated by out-of-control appetites (including for drugs), men and women who are irresolute and irresponsible and virtually incapable of serving other people—even if they wanted to.

Please understand this, for it is vitally important: *Your children will not grow up when they can take care of themselves. They will really and truly grow up only when they can take care of* others—*and want to.*

So, to work change in your children, to lead them to become men and women of strong character is your great challenge as a father. It is the greatest responsibility of your life as a man. And, no matter what else you accomplish in your career, to succeed at this—to have your children grow up this way—will be your life's greatest achievement.

Forming Character

I have sketched these great character strengths in outline here, but they are real. To flesh out your understanding, please pause for a moment to think about those people you have most esteemed in life—parents, relatives, neighbors, bosses and co-workers, figures in public life. List them by name and think about their outstanding qualities.

Didn't you admire them for their powers of mind, will, and heart? Didn't they show excellent judgment, wisdom, a refined conscience of right and wrong? How did they show their ethical uprightness? What kind of courage did they bring either to solving problems or to living with them patiently? Didn't they show thoughtfulness for others' needs and sensibilities? Weren't they on top of life, enjoying life to the fullest but without going overboard? Didn't they always seem to put people ahead of things? Weren't they fun to be with, enjoyable to work with?

Your children can grow up to become like these admirable people.

How do parents do this? How do young people grow in character at home? The collective experience of family life everywhere shows that children learn character in three ways, and in this order:

- First, *example*: what children witness in the lives of their parents and other adults whom they respect.
- Second, *directed practice*: what children are led to do, or are made to do repeatedly (despite their resistance), by parents and other respected adults, such as coaches, grandparents, and mentors.
- Third, *word*: what children hear from parents and others as *explanation* of what they witness and are led to do.

Let me focus in more closely on these three ways of learning. They are an outline of your role as an effective father.

EXAMPLE

You teach character to your children mostly through your own example, and, if I may put it this way, when you are least aware of it.

You have probably noticed already that children have selective hearing, a kind of filter that screens out unpleasantries such as their parents' scoldings and corrective criticism. They sometimes listen, sometimes do not, and it's often hard to tell how much of what you say is sinking in.

But—and this is the main point—they see everything. They miss nothing in their line of sight. Their eager young eyes, like their lithe little bodies, are constantly in motion, roving and scanning, noticing every detail of their parents' lives. Children are wired this way: to observe how adults, mostly their parents, go about the business of living.

If what they witness in you and your wife are your powers of character—your judgment, responsibility, toughness, self-control, generosity—they pay serious attention. They perceive confident, adult-level strength in you, and this perception leads to their respect for you. Children must, above all, deeply respect their parents, and (I cannot stress this too much) all respect derives from perception of strength.

This respect, in turn, leads children unconsciously to imitate their parents, to emulate their thinking and behavior, their attitudes and values. In this way, over the course of years children grow unconsciously, gradually, to adopt their parents' character.

In other words, you and your wife are teaching most about the virtues when you scarcely recognize it. Your snatches of conversation, your reactions to events (good and bad), your exertion in work and play, your comments on the news, your humor, whatever angers or delights you, even the look in your eyes—all these perceptions seep into the minds and hearts of your children. In fact, what children *overhear* at home is at least as important as anything you say to them directly, often more so.

So, please think about this.

Where, under what circumstances at home, do your children witness you living responsibly?

In what ways do they see you stick with a task, refusing to quit?

How do they learn about your thoughtful judgment, your ethical principles? What do they overhear at home—or is TV noise drowning you out?

How do you *show* them that your consider their mother the greatest woman alive? Where and when do they see you exercise self-controlled moderation in food, drink, and entertainment, even work itself?

Do they ever see you work, when your character strengths are on full throttle?

Do they see you practice courtesy (*please, thank you,* and actions that convey these attitudes) toward your wife and guests?

Under what circumstances do they witness other adults showing respect toward you?

In sum, no man can teach character effectively unless he first sets an example for what he expects of his children. If you want to be a good father, you must first struggle to be a good man.

DIRECTED PRACTICE

Let's not forget, virtue is a habit of living rightly—and all habits are built by repeated practice. You, as a father, must lead your children to *act,* to learn by doing.

A wise and savvy father is shrewd enough to understand this rock-solid reality: Kids are acquiring habits, whether good or bad, all the time. Children form habits from whatever they practice over and over again, whether virtue or vice.

Think about it: If they're inert every day, they grow up lazy. If they wait for adults to clean up their messes, they will never clean up after themselves. If they're pressed to read every day, they become readers. If they absorb large daily doses of TV, they grow up as couch potatoes and fervid fans of "celebrities." If they always get their way, they never learn self-control. If they say "please" and "thank you" often enough, they come to voice these words on their own; if not, they remain callously rude. If they make their beds each morning, they turn this into an unthinking part of their daily ritual. If they redo sloppy homework each night, they learn to do it right the first time. And on and on. *Every single day, the kids are forming permanent habits—the question is, which ones?*

This is where your real work comes in as a father. This is where you make sacrificial effort every day, for years, to turn your children's daily habits of living into lifelong virtues.

You lead children to become responsible by directing them to live responsibly—to carry out their chores and do their homework to the best of their ability, to clean up their own messes, to live with the consequences of their neglect, to practice good manners in the family and outside the home, to tell the truth and keep their word.

You teach them justice by correcting their rudeness and selfish disregard for others' rights, especially with their siblings. You teach right from wrong by giving swift, just punishment for wrongdoing—and sincere praise when they do right. You make them apologize.

You teach them fortitude by encouraging them to persevere in a tough task, not to be a whiner or quitter. You do not manage their affairs but rather *direct* them; that is, you do not do their work for them or micromanage their efforts. Instead, you show them what to do and then say, "Try it this way; you can do it on your own." You do not step in unless they've first given an earnest best effort; then you show them how the job is done and help them learn from mistakes. As someone wise once said, "Courage is the memory of past successes." In this way, you lead them to grow in confidence from putting their powers up against challenges. Their self-confidence grows from your confidence in them.

You teach healthy, realistic self-esteem from work well done, and so you engender in them the beginnings of a lifelong sense of professionalism. If their work is messy and careless, you press them to do it over again, and then praise them when it's done right.

In short, you teach them an all-important lesson about life: comfort and convenience are only by-products of a successful life, not its purpose. We are here to serve others with our powers—that's what adult life is really all about. You lead them, through concrete directed action, to forget about their self-centered interests—as you do—and contribute to the needs and welfare of the family. All this, you foresee as a father, is practiced preparation for their later lives as husbands and wives, fathers and mothers, workers and citizens.

As a father, you never let up and never give up until your children have the powers to live rightly on their own.

One smart father told me his experience teaching his two daughters to pick up the mess in their rooms. He said: "I kept telling my girls that they were old enough by now (ages nine and eleven) to keep their rooms clean, but the messes continued. Their habits of sloppiness from childhood remained unchanged, and this was driving my wife crazy.

"It occurred to me that my girls may not understand the starting-point concept of 'clean room,' so I decided to teach them myself. I set up what I called 'the Ten-Minute Drill.' That is, I went into their room and picked up their things with them—the three of us together, working to finish the job in ten minutes. At the end, when everything was shipshape, I pointed around the room and said, 'This, girls, is a clean room. Understand?'

"This I did with them two or three nights a week for a couple of months. At one point, then, I told them to go do it on their own. By then they knew what I was talking about; I showed them my standards for order. When I inspected their room, naturally I praised them for their work, told them I was proud of them, which pleased them a lot. I also showed them how little time it takes to accomplish something when we really set our minds to a job. Their work wasn't perfect every time thereafter, but we made serious progress."

WORD

Finally, verbal explanation.

For some reason I've never understood, many fathers believe that talks—lectures, scoldings, reprimands, and the like—are the principal way of forming children's character. This is positively untrue. Parental example and parent-directed practice are far more powerful. Talk in any form is most effective, maybe only effective, when it acts to *explain* or *remind* children about what they witness and are led to do in family life.

In other words, verbal explanation works mostly to form children's judgment and conscience—to give a rational understanding, a due importance, to the parents' ongoing example and their requirements for living the other virtues: responsibility, persevering toughness, self-control, and a spirit of generous forgiveness.

For instance, you and your wife say *please* and *thank you* to each other and insist that your children do the same. Repeatedly you explain why: because other people have dignity, rights, and feelings, and so we're obligated to show respect.

Another instance: You and your wife put things back where they belong, and you make your children do likewise. You explain that grown-up adults dislike messes and no one should have to search for something mislaid through someone else's self-centered carelessness. Others' needs take priority, always, over our own sloth and sloppiness.

Another: You and your wife stick with a job around the house until it's done right, and you make the kids follow suit with their chores and homework. You explain the importance of work well done and the disgrace of being a slacker or quitter. Looking ahead to their futures, you explain how in the grown-up world of work, everyone is routinely expected to turn out high-quality performance. This adult-level power to put out our best work takes years of practice, and it must begin in childhood.

Yet another example: You and your wife refuse to watch programs or Internet sites that treat human beings as things, and you won't permit such programs in your house. You explain your ethical convictions and how you and your family strive to live by them. When the children are adults, you explain to them, they can direct their own families in light of their own convictions, which you hope will be the same as yours. But in the meantime, it's your home and therefore your decision about what's allowed and what's not—period.

The rest of this book will spell out many other examples of these lessons to give your children. The point here is that you and your wife must rely on talk to help the children grasp *why* you live the way you do and *why* you press them to do the same: "This is the way competent, responsible, considerate adults behave before God and others—the way you must live when you grow up as adolescents and adults. Your mother and I direct you and correct you because we love you."

As any parent who has spent time in the trenches will tell you, children often resist this lesson giving; they will not understand, or will heatedly refuse to understand, what you tell them. This rebellion flares up especially during the two most troublesome times of children's lives: at ages two to five, and again at thirteen to seventeen. These are emotional times of life, and strong feelings skew perception and mess up motivations. All the same, you and your wife steel yourselves and patiently persevere. You live by the granite faith that someday, sooner or later, your kids will understand. At some point, maybe years from now, they will remember what you said, and your lessons will finally sink in, especially when they start their own families. (Hasn't this happened to you already? Don't you have a clearer grasp and appreciation now for your own parents' loving corrections?)

What I want to underscore here is that directed practice builds habits, while verbal explanations—heart-to-heart talks, strong corrections, scoldings, and the like—build judgment, conscience, attitudes, values. Talk alone can never replace parental example and directed practice. Rather, it strengthens good habits, and roots them in place for keeps by explaining the reasons behind them.

So, conversation between parents and kids is hugely important, and this takes stretches of time. This is why the electronic media—the biggest thief of time in family life—must be kept under reasonable control. A father needs all the time he can get to talk with his kids, especially in matters that will form their consciences.

It seems to be a fact of life: *For most people, the voice of conscience is the voice of their parents—the memory of their parents' lessons about right and wrong.*

A good father teaches his children, in the first place, to love and honor his wife. Your children should hear you explain what a wonderful woman their mother is, and why you think so. Draw your children's serious attention to the great qualities and beauty you see in her: why you came to love her, and still do.

Every time you do this, you strengthen her authority over them, especially when you're physically away from home. The effect seems to be proportional: the more a man honors his wife, the more the children respect her authority and give way to it.

In subtle and indirect ways, too, you direct your daughters to imitate their mother's character. And you show your sons the kind of great woman they should someday hope to marry.

Your conversations with your children should lead them to grasp the whole range of your judgment, values, personal convictions, and sense of family honor. You explain your family's history as best you know it: how the children's forebears were such strong, courageous people. (The generation who struggled through the Great Depression and World War II were truly heroic.) You tell them stories about your work, what you do for a living each day. (Because they probably don't see you on the job, you must tell them about it. If you fail to do this, how will they know?) You explain current events, your impressions of prominent figures in the news, and people past and present whom you respect—and why.

Children should grow to know their dad's thinking so well that they can predict how he'd react to almost anything.

And, of course, you should *listen*. You can learn so much from listening closely to your children—their own growth in judgment and conscience, their worries and self-doubts, their problems. Kids' problems seem small, even laughably petty to adults, but they're big burdens to children; when you listen, you can better understand and explain and encourage.

Many fathers have had this experience: If you listen to your children when they are small, they will be open and sincere with you when they're adolescents, and this is vitally important. At the time of their lives that's most uncertain and fearful, they will turn to you for guidance, lean on your manly strength, rely on your judgment, draw confidence from your fatherly love.

Please bear this in mind: In my long experience with teenagers, I've found that adolescents who deeply love and respect their fathers remain virtually immune to dangerous peer pressures and untouched by the rock-sex-drugs culture. Their dad's character is the measure by which they judge their peers.

Another important thought here: When you chat with your children, be sure to *listen with your eyes*. Children are sensitive to what they see in their parents' eyes. Make eye contact with them, your daughters especially, to show you give them your whole attention; that's how important they are to you. When they look into your eyes, let them see your manly affection for them, your hopes for their future, your pride in their growing character.

5 | *More about Character*

We're still looking at the big picture of a father's mission here—to build up his children's character—but now I want to sharpen the focus, show the virtues in clearer detail, make the job description more specific.

Every serious job calls for some sort of conceptual framework—a way of considering the overall project from several fixed, diverse points of view. An architect has to think of clients' needs and preferences, budget limits, layout of the land, zoning restrictions, access to utilities, and so forth. And any entrepreneur starting up a company has to look at financing, accounting, marketing, personnel requirements, and operations management.

What I'm outlining here is a useful frame of reference for a man's mission as a father. If you are like most men today, you need a framework for seeing your way clear to your children's growth in maturity and then smartly acting within that framework. Life today is so frenetic and confusing, a man needs some rational, sensible approach to separating out his mission's components.

I've already outlined this fivefold framework: sound judgment, a sense of responsibility, courage, self-mastery, and greatness of heart. For years I used this breakdown to advise and encourage fathers about their family job, and many men gratefully told me how much it helped them.

Once you see these commonsense components (all interrelated, of course), you can start to act effectively and confidently. After this chapter, the rest of the book will show *how* fathers and mothers work to build each of these virtues. But before we move into the *how*, we need to finish mapping out the *why*—What are we trying to accomplish here?

Veteran fathers will tell you: If the *why* is strong enough and clear enough, you can figure out most of the *how* for yourself.

In family life as in business or even war, if a strategy is clear and the goal passionately sought after, then tactics don't matter so much. If you know what you are after, you can afford to improvise, experiment, approach from different angles, try what other men have done, and even make mistakes along the way. As long as you keep moving toward your objective—relentlessly, courageously, without giving up or letting up—you have a fighting chance of winning in the end.

One smart father explained his philosophy to me like this: "When I was taking driving lessons a long time ago, my father gave me some good advice. He said that when a driver is approaching a tight squeeze—with only a foot or so of space, or less, on each side of the car—he should aim ahead, look past the obstacle, and keep driving. He shouldn't be so overcautious as to slow to a crawl and fearfully glance back and forth between the sides, struggling to gauge the space in fractions of an inch. If you do this, he said, you might hit something or get hit from behind because you're moving too slow. He said that as long as you look straight ahead and keep moving, then somehow, mysteriously, you'll pass safely on through.

"I've found that this works with being a dad, too. Don't get hung up and paralyzed by problems along the way. Just look ahead to your kids' future and keep heading there, no matter what. Somehow, mysteriously, it works; you bypass the obstacles and forge ahead. In parenting as in driving, I think, it's confidence that keeps you going."

So, here, one by one, are the strengths your children should have fixed like granite in their minds and wills and hearts before they leave your home for good.

SOUND JUDGMENT

Want some examples of bad judgment, unbelievably dumb mistakes made by teens and young adults? Read your newspaper, or talk with a few teachers and marriage counselors, or look carefully around your workplace. Here is a dismal sampling:

• A middle-aged woman executive (from a fatherless home) gives a sworn deposition for a lawsuit her company is fighting. During the questioning, it's revealed that she had lied on her résumé: she never received the MBA degree she had claimed for years, ever since starting her career. The next day she is fired, her career ruined.

• A young woman marries a man whom her parents and friends had warned her about—a lightweight, lazy, selfish, barely employable jerk. Her emotions blind her to what everyone else can see. Two years later, the man dumps her for somebody else and leaves her to care for their newborn son.

• A sixteen-year old boy gets his license and drives his family car for four months, each time with increasing speed and recklessness. Since he was about ten, he had a habit of tinkering with the car's radio and tape deck while riding as a front-seat passenger. Despite his parents' warnings, he keeps up this habit, even though he is now a driver sitting behind the wheel. One evening, while driving alone at high speed, he takes his eyes off the road for a few seconds to fiddle with the tape deck, trying to find a favorite song. He smashes into an oak tree and kills himself.

• Two fifteen-year-old girls from fatherless homes are hanging out on a street corner at 2:30 in the morning (something no normal father would allow) and are approached by a group of low-life youths in a car, all strangers to them. After a brief conversation, the girls accept their invitation to go for a ride. An hour later, both girls are raped and then dropped on the street.

• A bright and popular college student serves as class officer and controls large sums of money allocated by the university for student government expenses. He "borrows" several thousand dollars to pay off hefty debts run up on his credit cards. His embezzlement is discovered, and he is expelled from college. His future career chances are, to say the least, in doubt.

So much for bad judgment. How can we understand its opposite: thinking like a mature, responsible adult? Here are some ways of looking at it—ways that you can explain to your children:

(i) Fundamentally, sound judgment is the power of *discernment*. That is, it's the *acquired ability to make distinctions*, especially the great distinctions in life—truth from falsehood, good from evil, right from wrong. (More on this below.) On the moral plane—that is, in the interplay between rights and duties—it is our conscience.

Related to this, judgment is the power to understand human nature and life experience: to discern what is important in life from what is not, what is important in people and what is not. We have good judgment when we have the power to assess people's motivations, values, and priorities in life. It is the power to recognize the good, the true, and the beautiful in life and in other people—and to distinguish these from the evil, the false, and the sordid.

Someone once asked an Oxford professor what he thought was the purpose of education. His answer: "Why, it's so young people can recognize rubbish when they see it!" Not a bad definition. As a result of their upbringing at home and in school, young people should know lies, propaganda, and phoniness of all sorts when they see these things.

(ii) Sound judgment is also *shrewdness*. It's the ability to appreciate the good in people, to grasp deeply what moves them most in life: that is, their values. It's the power to size people up quickly and deeply, but without the desire to dominate them. Aristotle said (to paraphrase him) that a philosopher—someone who loves truth and goodness—combines shrewdness and kindness. Someone who is both shrewd and good-willed has the essence of wisdom. A great father has within him this kind of lynx-eyed, benevolent shrewdness, and his children learn from his wisdom.

(iii) Sound judgment also means a respect for learning and intellectual accomplishment. In a word, *culture*. This is a cordial familiarity with the greatest achievements of the human spirit: those accomplishments of mind, will, heart, and body that inspire us and prove that humans are not mere beasts. Great art, it is said, makes us proud to be a human being.

(iv) Conscience, the moral dimension of sound judgment, is the framework for judging the right thing to do in a tangled situation. It tells us what we *ought* to do so that we live ethically, honorably, at peace with others, respecting their rights and dignity and sensibilities. This power of conscience is not a bundle of shapeless sentiments; it's an intelligent understanding of good and evil, right and wrong, built up through a lifetime of learning, but especially during the years of youth.

DISTINCTIONS

One smart father I knew in Washington, D.C., is a gifted teacher and writer. He said this to me:

"I think one of the roles of parents is to teach children the *vocabulary* of right living. That is, kids don't simply need to be taught right from wrong; they need specific words and terms to put these concepts into their judgment and keep them there. They need to know the *names* for important concepts. Otherwise, their judgment stays fuzzy and sentimental. They use 'cool,' 'awesome,' 'bad' and other slipshod terms—which are only bubbles of sound surrounding a shapeless, even mindless, feeling.

"Over several days, I made a list of such words to keep coming back to when teaching and correcting my two boys. It included terms that kids seldom hear these days and only dimly understand. Examples: *honor, integrity, ethics, professionalism, magnanimity, charity, healthy skepticism, self-respect, vanity, etiquette, self-indulgence, considerateness, boorishness, commitment.*

"So, when one of my sons tries to fib his way out of trouble, I refer to his honor and integrity (terms we've discussed before), and he grasps what I mean. If his teenage brother tries to weasel out of a promise, we talk in terms of commitment. When I'm checking their homework and see that it's slapdash, I correct them in terms of professionalism—because they know I consider schoolwork as a ramp-up to serious professional work. And so on.

"When I was a debater in high school, we used to start each debate with a so-called 'definition of terms.' We'd define each important word in the topic under discussion. I took this sound idea, which cuts off futile semantic arguments, and extended it to teaching my sons mature ethical standards. Once parents teach these terms and what they mean, they can keep on referring to them. It works."

As this wise dad saw, judgment deals mostly with the ability to make important distinctions in life. Children learn these distinctions from their parents and other adults they respect. To list only a few that a man's children need to learn:

— *real grown-up life* from *life as depicted on TV and in the movies*
— *humor* and *wit* from *mean-spirited ridicule*
— the *noble* and *beautiful* from the *sordid* and *squalid*
— *responsible spirit of service* from *immature egoism*
— *shrewdness* and *healthy skepticism* from *cynicism*
— *heroes* from *"celebrities"* and *entertainers*
— *courage* from *cowardice*
— *calculated risk-taking* from *recklessness*
— *professionalism* from *careless sloppiness*
— *reasoned opinions* from *"feelings"*
— *proven fact* and *certain knowledge* from *assumptions* and *"impressions"*
— *healthy self-respect* from *vanity* and *pride*
— *reasonable enjoyment* from *self-indulgent excess*
— *love* from *eroticism*
— *courtesy* and *good manners* from *boorishness*
— *integrity* from *pragmatic disregard for truth and keeping one's word*
— *honorable competition* from *ruthless ambition*
— *love for family and friends* from *selfish individualism.*

This is a short list, but I'm sure you get the idea. Try adding to it from your own experience, and from the details elsewhere in this book. How many more distinctions can you think of—moral discernments that your children need to learn before they're out of their teens?

UNDERSTANDING EVENTS: LOOKING BACK AND AHEAD

The power of sound judgment is never a static state of mind. It's vigorously active, alert, probing for clearer understanding of events and people.

So, people of good judgment are interested in current affairs. They read as much as they can to stay well informed.

Their minds work to understand the past causes for present-day events. They habitually ask questions, of themselves and others, to try to *account* for things. They like the question *"Why?"* People of mature judgment also speculate about the future. They look for future directions of today's trends, and this line of thought leads to decisions and actions now. They ask big questions about life a generation from now, the future their kids will live in. Some examples. . . .

• At what point in our history did politics, show biz, and advertising all blur into one—so that public figures take on the looks and blather of Las Vegas celebrities? How can I help my kids to know glib-talking airheads when they see them? When they hear some public figure prattle on, how can I help them tell that "there's less here than meets the eye"?

• Children's toys and games used to relate somehow to grown-up work and life: chemistry sets, model planes, microscope sets, kits for constructing things, and the like. Now a huge percentage consist of weird aliens, grotesque monsters, creatures of escapist fantasy, and video games where kids practice killing people for fun. What does this development mean? Are kids being rushed into adult life—or cut off from it? How does all this relate to what we so often see: young adults living a "comic book" existence, seemingly trapped in a perpetual adolescence?

• All cultures used to put heroes before young people to imitate: outstanding men and women presented in folklore, literature, history, religious stories. At what point did our society begin presenting clownish "celebrities" and jerks instead? Who are my kids' heroes? Which people do my children respect—and why?

- Why so much marital break-up? What is pulling families apart? How has family life changed since the time of our grandparents and forebears? Is the core problem one of money and time constraints, or one of moral commitment? How can parents live traditional moral commitments in present-day family circumstances?

- On average, it seems, about half of my children's generation will be divorced by age thirty-five. What can my wife and I do now, here at home, to ensure a stable, permanent marriage for our children—so our kids will be on the right side of that 50 percent statistic, the one that stays married?

- It's sadly quaint to see monuments and plaques put up shortly after World War I; they refer to "The World War" or "The Great War," as if there would never be another. And yet today we still speak of *The* Great Depression, as if there could never be another. Do my children understand that peace and prosperity (which is all they've ever known) are not a state of nature, that wars and depressions reappear in historical cycles—and may come again in their lifetime?

- If my children must someday confront the ravages of a severe economic downturn, another Depression (which is possible, some say likely), what inner strengths will they need to succeed, or even only to survive? How important will it be that they have realistic self-confidence, strong drive, a marketable skill, religious hope, resilience in the face of adversity, and an ability to live simply and modestly?

- If our country's economy will increasingly link with that of other countries, how important will it be that my children master one or more foreign languages? Will they know how to appreciate and get along with people who are different?

- If children today are constantly bombarded with a glamorous, superficial way of assessing the opposite sex, how could this damage their later choice of a spouse? How can my wife and I teach our kids to weigh the real character of men and women, to grasp the difference between "romance" illusions and real love?

As mentioned before, in business and professional life, it seems, the esteem anyone receives from colleagues is directly proportional to his or her future vision. Those professionals who think ahead five, ten, twenty-five years—and who act now to control future events—are the ones who emerge as respected leaders.

The same takes place in family life. When parents think deeply about their children's future lives—in terms of character, not only careers—they win their children's respect. A father who thinks deeply about the future is a leader to his children. And over time, his kids quietly grow to regard him as a hero.

LEARNING FROM MISTAKES

Any father wants his growing children to be active. (If they're sluggishly lazy, he knows, they'll be shoved aside by their competitors.) And if he is a smart father, he knows that active people—kids as well as adults—make mistakes. Only the bone lazy commit few active blunders in life, but they fall headlong into the biggest mistakes of all: neglect, bad timing, missed deadlines, and lost opportunities.

So, if you taught them to be active self-starters, your children will make many mistakes along the way. You expect this and allow for it. You take advantage of your children's blunders, in home life or school or sports, as a chance to firm up their judgment. How should you react?

In two ways:

First, judge whether they were honestly trying to do the right thing. Give them credit and sincere praise for their earnest best efforts. Make clear to them, always, that you don't expect perfection or even success; but you insist that they try their best to surpass themselves.

Second, teach them a truth about adult life: mistakes are valuable if we learn from them. Sit down and talk with your children, and lead them to think through what happened . . .

—What were you thinking when you did this? What did you expect to happen?

—What exactly went wrong?

—What was your reaction? What did you think and feel?

—What did people around you say and do? How did your mistake affect them?

—If your mistake caused a problem or offense to someone else, how do you think they feel right now?

—What can you do now to repair this mistake? If you offended someone, even without meaning to, don't you think you should say you're sorry?

—If you're ever in this situation again, what will you do differently? What have you learned?

I once knew a smart father who worked as a professional pilot for a large commercial airline. He told me this: "From what I can see, most serious teenage problems come from crummy judgment, not malice. Even well-intentioned kids get into trouble because they don't know any better.

"We use a flight simulator in our flight training, and for obvious reasons. Better to goof in virtual reality than in a real 737 at take-off. I see my home life as a kind of simulator for my kids' lives as adults. What is training, after all, except learning from experience harmlessly? When they make mistakes, as we all do, it's better to do this at home when they're small and damage is minimal. Better small mistakes now than big mistakes later."

He's right. A healthy family is where kids can *experience mistakes harmlessly.*

Better to correct bad habits and attitudes now, at home, before these lead to serious and even lethal blunders—mistakes that can hurt their marriages and careers, or even kill them. Think what can happen to children if they grow up with their present faults uncorrected:

Kids can explode in anger if they don't get their way. If they later try this with their bosses, they could sidetrack their careers.

They can get used to being waited on hand and foot. If they demand this from their spouses, their marriages will implode.

They can have a careless attitude toward time and deadlines. If they do this at work, they'll get fired.

They can try to tell lies at home to avoid blame and punishment. If they lie to their bosses, they're through.

They can sit around at home waiting to be amused, impatient with boredom, counting on their parents to repair damage from their blunders. If they don't accept responsibility for themselves later, they'll be swept aside by their competition—and never amount to anything.

They can have an aggressive, "me first" pushiness at home. If they later drive a car this way, they could kill someone. If they treat their spouses this way, they could crack up their marriages—and your grandchildren will grow up in a fatherless home.

So, correct your kids' mistakes now, while they're still relatively harmless—while you still have time.

WISDOM

One additional thought here about sound judgment and how a father passes this power on to his children:

There is a collection of truths about life that each generation passes on to the next. This type of understanding goes way beyond skill instruction or piling up masses of information, the standard stuff of most schools. In one word, this is *wisdom*. It normally goes untaught in schools or universities, unless some teachers are exceptionally gifted and dedicated. Life knowledge is taught and learned mostly at home, from the example and advice of our parents.

These life lessons are reinforced later, not in school or college but on young peoples' first job, their first real experience with grown-up responsibilities. Later still, these parent-founded lessons really hit home during the first few years of marriage. "Dad and Mom were right . . ."—this is what young people come to see.

Here's a real-life example of this shrewd, wise lesson-giving in action:

I was once talking with a mother about how young adults of marriageable age need to size up the character of a prospective spouse and how hard this is when, as they say, "love is blind."

She told me this story: "When I was leaving home to start college, my dad gave me one of the best pieces of advice I ever received. He said that someday I'd fall in love with a young man and seriously consider marrying him. At that time, he warned, I'd probably find it hard to be objective about the man, to read deeply inside his character. So this was his advice—Look closely at the way this man treats his grown brothers and sisters. Is he affectionate with them? Does he like and respect them? Does he remember their birthdays? Is he proud of them, glad to be around them, does he stay in touch with them? . . . Or, on the other hand, is he indifferent to them? Does he quarrel with them, bear grudges, keep them at a distance? . . . Chances are (he said), this is a preview of the way he will treat his wife: The way a man treats his siblings is the same way he'll treat his spouse.

"I took my dad's advice. I went through several brief relationships until I met a young man who was proud of his own family and affectionate with all of them. He's now my husband."

What are some of these important truths about life that parents need to teach their children, especially from early adolescence? Here are a few:

• The word *integrity* is related to the words "integer" and "integrate" and "disintegrate." It refers to oneness, to unity.

Integrity means a unity of our intentions, word, and action—that is, we mean what we say, we say what we mean, and we keep our word. Our integrity is our honor, our most valuable possession.

- We should never make promises lightly, but if we make them, we must keep our word.
- Honesty is the best policy—always.
- Time is a resource, not a passive environment. If we waste it, we lose it. Neglect—failing to act in time—is often a huge mistake; to do nothing is itself a blunder.
- Mind your own business. Stay out of matters that lie outside your responsibilities and therefore your authority.
- Authority and responsibility must always be in balance; otherwise, the result is trouble. Because parents bear an enormous responsibility, they possess a proportional authority. Young people who disrespect their parents' rightful authority grow up to have problems with all other authority—teachers, bosses, the law, their own conscience.
- If we have self-respect, we win the respect of others.
- Popularity is not nearly so important as respect. If we strive too hard to make people like us, they probably won't. But if we strive to win their respect, then they will both like and respect us.
- Nobody respects a liar, a gossip, a cynic, or a whiner. If we act this way, people come to mistrust us and hold us without honor.
- If we read a lot, and discerningly, people grow to respect our judgment.
- Sometimes it requires more wisdom to take good advice than to give it.
- A shortcut to personal happiness: forget about your ego and give yourself generously to serve the needs of those around you, starting with your family.
- Love is not sweet sentiments. It is really the willingness and ability to sacrifice for the welfare and happiness of others. In a sense, love *is* sacrifice.
- Hard work without some motivating ideal is merely drudgery; but that same hard work, done for some great passionate love, turns into noble sacrifice—and life becomes an adventure.
- Money is an instrument for the welfare of our loved ones and those in need, and that's all it is.
- The real riches in life are family, friends, faith, and a clear conscience. Everything else is gravy.

There are scores, maybe hundreds, of truisms like these, succinct expressions of truth about life derived from experience. In many cultures, wisdom of this sort was passed on from parents to children through short maxims like those of Benjamin Franklin or those in the Bible's Book of Proverbs. My point here is that parents were and are the foremost teachers of wisdom, what's really important in life.

Note that most of the life lessons listed here are themes in the world's greatest works of literature. Great literature should teach wisdom; it ought to build sound judgment in young people. The humanities should teach us about people, about the richness of human experience. In today's schools, sad to say, literature is almost never taught this way or for this purpose.

RESPONSIBILITY

Irresponsibility basically means growing older without growing up—trapped in the compulsive "me first" attitudes of childhood. If a father fails to act on purpose to reform his kids' selfishness, they'll remain irresponsible for life, or until they meet with real-life consequences, some of them disastrous.

You can probably think of dozens of examples like these:

• A talented computer whiz hacks his way into a nationwide network and inserts a virus for the fun of it. He causes millions of dollars in damage before he is caught. His fun comes to an abrupt halt when he is sentenced to a year in jail.

• A young salesman, new to his job, enjoys very long lunches. He enjoys them so much he's routinely late for afternoon appointments. His boss is not amused and lets him go.

• A high-school girl has so much fun in senior year she puts off doing her college applications until days before the deadline. She loses out on financial aid, and so her parents must take out massive loans to pay full tuition.

• A group of college students set up initiation rites for introduction into their fraternity. Just for laughs, they require a freshman to drink a quart of vodka in one sitting. He collapses into a coma and dies.

• A husband and wife, both raised to see life as pure amusement, grow bored with each other and annoyed with each other's faults. They call it quits and break their children's hearts.

What, then, is responsibility? The Greeks called it *justice* and said it meant giving others what is due to them. (The word *duty* is related to *due*—a duty is something owed to others by right.)

If any of the great virtues comes naturally to kids, it would seem to be this one. Children call it "fairness," and they have a keen, powerful sense of what's fair. For this reason, you can usually correct kids effectively when you strongly appeal to their sense of fairness: "It's unfair to your mother to leave your chores around the house undone; she shouldn't have to clean up messes you have made." Wise parents discover this early on, and so they put correction to the kids in terms of what's fair. This lays a solid ground for more complex lessons of ethics later in the children's lives, especially during adolescence.

This virtue of responsibility is rich with meanings. Here is how you can explain it to your children:

(i) Responsibility means acting so as to respect the rights of others, including their right not to be offended. (So it overlaps with charity, thoughtfulness for others' needs and feelings.) *Because other people have rights, we have obligations.* Our right to swing our fists stops at someone else's face. I have a right to scribble a big drawing, but not to smear graffiti on somebody else's wall. I have a right to stand in line, but not to butt in. I have a right to speak my mind, but not to interrupt or offend someone. The whole moral development of children consists of moving them from *self* to *others.*

(ii) Responsibility is a *habit of doing our duties whether we feel like it or not.* In family life, it is sacrificial love. Love means shouldering and carrying out our family obligations; in family life, love *is* responsibility.

And in the world of work, responsibility means professionalism—the power to perform at our best no matter how we feel. Real professionals carry out their responsibilities, perform their services as best they can, even when they don't feel like it. Headaches, personal concerns, emotional ups and downs—none of these things deter really effective professionals (or parents) from fulfilling their duties of service.

(iii) Responsibility is *respect for rightful authority.* Authority means, among other things, the right to be obeyed. Great parents may be unsure about many things in their children's upbringing, but they have no doubts about their rightful authority. Successful parents are conscious and confident of their authority. They take for granted, so to speak, that their children will respect and obey them. As a result, their children, over time, grow to have *confidence in their parents' self-confidence.*

To look at it another way: effective fathers and mothers see their parenthood as a kind of office, like the office of a President or Supreme Court Justice. Whoever carries the burden of a highly responsible public office, regardless of personal shortcomings, has a right to be respected and obeyed. So, too, no matter what personal faults or self-doubts they may have, parents—by the very fact of their parenthood—have a right to their children's respectful obedience.

(iv) Responsibility also means *living with the consequences of our decisions and mistakes, including our neglect.* How many problems in our society derive from people's attempts to escape responsibility? Responsible people do not shift blame; they refuse to see themselves as victims. They admit their mistakes honestly and shoulder the consequences.

(v) Responsibility is the *willingness and ability to honor our promises and commitments even when this involves hardship.* Responsible people will endure hardship to keep their word. Because their given word means much to them, they do not make promises quickly or carelessly.

(vi) Responsibility is the *habit of minding our own business, staying out of matters that do not concern us.* Mature people do not snoop, gossip, or meddle. Consistently, they give people the benefit of the doubt and they respect peoples' right to presumption of innocence.

Responsible children learn from their parents how to put their powers up against problems for the sake of contributing to family welfare. They receive encouragement as well as correction from their parents, and so they grow in confidence. In a real sense, *responsibility is another word for maturity.* A man's children become mature not when they reach puberty and grow in physical stature, but when they think and act consistently like altruistic adults.

Here's a story about responsibility told to me by another smart father:

"My eleven-year-old son Kevin is a great kid, but for many years he had an annoying problem that drove his mother and me crazy. He would lose money. I don't mean he'd misspend it; he would somehow let it drop out of his pocket. I gave him a couple of wallets along the way, but he also lost those. This was exasperating, but I kept hoping he'd outgrow it.

"He also loved collecting baseball cards, as I do, and one day we both attended a baseball card convention that opened in our town once a year. Kevin looked forward to it for weeks and my wife and I let him take out $10 from his bank account to buy some collectible cards.

"Kevin and I spent the afternoon poring over cards, and he selected a few choice ones that would come to about $10, his limit. When we arrived at the checkout counter—you guessed it—Kevin had dropped his $10 bill somewhere. Suddenly he was broke. He turned to me pleading for a loan, begging me to advance him the money to buy the cards he had in hand.

"I gathered up my courage and told him no. I explained the reasons: a deal is a deal; you lost your money through careless-ness and so now you have to live with the consequences—that's what happens in real life. He pleaded and pleaded, but I wouldn't give in. Finally, he had to leave the cards at the counter, and he cried all the way home. This was very, very tough for me . . . but I saw no other way to teach him this lesson. I could not let him grow up with this slipshod habit.

"Believe me, he learned it in spades. For both of us, the pain was worth it. He started carrying a wallet, and he's never lost any money since. That was twelve years ago."

You can explain it this way to your youngsters: *Responsibility means this—if we don't do what we're supposed to do, somebody else gets hurt. We do our duty so that other people won't suffer.*

PERSONAL COURAGE

Personal courage is the third great virtue. We also know it by other names: *fortitude, perseverance, toughness, "guts."*

Outside of war or some physical threat to our safety (as in our poorest neighborhoods), physical courage isn't much needed in civilized suburban society. But moral courage certainly is. Life means taking risks and grappling with all sorts of hardship—including the problem of looking different from our peers. Many young people never learned the concept, never knew firsthand any sort of adversity. For this, they suffer.

Look at these examples:

• Teens at a party or dance are enticed by friends to try drugs or get wasted on beer. They are afraid to seem different ("uncool"), so they give in.

• A young man is grotesquely overworked by his firm. Through obsessive fear of failure, he puts in sixty to seventy hours of work a week. He agonizes because his marriage is unraveling, but he will not risk searching for another job. On all sides he is trapped by his fears.

• A young mother struggles with the savage misbehavior of

her three-year old son. She reads scads of books and tries everything from pleas to bribery, but meets with never-ending frustration. Her problem? She's afraid that if she punishes him, her child will "hate" her. She fears losing her son's affection.

• A college senior is still clueless about what to do for a living. He's afraid to choose, decide, take risks with a commitment. Solution? Put off the decision with a couple more years of grad school. But first take a year off to travel and "think things through."

• The first two years of marriage are the toughest. Each spouse discovers that the other has faults, some of them insoluble—shortcomings, annoying habits, flaws in thinking or conduct, gender differences. Strong people shrug these off and let love cover them over. Weak people, with their low threshold for inconvenience, exaggerate these faults and come to view them as absolutely intolerable. Solution? See a lawyer, go to court—and escape.

You can explain courage this way to your children:

(i) Fortitude is the *acquired ability to overcome or endure difficulties: pain, discomfort, disappointment, setbacks, worry, tedium.* It is the strength of will to solve a given problem or simply to live with it—but in no case to seek escape.

How many serious problems among teens and young married couples stem from a fixed resort to escape, from a low tolerance for hardship or even inconvenience? How is this weakness related to our problems with drugs and alcohol abuse and so much of our staggering divorce rate?

(ii) *Personal toughness is a habit of overcoming anxiety through purposeful, honorable action.* We turn our worries into action. It is the opposite of whining inertia in the face of problems, a compulsion to feckless complaint. Courageous people, in fact, see escapism—fleeing from inconvenience—as unworthy, even dishonorable.

(iii) Personal courage, enhanced by sound judgment, is a firm grasp of an unavoidable fact: life always brings hardships, and many of these are unavoidable, even insoluble. But we adults learn to live with them as best we can; we put them behind us and get on with life. Related to this is the realistic understanding that expectation is more painful than reality: anticipated problems nearly always seem worse than they really are once we tackle them.

(iv) To look at it another way, this strength is a *confidence in our problem-solving abilities, built through a lifetime practice in solv-*

ing problems. Athletics, jobs around the house, schoolwork and homework, meeting deadlines, working at our best under reasonable pressure—all these build courage and self-confidence. So does steady, affirming encouragement from parents: "You can do it if you try" . . . "Stick with it and you can lick it" . . . "You're stronger than you think."

It seems to be a fact of life in youngsters' upbringing: Some adversity is healthy for children. There is such a thing as good stress. Outside of certain misguided schools, nobody in society "works at his own pace." If our forebears had worked at their own pace, we would still be riding in donkey carts and lighting our homes with candles. It took gutsy risk-taking and sustained hard work to produce all our wonderful labor-saving devices. When faced with reasonable stress and adversity, we all do our best work.

(v) Fortitude is also our *determination to overcome personal shortcomings.* If we are shy, we learn to be a friendly, attentive listener, for a "good listener" usually attracts good friends. If we're impulsive, we learn to restrain ourselves and foresee consequences; we direct our energy to achievement. If we are lazy, we strive toward purposeful action. If we fail to understand something, we seek advice from people we respect and otherwise think matters through. And so on.

In a sense, the power of fortitude is the exact opposite of "getting in touch with our feelings"—a woefully common approach today in too many schools and families. To be sure, sentiment has its place in life. Powerful feelings of love and loyalty—directed as they are to others' welfare—can move us to greatness. But in real life, self-centered feelings must give way to duty; if they do not, then young people have practically no capacity for *sacrifice,* which is the absolute essence of real love. Genuine love often means *ignoring our self-centered feelings for the sake of others.* In real life, love means serving others courageously.

An example of quietly heroic courage in family life is the way great parents persist relentlessly in teaching manners to their children. Dad and Mom say to their kids over and over again, hundreds of times: "Say *please.* . . , say *thank you* . . . , say *excuse me.* . . ." They keep at this for months and even years without let-up until finally, miraculously, their children voice these terms on their own.

One couple told me how they saw this task: "It's like hammering a nail into a very hard wall, like cinderblock. You keep tapping and tapping with the hammer, putting a little bit of pressure on the nail over and over again. For a while, sometimes a long while, you see no progress at all. Maybe you're moving a few molecules out of the way with each hammer tap, but you don't see much to show for your effort. After a while, the nail starts to settle in. Eventually, after a long time, it's solidly in the wall—it's in for keeps, and you can hang anything from it.

"And that's the way it is with the kids. You teach *please* and *thank you* over and over again, even when you see no change, even when they keep falling back into thankless grabbing. You have faith that, if you keep at this no matter what, then somehow, sooner or later, they'll get the message and change. Eventually, at last, they do exactly that—and the habit's in them for life. . . ."

SELF-MASTERY

The fourth great virtue, *self-mastery* or temperance, is one of the character strengths we admire most in people. In our self-indulgent culture, a temperate man or woman stands out from the crowd. Sometimes, especially in teen years, it takes real courage to resist peer pressures and stand apart as one's own master.

Children grab for pleasures and power. They give free rein to their appetites and passions while doggedly resisting the word "no." So they are enslaved to their fears and feelings. If they grow up this way, they are headed for serious trouble—like these young people. . . .

• A fifteen-year-old girl attends a party at her boyfriend's house. The boy's parents are away in Florida, and the kid disobeys his parents' warning not to run an unsupervised party while they're gone. Twice before he had done this. The kids drink alcohol, and then someone passes around drugs bought that day on the street. The girl and other friends take the drugs, which are bad. (Drug dealers don't care about quality control.) Within minutes, the kids collapse in epileptic-type seizures and pass out in a coma. Paramedics rush them to a hospital. Over the next week, three die. The rest, including the girl, later regain consciousness, but their minds are permanently shattered. For years, they suffer from amnesia and psychotic hallucinations, and they probably will never recover.

• A college freshman invites friends into his dorm room on a Friday night and consumes seven or eight beers over a couple of hours. He sits on the window ledge of his room laughing and chugging his last drink. Reeling drunk, he loses his balance and falls four floors to his death.

• Two men in their early twenties are driving to work in their powerful new sports utility vehicles. One abruptly cuts the other off, nearly causing an accident. Enraged, the offended driver speeds ahead and does the same. For several miles, both drivers, now in furious frenzy, cursing and yelling at each other, dodge and weave through rush-hour traffic at a speed of more than 80 miles per hour, cutting in front of each other. They both lose control and crash in a fireball that kills one of the drivers and a woman driving on the other side of the road. She was a mother of two children, heading to her first day of work on a new job.

• A young woman in her junior year of college goes to a crowded party at someone's house and passes out drunk. Next morning, she wakes up with a hangover in her own apartment with no memory of how she got there. Total blackout. Weeks later, she finds she is pregnant.

• From a morbid fear of failure, a man works seventy-plus hours a week at his job, comes home late every night, goes in to work on weekends. His wife bitterly complains about his priorities; he leaves her to care for their five-year-old son all by herself—and the boy almost never sees his father. She leaves her husband, sees a lawyer, and the marriage is through. He returns home late at night to an empty apartment and an empty life.

• A young salesman puts on forty pounds over two years and has to refit or buy a new wardrobe every few months. Since childhood he has always been slightly pudgy from overeating and physical inertia. Now, with disposable income, he really lets go. He eats rich foods, consumes quantities of beer, watches a lot of sports, but never exercises. When his company has to cut back on its sales force, he is among the first to go. The firm wants to convey an image of quick, competitive, cutting-edge service. And though he's a nice enough guy, his tight-fitting clothes and his bulging, button-popping gut make the wrong impression on clients.

• A young man, early thirties, retains the same short-fused volcanic temper he has had since childhood. As a teen, he was suspended from games for flying off the handle at referees. His wife is exasperated with his tantrums. His kids are scared of him. One day he loses it with an important client. When his boss learns about this and tries to set him straight, he reacts with yet another blow-up—his last at that company.

No question about it, there's a lot riding on how well or badly a father leads his children to control themselves, to curb their passions and cravings by his artful use of the word "no" and action to back it up. I will explain the how of this teaching in the next few chapters, but for now let's focus on the strategy. What does temperance/self-control mean? What should you teach your children about it, and its urgent importance?

• Temperance is the power to say *no*, at will, to our laziness, passions, and appetites. It is the power, built up through practice, to *wait* for rewards and to *earn* them. A self-controlled man or woman, like everyone else, wants instant gratification—but does not expect it or need it. Temperate people do not turn wants into needs, and they know the difference.

Self-indulgent people grab for gratifications now and put off hard effort for later. Self-controlled people do exactly the opposite. They have a lifetime habit of *earning* what they want.

• Self-controlled people enjoy pleasures of life in moderation, never (or hardly ever) to excess. They don't go overboard in food, drink, entertainment, or even work. Because they are self-directed, they appear quietly self-confident, on top of life. Their enjoyment comes from other people, not merely from things. To the extent that they take pleasure in food, drink, entertainment, and work, it's because of the company—family and friends—with whom they share these things. They are affable, fun to be with, enjoyable to work with. Their greatest delight is to delight their friends.

• Self-controlled people do not use coarse language gratuitously. Only some rare, outrageous provocation prods them to a cussing outburst, and they follow up with apologies when called for. The point is, they have a habit of controlling their speech, and thus they show respect for the people around them.

• Self-controlled people know how to manage time. In fact, the business catchword "time management" is merely another name for self-control. Self-disciplined people know how to plan ahead, set their own deadlines, and stick to them. They neither exaggerate nor underestimate the size of a task and the time needed to complete it.

• Self-disciplined people have a lifelong habit of saying and meaning *please, thank you, I'm sorry,* and *I give my word.* . . . If they offend anyone, even unintentionally, they are quick to apologize. They extend courtesy to everyone, and they can do this even in the face of rudeness or provocation.

In a word, temperate people have "class." Self-restraint, etiquette, healthy self-respect, an active spirit of service, an ongoing and active concern for the dignity and needs of those around them mark their character. To everyone who knows them, they are esteemed as great friends.

Habitual self-control does more than give grace to our lives; it's also absolutely vital to physical safety. Kids who grow into adolescence with little self-control—driven to act on thoughtless impulse—can injure or kill themselves, along with their friends.

Consider this. In the mid-1990s, the U.S. government released results of a ten-year study on the causes of teenage automobile fatalities. Results were surprising: only 5 percent of these fatal accidents were caused by drunk driving. (For adult car fatalities, the figure is almost 50 percent.)

What caused 95 percent of these deaths among teens? You can guess. Speeding, showing off, road rage, reckless driving, ignoring stop signs and other warnings, and general inexperience. In other words, nearly all these kids were killed through uncontrolled impulsiveness, irresponsibility, or poor judgment.

The power of self-mastery prevents tragedies. It saves lives.

HEART

Last of all, *greatness of heart*. This is the all-important spiritual power that gives force to all the other virtues. It directs our powers of judgment, responsibility, toughness, and self-control toward the well-being of other people, starting with our family and radiating out to friends, colleagues, acquaintances, strangers, our country.

The ancient Romans called it *magnanimity*, "greatness of soul." To us it goes by other names: *charity, compassionate understanding, awareness of others' needs, a spirit of service, sacrificial love*.

It is the capacity and desire to surpass ourselves, to endure or overcome anything for the sake of somebody else's welfare and happiness. It's *generosity*—the drive to give others the best of what we have for their sake and to expect little or nothing in return.

VALUES

Where does someone put his heart? What does he love most in life? Answer these questions and you put your finger on that person's values.

This word "values" has swirled in a lot of controversy lately. It has cropped up in heated political wrangles over classroom curricula and media censorship. Here I want to stay clear of these public-policy thickets and look rather at values as they're taught at home.

The fact is, everyone has values. Everyone puts something closest to his heart and leaves other things at a distance.

To speak of people's values is to speak of their *priorities* in life: what comes first to them, then what comes second, third, and on down the line. Where, in what order, do people put their passions? What do they love most? That's the question.

People differ in their values because they differ in what they love most and least. Look at this list of things that people love and live for—what they passionately pursue as the object of their heart:

- God
- family and friends
- country
- money
- truth
- fame and glory
- satisfying, service-oriented work
- career advancement
- comfort and convenience
- substance addiction
- pleasure and amusement
- power over others
- safety and security
- conformity: acceptance by others
- vengeance

Tell this to your children: You can tell people's values by which of these loves they hold closest, and which they belittle or ignore.

Some fathers give their hearts to God, family, friends, truth, and service-directed work. Everyone who knows these men considers them great. When their children love and respect their parents, they grow to adopt the same loves and in the same order—their parents' values.

Other men put power, career, and comfort ahead of anything else—and their families suffer.

In adolescence, teens are strongly tempted to put conformity and pleasure ahead of their family. But if their parents won their hearts in childhood, if teenagers' love for family comes first, they can push these allurements aside. They love their parents deeply, and so they will never betray or disgrace them.

So, then, do your children know your priorities, the loves you hold above all others? Tell them. Urge them to follow you, to embrace your values and live by them. And warn them about one of life's greatest disasters: to marry someone with mismatched priorities—whose values conflict with their own.

PERSONAL GREATNESS

In the third century B.C., the Chinese philosopher Mencius said, "A great person is one who never loses the heart he had as a child."

It's obvious (once we see it) that the great character strengths have to be formed from scratch in children as they grow up, for kids do not enter the world with judgment, responsibility, courage, or self-control. But, no question about it, children do have beautiful qualities that must survive intact throughout childhood and into later life, and the greatest of these is charity.

It's true, parents must patiently lead their children to become competent, learned, tough-minded, responsible, shrewd, savvy, and nobody's fool. But, at the same time, in their hearts children should never lose the same great loves that they had as small children—loves they see still alive in you.

What are these great loves of childhood?

Love for family. A natural and abiding affection for parents and brothers and sisters—who are the compass of children's young hearts, the center of their existence. All their lives, young people should hold onto their loving trust in Dad and Mom, loyalty to their grown brothers and sisters, and devotion to the families they form themselves.

Love for God. A humble, sincere, and beautiful trust in God, whom children see as an all-powerful, all-loving Father.* Great people never lose this vision and faith, seeing themselves as children of God all their lives, watched over by the Creator's loving protection. This hope-filled confidence empowers them to withstand any hardship in life and steels them with a stalwart sense of responsibility—ethical uprightness, a clean conscience, what the Scriptures call "righteousness." God lives in the home,

---

* I have discussed the religious formation of children in my books *Lifeline: The Religious Upbringing of Your Children* and *Anchor: God's Promises of Hope to Parents* (Scepter Publishers). See also my Web site www.parentleadership.com.

not only in church. If children do not find God in their parents' lives, they may never find him at all.

Love for life, friends, laughter. Children arise each morning seeing the day as an adventure, a call to fun and achievement with family and friends. With their loved ones they share the gift of laughter, that splendid sign of a light, clean heart. So, too, as adults they should be moved by that same vision of life as adventure, enjoying each day as a gift, delighting in the companionship of friends. They should take their responsibilities seriously, but not themselves.

Love for those in need. At their best, youngsters have an exquisite quality of mercy, a capacity for compassion. We see this in their tender care for a wounded little animal or their heartfelt sympathy for a grieving friend. This capacity for mercy, feeling sorry for someone, must never be snuffed out. All their lives, great men and women show mercy to others, extend their hearts and help to strangers in trouble. They hate sin but love the sinner. They strive for peace, forgive injuries, bear no ill will or grudges toward anyone. They know that charity does not mean donating old clothes—it means mostly compassionate understanding.

Love for the truth. Tiny children, it seems, are naturally truthful; when they first try to lie, they are laughably inept. They have a way of putting their small fingers right on the truth, often with startling insight, like the little boy in "The Emperor's New Clothes." Instinctively and oftentimes with astonishing accuracy, they can judge people's character. So also in adulthood, they should shun all forms of phoniness; they should know falsity when they see it. They should have the guts to tell the truth and to admit when they're wrong. They should never enslave themselves to the worst lie of all: self-deception. They should know who they are and what they stand for—lessons learned from their dad and mom.

Great people, then, are those who possess within their souls the powers of adults and the hearts of children. Generously, they direct their lives to the needs of others, and they have the inner strength to serve people effectively, starting with their families. To all who know them, they are "wise as serpents, innocent as doves"—great men and women.

Your job as a father, your mission in life, is to raise your children to this ideal—to form generosity and character so deeply within them as to direct the course of their lives to greatness. This is what a great father does.

6 | *Rely on the Power of "We..." in Family Life*

The word "we" is a powerful force in family life. It's what anchors children's loyalty to their parents and brothers and sisters—and lifelong fastness to their parents' convictions of right and wrong. It empowers children's inner voice of conscience for life.

I have seen this so many times. Loyalty to their family is what rescues many teens and young adults from calamity. Adolescents will shun drugs and drunkenness and reckless driving, not only because these are wrong but because, if they are caught, the teens would disgrace their families. Fear of causing shame to their family can steel the will of young people, lead them to shrug off peer pressures, say "no" to selfish impulses, and live rightly.

Every healthy "sporting adventure" family I've known, without exception, has lived by a set of clear rules in the home, some high standards for selfless conduct. When kids lived by these standards every day for years, they gradually—with fits and starts along the way—internalized powers of judgment, ethical responsibility, gutsy perseverance, and consideration for others. Active family rules cemented the kids' rock-hard foundation in place and formed the framework for their structure of character.

Why does a healthy family have rules? For one reason: because it has a *job* to do, a *service mission* to carry out. A picnic-like consumerist family, by contrast, has no job at all—for entertainment is a static pastime, not an achievement—and so it has no reason to lay down standards for performance. No expectation of workmanlike performance means no need for standards.

I think you, as a father, will see your challenge more compellingly if you look at your fatherly task from a professional point of view, the way things work in any serious business enterprise. Here's how I see it: Every serious enterprise—whether a business, a nonprofit service, a society and its government, or a family—has three basic elements that distinguish it from a loose and pointless or amateurish operation:

First, a *mission*. This is some long-term goal of service, some task carried out for the betterment of others.

Second, a *responsible chain of command*. In any group, some people assume the burden of responsibility and consequently hold the authority to lead; they teach and direct others to carry out the institution's mission and deliver its service. In this way, responsible leaders direct those who work with them, not only under them—for a real leader has *joiners*, not followers.

Third, a *set of performance standards*. These are clear directional rules by which those in charge show others what is expected of them, the ways they most effectively contribute to the overall mission. This includes a job description and some sort of protocol that sets standards for acceptable performance—office rules, by-laws, contractual obligations, and the like.

Every healthy family is a serious enterprise, and so it displays all three elements outlined here: mission, leadership, and performance standards.

Because the picnic family is going no place—has no real directed mission—then the parents are weak leaders (lead where?) and rules, if any, act only as ad hoc bandages to keep hassles and damage to a minimum.

As we've seen so far, a man and his wife take on a serious mission in family life—to form children's conscience, character, and spirit of service for life. Because they assume this huge responsibility, Dad and Mom have the right and duty to lead. All children need leadership, and if both parents do not lead them to do right, then someone else may lead them to do wrong.

In my many talks with great parents and their children, I used to probe from time to time to learn what rules each healthy family lived by. These odds and ends I scribbled down and set aside in a bulging folder. Sometimes I would lay them out on my desk, group like things together, and hunt for patterns.

Here is what I noticed—

(i) *All the rules, directly or implicitly, began with the word "We" not "You."* For instance, the rule for chores was not "*You kids* must clean your room," but rather "*We* all pitch in to keep this house in decent shape." Not "*You* must call if you're late," but instead "*We* call if we're going to be late." It wasn't "*You* have to put toys away," but "*We* all return things where they belong."

In other words, *the parents lived by the rules themselves, the same ones they imposed on their children.* The parents lived at home like responsible, considerate adults, and they insisted their kids do the same. Dad and Mom, like any other real leaders, demanded as much of themselves as of their children. They practiced what they preached and led the way by their personal example. Consequently, every day, their children witnessed the parents' convictions alive in ongoing action. (And so, later as teenagers, they could never justly accuse their parents of hypocrisy.)

(ii) *Abiding by these rules led the kids—or forced them—to practice each of the virtues.* Repeatedly, every day, Dad and Mom pressed their kids to live rightly: to take responsibility, manage their own affairs, work conscientiously, discern right from wrong, respect their parents' authority, and consider the needs and rights of others. Right living permeated the whole spirit of the family—and seeped its way inside the kids little by little, day by day.

(iii) *All the rules seemed to fall into five separate but interconnected categories:*

—We respect the rights and sensibilities of others.

—We all contribute to making our home a clean, orderly, civilized place to live.

—We give people information they need to carry out their responsibilities.

—We use electronic media only to promote family welfare, never to work against it.

—We love and honor our Creator above all things; we thank Him for His blessings and ask His help for our needs and those of others.

▲ ▲

For whatever use they may be to you, I list these rules for you here.* Let me stress that what I lay out below is *de*scriptive, not *pre*scriptive. That is, I am describing what I've seen work in one great family after another. I do not presume to be dogmatic about details here, or insist that every family should adopt these standards wholesale. I couldn't rightly do that even if I wanted to.

It's up to you to weigh each one, in teamwork with your wife, and judge what might work best for you and your children. It's your family, and therefore your call.

Here they are:

(1) *We respect the rights and sensibilities of others.*

—We say to everyone, when appropriate: *please, thank you, excuse me, I'm sorry, I give my word of honor.*

—We do not insult people with words or affront them with rudeness.

* A copy of these rules is available also at www.parentleadership.com.

—We do not tattletale or gossip about people, or otherwise negatively criticize people behind their backs. (Though if someone we know is getting involved with drugs, then for their sake we report it to whoever can help them in time.)
—We keep our family's affairs within the family. No "airing dirty laundry in public."
—We make no disparaging remarks of a racist, sexist, ethnic, or religious nature, not even as a joke. We have no place in our home for humor that hurts.
—We do not use profanity or vulgar language.
—We never ridicule or belittle anyone who tries.
—We do not interrupt; we wait our turn to speak. We do not distract people when they're speaking with someone, either in person or on the phone. If there is an urgent situation and we must interrupt, then we first say, "Excuse me, please."
—We respect people's right to presumption of innocence. Before forming a negative judgment, we first listen to their side of things.
—We never lie to each other. Unless we have solid evidence to the contrary, we presume other family members tell the truth.
—We do not argue back when we are corrected.
—We do not make promises unless we commit ourselves to carry them out. If we can't keep a promise for reasons beyond our control, then we make a sincere apology.
—We respect each other's property and right to privacy. We knock before entering a closed room; we ask permission before borrowing something.
—We do not bicker or quarrel during meals.
—If we must get up from the table at meals, we first say, "Excuse me, please."
—We greet adult friends of our family with good manners, a warm greeting, a friendly handshake, and a look in the eye. We give our guests the best of what we have. (But children do not talk with adult strangers without their parents' okay.)
—We show special respect to older people. We offer to give them a seat, hold doors for them, let them go first in line.
—We celebrate each other's accomplishments. But win or lose, we appreciate each other's best efforts.
—We practice good telephone manners and thus bring honor to our family. We keep use of the telephone under reasonable control: • No calls during dinner or homework or after 10:00 P.M. • No outgoing calls after 9:30 P.M. (except for emergencies). • Calls generally limited to fifteen minutes.

(2) *We all contribute to making our home a clean, orderly, civilized place to live.*

—We do not enter the house with wet or muddy footwear; if we track in a mess, we clean it up right away.

—We do not bring "outdoor" activities indoors: no ball-playing, running and chasing, missile throwing, rough wrestling, or excessive shouting. Males in the family wear no hats or caps indoors.

—We open and close doors quietly; if we accidentally slam a door, we say, "Excuse me, please."

—We do not shout messages to people in other rooms. We walk to wherever someone is and then deliver the message in a normal voice.

—We do not consume food outside of designated eating areas: kitchen, dining room, play or TV room.

—We do not overindulge in food or drink. No unauthorized snacks between meals, especially right before meals.

—We try to eat all the food set before us.

—At night, we lay out clothes for use the next morning.

—We put clothes where they belong when not in use: clean clothes in closet or drawers, dirty clothes in laundry.

—When we're finished with them, we put toys, sports gear, and tools back where they belong.

—If we've used a plate or drinking glass, we rinse or clean it and put it where it belongs.

—If we've borrowed something, we return it. If we've lost a borrowed item, we apologize and either try our best to replace it or we pay for it.

—We do our house chores promptly and to the best of our ability; we start our homework at a set time and stick with it until it's done right.

—We do not return a car home with less than a quarter tank of gas.

—We can all make suggestions about many affairs in family life, but parents make decisions in serious matters. And they decide what's serious.

—We do not aim for "results" as such, but rather for *personal best effort.*

(3) *We give people the information they need to carry out their responsibilities.*

—When we're going out, we always inform: where we are going, with whom, and when we plan to return.

—We get prior permission, with at least one day's notice, for important and potentially disruptive activities: sleepovers, camping trips, long distance trips, and the like.

—We come straight home from school, work, social events—except with prior consultation.

—We return from social events at a reasonable hour, one previously agreed upon.

—If we're going to be late, we call.

—We take phone messages intelligently: caller's name and phone number, summary of message (if any), time and date of call, name or initials of person who took the call.

—In general, we work to avoid unpleasant surprises and unnecessary worry in the family. (We have enough as it is.)

(4) *We use electronic media and games only to promote family welfare, never to work against it.*

—We have one television in the house, so as to monitor it and keep it from fragmenting the family.

—We use TV and video gadgets sparingly and discerningly. Most of our recreation will be non-electronic: reading, games, hobbies, sports, or conversation.

—We permit nothing in our home that offends our moral principles and treats other human beings as things: no pornography (treating women as objects), no racist or sexist or ethnic disparagement, no gratuitous violence, no coarse language, no glamorous depictions of disrespect and rudeness.

—We will usually—not always, but much of the time—watch TV and movies together: sports, high-quality shows and films, news, and documentaries. That's it.

—We do not watch TV on school nights, unless we watch together or with prior consultation, as noted above.

—If we bicker over TV or games, we get one warning to stop; if quarreling persists, the activity is terminated.

—We keep the noise level within reason so as not to distract or bother others.

(5) *We love and honor our Creator above all things; we thank Him for His blessings and ask His help for our needs and those of others.*

—We thank the Lord by worshipping Him together as a family.

—We strive to live by His commandments of right and wrong.

—We respect the conscience and rights of others who worship Him differently.

—We pray before meals and bedtime. We pray for the needs of our family and country and those of anyone suffering in sorrow. We serve the Lord by serving others.

—We live in the confidence that God watches over us with His loving fatherly protection. Parents treat their children the way God treats all of us—with affectionate and protective love, attention to needs, clear standards of right and wrong, compassionate understanding, and a ready willingness to forgive.

—We know that God commands all of us to honor father and mother. The finest way we do this is to adopt our parents' values, live by them all our lives, and pass them on to our own children whole and intact.

▲ ▲

There you have them, the rules most commonly found in great families.

To live by these rules perfectly every day is, of course, an impossible ideal. Some amount of backsliding and flawed performance is absolutely normal. Nobody's perfect. All the same, these rules are fixed in place as what we try to live by, a "resting place" for our conscience—like the keys on a piano or keyboard to which our fingers always return. People in a great family never attain perfection, but they never stop trying. To keep trying, no matter what, is the essence of greatness.

Of course, you may not agree with everything listed here. You and your wife may want to add or delete. It's your family, and the two of you may share different approaches, varying values all your own that you want to put into family life.

In any event, I urge you—as a responsible father—to work with your wife to set high standards for yourselves and your children, and then act on them every day.

If you do, you will probably see your grown children, twenty or more years from now, set these same high standards—even the exact same rules—to raise your grandchildren as great men and women. This will be part of the payoff, the final return on investment for your years of hard work: to see your grandchildren raised by the values you shaped so patiently in your children's minds and hearts.

YOUR WIFE AS YOUR PARTNER

I was talking with a group of men about a father's role in the family, passing on what I'd learned, spelling out the lessons that I've laid out in this book. One middle-aged man, one of the best fathers I've ever known, said this to me, and quite strongly: "Everything you've said is true, Jim. But the key thing, more important than anything else, is to work as a partner with your wife. Unity! That's what it's all about. Get united with your wife and everything else falls into place."

He had a point, and I have to emphasize it here: *The power of "We" starts with leading your children to honor their mother.* If you win here, you win half the battle.

Make no mistake about it: your wife is the cornerstone of your family life. Her life of endless sacrificial service is the basis for all the good and great things the two of you will teach your children.

I've said it before, but I must say it again: Though children hear things selectively, their roving eyes scan everything. From the corners of their eyes, they soak up everything that passes between you and your wife. And they learn from what they see.

When kids see Dad show affectionate respect toward Mom, then they grow to honor her themselves. But if they sense Dad's apparent laxity or indifference toward Mom, they steadfastly ignore her authority and increasingly treat her with sass. They imitate what they see.

In other words, a mother's authority in the home, her ability to teach and to lead, depends enormously on her husband's obvious respect and support for her. So a good father is above all a loving husband. He is a man who leads his children to love and honor their mother, his beloved wife. Where the children are concerned, he *insists* that they respect and serve her, exactly as he does.

As I explained above, every healthy family sets rules in place, some standards to direct the children's attitudes and comportment. These I've spelled out. But the number-one rule among smart, effective fathers is this: *Mom comes first.*

That is, whatever pleases Mom—whatever gives happiness, comfort, enjoyment, and honor to Mom—is what we will do, period. It's what we, the children and Dad together, will carry out. Notice the *we*: all of us in the family, with Dad in the lead.

In light of this, here are some questions for you to think about:

• How often, and in what ways, do your children see you show affection to your wife? Do they see you hug and kiss her, give her flowers and other little surprise gifts? Do they see you remember her birthday and your wedding anniversary, and celebrate these in a big way? Given the many distractions pulling at the children today (TV, video games, busy schedule, the Internet), do you go out of your way to get the message across to your children?

- Do you tell her, often, how much you love her?
- In your casual conversation with your children, do you sometimes remind them of what they see in your actions—that their mother is, in your estimation, the greatest woman in the world?
- Do you point out to your children her special beauty, her courage and character, her mastery of detail, her incredible stamina, her constant sacrificial love for the family? Do you show your kids that you're proud of her and consider her as your best friend?
- Are you sensitive to her needs? Do you make time to listen to her when she wants to talk, *needs* to talk? Do you ask her opinion and value it? Do you ask how you can help out around the home? Do you sense when she needs a rest, a break—and what do you do about it?
- Do you make clear to your daughters that their mother is a model for their future lives as great women?
- Do you explain to your sons why their mother is the standard for the kind of woman they should someday seek in marriage? And if they succeed at this, as you did, they can count their lives a success?

Naturally, this list of questions works in reverse, as well. That is, your wife's signs of love and honor for you will enhance your authority as father, even if—or especially if—you must work long hours away from the home. But that's not your problem here. We're talking about what you do for her.

Remember, marriage is not a 50–50 proposition, a mere business deal, like a contract with a plumber. A really healthy marriage is more like 80–20 or 90–10. If you count on giving more than you receive—to weigh your wife's needs and feelings more than your own—then you will be a great husband and father. When you show more love for your wife, on purpose and sincerely, you will see her return it to you in even fuller measure. (In fact, maybe this is already happening, but up to now you've failed to notice it.)

I cannot emphasize this point too strongly. The affectionate honor you and your wife show to each other is more than half the task of raising your children well. After all, your long-range ideal is that each of them enter into a solid marriage and raise a great family. So every day, together with your wife, you teach your children what family life is really all about—generous, self-sacrificing love.

The French writer Antoine de Saint-Exupéry said: "Love is not two people looking at one another. Love is two people looking together in the same direction."

Great parents look together toward their children. Though they may differ in any number of other things, a great husband and wife share one mind and will concerning their children's upbringing. They share the same long-term vision about their children's future as responsible men and women, and they're determined to work together, no matter what, to make this happen.

Great parents hold this truth ever before them: each child has only one mind and one conscience—and therefore needs one direction, and only one, coming from each of the parents. Children raised in a united family learn from infancy that each parent is "the boss." What's more, if asked about it, they would say, "My parents always stick up for each other."

No doubt about it, children whose parents work hard at this *directional consensus* grow strong in character more quickly. As they grow through the teen years, they cannot play one parent against the other and then scoot through the gap. (Look around and you'll find families where canny teens manipulate their parents this way.)

Parents who can count on each other's support are much more confident in acting as leaders. Knowing you're not alone, that you can rely on strong backup, always enhances courage and confidence. So children led by united parents know only confident, clear direction at home. With this sort of guidance, they grow in confidence themselves.

As a father, you should never forget: Confident kids resist drugs. Confident teens resist peer-group pressures. Confident workers go places in business—they receive respect, raises, and promotions. Confident young people tend to marry wisely and then raise confident children themselves.

A large part of our courage in life, probably most of it, derives from growing up in a loving, supportive family. It comes from the purposeful, affectionate direction of mutually supportive parents—a man and woman who are confident in each other.

How can you and your wife work at strengthening this mutual support? Here are five approaches that other smart parents have relied on.

First: Set some time apart each week, even only a half hour or so, to talk about each of your children—strengths and shortcomings, personal needs and problems, dealings with siblings, possible courses of action, what to do next. Sunday morning seems to work best for this sort of family shoptalk. Pay attention to your wife's judgment in these matters. Almost certainly, she has sharper, more sensitive insight than you do. Mothers are gifted this way.

Second: Determine that you will never, ever, oppose or demean each other in front of the children, especially when one of you is correcting a child. If either of you thinks the other is wrong, save the discussion for later and work it out privately.

Third, and related to the first and second: Don't ever carry on a heated quarrel in front of the children. You can express a difference of opinion or even an argument in the harmless sense. But any sharp clash with a jagged personal edge should be quickly followed by apologies and return to normal affection.

In fact, it's healthy for kids to see that sometimes even loving parents will argue but then swiftly reconcile. Nobody is perfect; anyone can have a bad day. Spotty flashes of anger flare out in nearly all marriages, but apologies swiftly cover these over. "I'm sorry . . .please forgive me . . ." is one of the strongest bonds of marriage.

What is terribly frightening to kids and corrosive to family life is any prolonged and really heated quarrel. The two of you must avoid this at all costs, even that of your pride.

So, if you sense that a disagreement is getting out of hand, that an argument is going too far, then have some pre-established signal with each other (like tapping your watch or discreetly giving the "time-out" sign with both hands) that means it's time to drop the subject. That is, you both agree that—no matter how upset you feel at the moment—you'll put off the discussion till later when you're alone together. At that time you can thrash things out; but by then, of course, both of you will have calmed down. Whatever it takes, do anything rather than scare the kids.

Fourth: Set a policy that's helpful when your kids are small and extremely important as they enter their teens—namely: when your children ask your permission in a fairly important matter (sleepovers, camping trips, exemption from house rules, special use of the car, and the like), put off your decision until you've checked with your wife. And she follows the same deferred-decision policy with regard to you.

Each of you says, "Let me first check with Mom (or Dad)." Doing this consistently is a great boon. For one thing, it prevents misunderstanding and arguments between you and your wife later. It also builds the kids' concept of your mutual support; it underscores how you respect each other's judgment. What's more, it keeps wily teens from playing each of you off against the other, and it gives both of you time to reflect about the decision and impose reasonable conditions where necessary.

Another benefit is that it makes your kids *wait* for what they want, and this is healthy for them. Your children should not form the corruptive habit, as with many kids today, of expecting *instant gratification*, especially in significant matters. If your children cannot *earn* whatever they want, they can at least *wait* for it. Waiting is healthy for children.

Fifth: What should you do if you find it hard to agree on some specifics of discipline—in house rules, for instance, or types of punishment for serious wrongdoing? You can try several tactics that other parents have relied on.

You can work out a compromise: "Okay, we'll try it your way for three months (or whatever), and then we'll try it my way. Let's see how things work out."

Or, if you have time, seek out some arbitration. Agree to consult someone you both respect—a good friend, a relative, a teacher or member of the clergy, anyone with sound judgment and experience in family matters—and agree to abide by his or her advice.

As a last-ditch measure, or if time is pressing, flip a coin! I mean this. Any decision is better than none at all. No effective leader ever lets indecision lead to inaction.

No matter what you do, know that you (and your wife) may have to swallow your pride a bit for the sake of presenting a united front to your children. Experience shows that this unity, no matter how arrived at, is far more important than specific tactics. As long as you are together in mind and will, as long as you're both determined to remain united, you can afford to make mistakes along the way. Somehow, in the long run, it works.

7 | Direct Your Children with "Affectionate Assertiveness"

All right, you've set standards for your family, and you and your wife try to live by them yourselves—to set an example before your children's eyes. So far, so good. But that's only the concrete foundation, and you still have to raise up the structure inside your kids, within the mind and heart of each of them, not only loosely in the home.

Now we come to the tough part: directed practice—making the kids do the right thing, living by the family's rules, over and over again until "right living" is fixed firmly within them, and for keeps.

If they stray into wrong from time to time (and they will), they will at least *know* it's wrong. Within their consciences they'll hear the echo of your voice, remember your lessons—and this voice and memory can protect them from harm. Throughout the twisting course of their lives, as long as they hold on to what you taught them, you will never stop being their father.

How does a father go about this? Well, start with an absolutely basic principle: your right of authority in the family.

A smart father understands that parenthood is not an elective office; you do not have to curry favor with your children. Your rights as a father come with the job, with your responsibility.

In the picnic family, parents are unsure of their authority because they are unsure or clueless about their job. No job means no responsibility, which means no real leadership.

In the home as in business, authority and responsibility— rights and duties—must go hand in hand; you cannot have one without the other. They have to be proportional, of equal heft. If you were handed a tough assignment at work but were denied the power and resources to carry it out, you would gnash your teeth in frustration. You'd be stymied with the burden of your duties, and you'd seethe with resentment at this injustice. No-body—in any human situation—can bear responsibility without holding the power to carry it out.

As a father, you take on enormous responsibility. You are responsible for your children's welfare, and for this you answer to the law, to society, to your conscience, and to your Creator. In fact—and this is something men seldom think about—you will even answer later to your grown children; someday they will look back and judge you, up or down, for the way you dealt with them in childhood. (And, by the way, so will your in-laws.)

When a man becomes a father, he takes on rights. He confidently claims the authority—the power to choose and decide—that he must possess to lead his children responsibly, to keep them from harm.

Authority means, among other things, the right to be obeyed. A smart father may harbor quiet doubts about many things in family life, but he never doubts his right to his children's obedience. He asserts this right, as he asserts all his other rights, in a manly, no-nonsense way. But he does this with understanding and affection: he is "affectionately assertive," and this is the essence of fatherly discipline.

This is what some fathers have told me:

"I don't always know what's the right decision for my kids, . . . but I know I have the right to make a decision and to make it stick. My judgment may be sometimes mistaken, but that doesn't affect my right to make a judgment in the first place."

"I don't often have to put my foot down hard . . . but if I do, my kids know I mean business. They know better than to cross me when I've made up my mind about something that's important to them."

"My teenagers try to push the envelope, but I won't let them. I push back. . . . As I see it, if I give in easily to teenagers, so will they. That is, they'll buckle under peer pressures, follow along with the crowd. And a lot of teenage crowds these days are headed over cliffs to their destruction. My teens will not be among them. . . ."

"My kids aren't old enough to judge what's best for them. Until they are, my wife and I make the decisions. . . . We won't allow our children to hurt themselves through childish misjudgment."

"If kids won't respect their parents' rights, then they won't respect anyone else's, either. . . . A kid who rejects his father's authority will later have problems with his boss. This could be lethal to his career."

"I get only one shot at raising my kids. That's all, only one. And if I blow it, I could spend the rest of my life regretting it. I won't let this happen. . . ."

Discipline Is Leadership and "Joinership"

The word "discipline" has had bad press. It's widely misunderstood to mean punishment. But it does not mean punishment. Nor does it mean control for its own sake. And it does not mean enforcing rules only for the sake of minimizing hassles at home, a kind of "damage control."

Discipline certainly involves occasional punishment and some control as well as clear guidelines for behavior. But its real meaning is far deeper and more important. Discipline really means confident, effective leadership.

Look at it this way. The word "discipline" is related to the word "disciple," and it springs from the Latin word meaning "to learn." Discipline is what happens when some leader teaches and his "disciples" learn. Broadly speaking, discipline means teaching and learning, leading and joining.

To repeat the key idea here: Discipline in family life means teaching the children to acquire—by personal example, directed practice, and verbal explanation (in that order)—the great virtues of sound judgment, a sense of responsibility, personal courage, self-control, and magnanimity. These take root in the give-and-take of family life and then flower to healthy maturity through the steady nourishment of confident, unified parental leadership. All this takes years.

In other words, discipline (teaching) requires planning and patience as much as occasional swift corrective action. It calls for setting the example as much as rules, and encouragement and praise as much as loving denial and just punishment.

It means living in such a way so that children are made to do what is right—as the parents see this—and shun what is wrong, and to explain the differences so compellingly that the children will remember the lessons all their lives and then pass them on to their children. That's the long and the short of it.

AFFECTIONATE ASSERTIVENESS

Every effective father I've known practices what might be called *affectionate assertiveness*. That is, he *asserts* correct conduct and attitudes by his example, action, and words. At the same time he's unfailingly affectionate with his children. He corrects because he loves them, wants to protect them, and cares above all else for their future welfare and happiness.

He sets out to *correct the fault, not the person*. He "hates the sin, loves the sinner." He's willing, on occasion, to risk being temporarily "unpopular" with a wayward son or daughter—knowing that their future happiness is at stake (along with that of his wife), and that his children will someday thank him and revere him as a great father.

You can see this affectionate assertiveness at work when you bathe your infant children. Your little youngsters resist and scream rebellion against your rubdowns with soap and water. They do not understand how dirt and germs can harm them. No matter. Loving parents ignore the tearful, screeching protests and simply scrub away, cooing affectionate words of encouragement—until the little one's skin is clean and dry, and once again baby is happily at peace.

The same thing happens when the children are older. Because of their gross inexperience with life and consequences, kids will rebelliously, vehemently resist what is good for them. Smart parents know this, take it for granted, and are courageous enough to *resist their children's resistance.*

Effective parents ignore their kids' squawking and assert what's best for their welfare—by making them do their chores, clean up their messes, abide by rules of the house, obey instructions, respect other people's rights, make and accept apologies where called for, the whole gamut of lessons in civilized living.

When he's sure he is right, when he knows his kids' welfare depends on it, an effective father shrugs off his children's gripes and moaning (for, as he knows, nobody enjoys being corrected) and assertively presses his kids to do what he judges best for them, what will protect them, both now and later in life.

One man told me this story:

"My college-age daughter brought home her new boyfriend, at my insistence, and I sized him up. To be blunt about it, I didn't like what I saw. My wife also sensed a problem with the guy, and she's usually right about these things. Later, when my girl and I were alone, I insisted that she break up with him. I put my foot down, said I wouldn't take 'no' for an answer. . . . She broke into angry tears, wailing and carrying on, but I wouldn't budge. Finally she gave in. . . . Six months later, he got another girl pregnant. . . .

"My attitude has always been this: *I'd rather see her crying now than later.* Tears today come from disappointment and a frustrated will; but tomorrow's tears can come from a tragedy. Better she break up now, however painful, than get stuck with a pregnancy or a bad marriage."

Here's another man's story:

"My son Bobby was close to his sixteenth birthday and was eagerly looking forward to getting his driver's license. He'd taken the courses, talked about it night and day, bored us to death with it. But I had some serious doubts. Most of the time he was fairly cooperative around the house, but he still—at age sixteen—hadn't completely controlled his temper. He'd sometimes fly off the handle, rage around the house over trivial things, bother his mother. I corrected him every time, mostly with success, but sometimes he'd still fume for hours. . . .

"Finally, I sat down with him and laid it out calmly but firmly: I won't permit you to get a license or use our car unless you show us, over three months, that you've got serious control over your impulsive temper. Every time you explode around here, we push the deadline back another month. . . . Driving is for grown-ups and nobody else. I can't, in good conscience, let you on the road if you've still got the attitudes and angry impulsiveness of a child.

"Naturally, he hit the roof. . . . He stomped and bellowed, almost in tears. When he calmed down a bit, I told him softly, 'That, Bobby, is exactly what I'm referring to. . . . If you react like that when you're behind the wheel, you can kill or cripple someone.' He got the message and was almost like an angel for the next four months. Whenever he was on the verge of an outburst, all I had to do was stare daggers at him, and he understood. I made him prove he was really old enough to drive.

"That was twelve years ago, and I'm happy and proud to say he's never had an accident or even a ticket."

Somehow, mysteriously, normal children sense when their parents correct them out of love. Great parents correct because they love. Even though kids dislike the correction itself, deep down they grasp the love behind their parents' direction. Sooner or later, as they grow up, they understand that their parents' occasional wrath is aimed at their faults, not them personally.

Because you, as a father, show plenty of affection in normal, nonconfrontational situations in family life (which is most of the time), and because you always show willingness to forgive once apologies are made and punishment done, your children sense the truth—that your whole life, including episodes of corrective punishment, devotes itself to their happiness. Later, as young adults, and even before they're out of their teens, they will understand why your love moved you to act as you did, and they will thank you.

A few words here about manly affection.

In family life, you show your love most when you show affection to your wife. Your kiss with her when you leave home and return, your arm around her shoulder when you huddle together on a couch, your hand in hers when you walk or sit together, the way you look at her and listen when she's talking— all these and other signs of your love for each other impress your children enormously.

By these signs, your children sense that your love for them derives somehow from your love for their mother. Kissing your wife in front of the kids is like kissing each of them in turn.

But you should show affection to your children as well, and this is easy for a man when his kids are infants. Psychologists note that most men seem to have an irresistible urge to vigorous physical play with their toddlers—bouncing them, swinging them in the air, tickling them, making funny faces, anything to share laughs. Specialists say this natural play instinct helps to bond very young children to their fathers. Tiny children physically feel their father's power, his muscles and bodily strength, and they sense that this power is there to protect them. So they have nothing to fear when Daddy is around.

Affectionate heart, strong muscles, powerful mind and will— this is what "Dad" means to small children. This impression of "powerful Dad" leads youngsters to feel protected and therefore confident.

As the kids grow older, they need this impression reinforced by Dad's ongoing displays of affection. How do you do this?

You physically touch them. You welcome them on your knee and embrace them. You take their hand while walking together. You playfully squeeze them on the shoulder or arm. When walking by them as they're sitting someplace, you pat them on the head or ruffle their hair a bit. You invite them to sit next to you and pat them when they sit down. You give them a wink and a smile. You tell corny jokes and laugh at theirs. You tell funny stories and find other ways to share a good laugh, but without offending anyone. You whisper things in their ears. (Sometimes, when you feel like shouting something at your small children, have them sit on your lap instead and whisper it into their ear; this nearly always gets their attention. And your correction comes across affectionately, as it should.)

You show happiness and pride in their accomplishments. *You make praise every bit as specific as blame.* (Parents tend to make blame specific but to put praise in vague generalities: "You've been a good girl this morning. . . .") Praise them for a job well done, even when they've done it as punishment: "You did a great job making your bed this morning. . . . Your room is spic and span, the way it should be. . . . Your homework looks neat and professional, and I'm proud of you. . . ." Children need sincere praise from time to time. In fact, we all do. One of people's greatest needs, at any age, is sincere appreciation.

When you tuck them into bed, you linger a bit, a couple of minutes to make small talk. Bedtime is a great occasion to talk things over with children, and listen to them. All their lives, they will fondly remember their bedtime chats with Dad.

With your daughters, especially as they approach adolescence, you show *respectful* affection. That's warm fatherly affection combined with respect for their womanhood. That is, you avoid any physical contact that would even suggest improper intimacy. You do not touch or hold them in any way that would bother you if done by a male your daughter's age. Though you show affection with your voice and eyes, you maintain a certain physical distance—a respect for your girls' personal "space."

Very important: This fatherly respect is a preparation and, as it were, a model for the self-respect they should maintain in their dealings with other men. When girls receive this respectful affection from their fathers, it seems, they are more careful and self-respectful in receiving affection from men. On the other hand, girls who lack this fatherly guidance are far less sure where to draw the line with men, or they have poor judgment altogether in intimate situations—and they can fall headlong into trouble.

In effect, a father says to his daughters: The way I treat you is the way all other men in your life should treat you. Don't tolerate anything else. Because you've grown to be a young woman, it's no longer appropriate for you to sit on my lap. That means you don't sit on any other guy's lap, either! As your father, I give you a brief, gentle hug and a quick affectionate kiss—and that's as far as you should go with other men. In my eyes you see affection, pride, and my wish to protect you from harm. That's what you should look for in the eyes of other men; if you see anything else, especially a hunger to possess you and treat you like an object, then drop the guy permanently! When you find a man who looks at you and treats you as I do, then you can begin to consider him as a possible marriage partner. There are other character traits you should look for, too, but begin with this.

Most of all, with both sons and daughters, you show affection with your eyes.

You should *listen to your children with your eyes*. When you deliberately make eye contact with them, especially when they're speaking to you, you show how much you care for them. In your eyes they can read your fatherly soul—your love for them, your pride in them, and your hopes for their future.

COPING WITH WILDNESS

As any veteran parents can tell you, there are two fairly long stretches in children's lives when abrupt bodily changes—rapid physical growth and development—lead to emotional instability. Biochemical agents pummel the brain and provoke mood swings, crankiness, resistance to directive authority, lack of self-esteem, alternating physical exuberance and fatigue, and other outward signs of inner turmoil. At times like this, children are hard to deal with, sometimes exasperating to contend with.

The first of these stages lies between the ages of two and five. Ralph Waldo Emerson once wrote, "A child is a cuddly, dimpled lunatic." He had a point: kids really are nutty at this age. They are typically driven by wild impulses and they try to defy any outside controlling authority. They push the envelope, trying to tear it open. They seem bent on struggling with their parents to see who's "boss" in the house.

Lamentably, some picnic-type parents, weak-willed and clueless about their mission to form character, more or less give up—so their kids emerge on top as "boss" of the household.

Other parents, more savvy and confident, do whatever is necessary to civilize their children. By the age of five, their kids emerge with a clear understanding: Mom and Dad are in charge of things around here. Each of them is "boss."

This grappling and sometimes frustrating struggle in the youngest years prepares the way, for good or for ill, when the kids grow through the second unsettled stage, between the ages of thirteen and seventeen. In most respects, adolescence is a replay of the earlier wrestling match for domination. Once again parents contend with the same emotional ups and downs, the pushiness and insecurity, the need for clear, calm, confident, and affectionate direction.

Here's the point, and an extremely important one: Experience shows that those parents who won the earlier struggle—who, as "boss," managed to teach lessons of justice and self-restraint in the youngest years—have relatively few problems later with their teenage children.

You may have trouble believing this, but it's true. I've seen it countless times. With some exceptions, families where Mom and Dad gave firm character formation to their kids since infancy eventually turn out adolescents who are (despite occasional roller-coaster dips) fine, responsible young men and women, kids to be proud of. Often, in fact, parents find that life with their near-grown adolescent children is actually—surprisingly—enjoyable and rewarding. After all, these parents aimed for years to raise their children as adults; they always saw their kids as adults-in-the-making. Now they're coming down the finish line. They find they're sharing their home with enjoyable, interesting young men and women of high-school age—adults in everything but experience.

I wish I had a few dollars for every time I heard something like this from fathers and mothers who did their job with their kids: "We kept waiting for this so-called 'adolescent rebellion' to hit us, but it never did! Oh, we sometimes had our spats and flare-ups, especially if we were all worn out, dead tired. Who doesn't? To be honest, half the time it was my fault—I was short-tempered and unreasonable. We quickly made up and got on with life. So there were outbursts, yes. But wild rebellion? It never happened."

A great father, a wise man, once told me this: "As I see it, the drive for independence is absolutely normal in teenagers. In fact, it's healthy. I'd worry if my kids didn't want and expect to be independent some day. I think parents head off trouble with teenagers, long ahead of time, when they've always wanted their kids to grow up, as my wife and I did. From the time the kids were small, we told the kids that we expected them to think and act like responsible young grown-ups about halfway through high school, by the time they started driving. The more responsibly they acted as teens, the more freedom we gave them. The only time we imposed restrictions was when their inexperienced judgment could harm them. . . . My wife and I think kids grow in one of two directions: either *up* to their parents' expectations or *down* to them."

I can't leave off here without saying this: Psychologists note that there's yet a third time of life when bodily changes lead to unsettled psychological state and occasional mild wackiness. That's around the age of forty, give or take a few years—the so-called midlife crisis.

This "crisis" does not afflict everyone, and it's usually not so dramatic or vexing as the first two bouts, in young childhood and the teen years. All the same, it does happen, and it can happen to you.

In many families, unfortunately, while the children are careening through the ups and downs of adolescence, one or both parents are struggling through emotional problems of their own. Consequently both teens and their parents are insecure and edgy. Teens glare into the mirror and worry about acne and bulbous noses; their parents gaze in the mirror and fret about newfound wrinkles and gray hairs. Parents and teens can get on each other's nerves, and even in stable families, minor skirmishes sometimes skyrocket into emotional ego-centered battles for control.

I'm trying here to put you on notice, to give you some prior warning that you and your children may someday face this muddle. If you're aware of it, you can prepare for it in advance and brace yourself to ride it out. Try to be honest enough to admit frankly: it takes two to have a pointless argument, and sometimes I'm at fault.

You can take a lot of confidence from what's been noted already. Namely, if you've raised your children right in their youngest years, then even with complications of midlife touchiness, you can still deal successfully with your teenage children. Many men have won at this, and so can you. Sooner or later, the storms blow over. Teens and parents both have their bodies settle back to normal. They emerge from the valley of shadows and life goes on. You and your wife will enjoy a calm and confident middle age, proud of your grown children.

"MEMORABLE CORRECTION"

I said earlier that discipline does not mean punishment as such. All the same, discipline sometimes calls for punishment—and punishment is best understood as "memorable correction." Look at it this way and you'll seldom go wrong.

When kids do wrong in fairly serious matters (more on this below), they have to learn that wrongdoing in the family—as in society, as in normal life—leads to unpleasant consequences.

We're talking here about the virtue of responsibility, which means, among other things, having to live with the conse-quences of our decisions and actions, our goofs and injustices. So, what can we say about punishment? How can you and your wife effectively manage it?

(i) Be aware, first of all, that you both hold enormous power over your children. Too many parents underestimate their ca-pacity to direct and control. They don't recognize how depen-dent their children are on them. Even though children resist it mightily, they badly need outside control, for they have almost no self-control. If their life has no control whatever, neither from themselves nor from their parents, then their lives spin out of control—and this drives them crazy. It seems that much of the wildness among spoiled children stems from their fear, their quiet terror, that *no one is in charge*.

In healthy families, kids sense that their immediate environ-ment, the place where they live, is safely under control. That is, the parents' confident and loving direction of events fosters children's sense of security and therefore their growth in self-confidence.

To be sure, kids in the two-to-five age group will try to wrest this control away (as noted before) and impose their own wills. But smart, conscientious parents simply do not permit this to happen, no matter what.

You and your wife *must* be in charge—so that your children's insecurity and aggressiveness will be replaced by confidence in you now and, later, in themselves. In other words, though your children will resist it at first, they unconsciously depend on your strong leadership to put order in their chaotic lives. With order comes peace of mind. For them as for you and nearly all other adults, anarchy is frightening.

(ii) So, how do you get their serious attention in order to correct them memorably? Reflect first on what they most fear and respect.

To begin with, all children respect physical strength, and most often associate this with Dad. You can impose your physi-cal strength on your children without resorting to corporal punishment.

Moreover, children have an inborn fear of separation from their families. Child specialists say that the greatest terror chil-dren suffer is that of being separated from their parents, being left alone. Children's nightmares often center on this theme. (In ancient time, ostracism—banishment from society— was a se-vere, horrifying punishment, second only to the death penalty.)

(iii) Children from normal, loving homes fear angry disapproval from parents who are otherwise normally affectionate. When confronted with it, children want deep down to reestablish normal good relations and they're willing (once they've calmed down) to meet their parents' terms for peace. Parents need to remind themselves that all children misbehave occasionally, and that most of the time kids are at least reasonably cooperative. All things considered, children's misbehavior is really only a sporadic straying from the norm. Your disciplinary strategy is really to take matters in hand so as to *restore peace* between you and your children.

So, these things being said, what can you do to punish misbehavior in fairly serious matters? Here is a list drawn from parents' experience:

• Physically, but painlessly, restrain the children. Take them by the hand or arm and remove them to someplace private. Take both hands or wrists in yours, hold the children still, and look them in the eye. Say what you have to say in a low but "I-mean-business" way and keep at it until they've understood and said they are sorry.

• Remove them physically and make them spend what some parents call "time out"—a few minutes of isolation away from the family, even in a closed room. Don't let them return until they've said they're sorry. (For very young children, you may have to supervise their time in a corner or some other "punishment spot.")

• For older children, remove privileges. This means no games or television or use of the telephone. For teens it might mean no phone calls or going out with friends or use of the car. (Teens who display thoughtless attitudes and uncontrolled impulsiveness are a menace on the road and shouldn't drive anyway. You can make this clear to them: only responsible, mature adults may drive the family car.)

• Put them to work. Have a so-called "job jar" at home. This is a receptacle with slips of paper describing jobs to be done around the house. Let the malefactor pick out three slips and then choose one, which must then be done to your satisfaction. Also, if kids complain they're "bored" around the house, direct them to the job jar. Parents who do this hardly ever hear complaints from their kids about boredom. The word "boring" disappears from the family vocabulary.

• If two siblings are quarreling and won't stop after one

warning, put both of them to work on the same project: cleaning dishes, raking leaves, gardening, washing the car, whatever. This treatment usually brings about reconciliation. Misery likes company.

I have to insert a parenthesis here: For many kids in picnic families, being banished to the bedroom is scarcely a punishment at all. Typically, kids' rooms bulge with stereos, radio, television, and electronic games galore, and the kids live like pashas. Their rooms are essentially entertainment centers surrounding a bed.

From what I can see, many healthy families hold firmly to this policy: each child's bedroom is a place for study, reading, conversation with siblings, and sleep—period. Entertainment gadgets are only for common areas of the house, where people can enjoy them together. This policy has the happy side effect of eliminating distractions from homework. It works. And the kids learn a truth about life: When we try to work and play at the same time, we wind up doing neither—leisure is really enjoyable only when we've earned it.

In any event, whatever method of correction you use with your small children, see it as an investment that will later yield high return. Once you've established your authority in their youngest years, then you've won most of the battle. When they're older, a businesslike warning or flashing-eyed glare from you, or even your expression of "disappointment," usually works to restore cooperation. By that time, the kids know you mean business. In child rearing as in law (and especially with the IRS), there are few things as effective as a sincere threat.

LEVELS OF RESPONSE

A smart father—one who lives this affectionate assertiveness— works with his wife to plan out different lessons of responsibility (that is, punishments) in response to their children's varying types of misbehavior. This is important. The more carefully these responses are thought out beforehand, and thus made routine in family life, the calmer and more consistent both parents can be in handling their kids' provocations.

This rational structure avoids, or at least minimizes, the problem in many ineffective families, especially when dealing with teen-agers—impromptu punishments imposed in anger, often harsh and overreactive, and resented as unfair.

Remember, you can be tough with normal children and

quite effective with them if, and only if, they perceive that you're trying to be fair.

Here is a rational structure for imposing memorable correction on the kids for their wayward ways. It's based on a sound principle from military history: Those generals who chose their battlegrounds ahead of time usually managed to win—Hannibal at Cannae, Wellington at Waterloo, Lee at Fredericksburg, Eisenhower at Normandy.

Choose your battleground. Don't scatter your resources trying to correct the kids every single time they do wrong. If you or your wife tried this, you'd soon need to be fitted for a straitjacket.

Instead, establish three levels of misbehavior, each calling for proportionately heavy response. In rising order of seriousness, these are:

First, *misdemeanors*. These are minor infractions, misdeeds arising from childish inexperience, thoughtlessness, reckless impulsiveness—such as tracking mud in the house, noisy roughhousing, throwing missiles indoors, forgetting (that is, honestly forgetting) to do chores, failing to put things away. A lot of these habits the kids will outgrow anyway. These misdeeds call for quick but low-level response, or sometimes letting the matter go. It's like the quality control system in a factory: try to catch a sample every few times. You don't need to correct minor goofs every single time, and you might go crazy if you tried.

Second, *serious infractions*. These are actions where children infringe on the rights of others, especially siblings—causing offense by name-calling, taking property without permission, physical aggression, refusing to give or accept apology, using profanity, and similar deeds of barbaric injustice. Though you can occasionally overlook the misdemeanors mentioned above, you *must* correct these serious lapses of justice and charity practically every single time.

Never forget, every time you correct your children's injustices, their infringements on the rights of others, you are forming their lifelong conscience and ethics. You are preparing them for the way they will later treat their spouses, children, and professional colleagues. So there is a lot at stake here. Don't let up and don't give up.

Third, *felony infractions*. These are serious matters that endanger your children's welfare, either now or later in life, and they call for the severest punishment every single time, whatever this might be. The kids should have the roof fall in on them.

For the youngest children this category obviously includes whatever physically endangers them now: playing with fire, wandering into the street, poking metal objects into electrical outlets, and the like. Punishment should be swift and memorable. It seems that nearly all parents, even the most pacifist, react this way instinctively.

But equally important are those wrongdoings that threaten children's welfare later on as adults—those acts that imperil their basic concepts of respect for rightful authority and the importance of personal integrity. You must impose swift, serious punishment every time your children do the following:

—Show disrespect for you personally—call you names, try to strike you, raise their voice in anger at you.

—Attempt to defy your authority—say "no" or otherwise refuse to comply with your direction, or deliberately "forget" to do so. This pertains even in relatively minor matters, especially after you've given warning. If you direct your child to clean up a mess of his and he refuses or walks away, then the issue becomes one of authority, not cleanup. You must not permit him to get away with this defiance.

—Deliberately lie to you, especially after being put on their honor to tell the truth. (More on this later.)

These three areas are vitally important for your children's welfare. *Everything you have to teach your kids depends on their respect for you and for your authority and for their own word of honor. If you lose this, you lose them.*

To use a comparison, your insistence on these basics is like what happens in the criminal justice system. Disrespect for parental authority is like contempt of court, and deliberate falsehood is like perjury.

As you know, in our legal system we can lighten punishment through plea-bargaining for nearly all crimes—but never for contempt of court or perjury. The full weight of the law comes down on these offenses every time. Why is this? Because without people's respect for judicial authority and for telling the truth under oath, the courts cannot function at all. They might as well shut their doors and go out of business.

So it is in your family. You and your wife can't deal effectively with your children—cannot form their consciences, cannot even reach them—unless they respect your rightful authority and their obligation to tell the truth and keep their word.

Let me note here that ineffective parents generally fall into one of two extremes. They're either excessively strict or overly permissive. The "control freaks" treat all of children's misbehavior as felonies, and the weak treat all misdeeds, no matter how serious, as misdemeanors. The tyrants turn out teenagers who are either rebels or sneaks. The wimps turn out teens who can't control themselves; since the teens have lacked parental control, they never learn self-control—and so their lives spin out of control altogether.

Your approach—the one most effective in the long run—should fall in the middle and be qualitatively different: you are assertive without being harshly aggressive and affectionate without being sentimentally permissive.

If you and your wife deal with your young children by setting this hierarchy—misdemeanors, serious misdeeds, and felonies—you will, even with occasional mistakes, lead your children to grow in responsible attitudes and behavior. By the time the kids are adolescents, they'll have a lifelong habit of respecting your leadership and deferring to your judgment.

PEACE AT THE TABLE

Many effective parents I know maintain a rule that's strictly enforced: no fighting or squabbling at the dinner table, period.

Dinner is a very special time for families. For healthy families, it's positively sacred, one of the few occasions when the whole family draws together in unity. Consequently, it is no place for heated clashes or emotional tugs-of-war. If the kids have sharp disagreements, they can thrash things out (if they must) before or after dinner, but not at the table.

Why is this a sound policy? Why should a father enforce it?

For one thing, it's crucial to your wife's peace of mind. Few things bother women more than angry clashes among their children, especially at mealtime, when the family should be united. Your wife deserves freedom from hassle during this sacred time, and she leans on you to enforce it.

Second, as we've seen before, your children absolutely must learn to restrain their impulses, to put a brake on their passions. This habit is vital for their growth in self-control and their sense of family loyalty. If they practice self-restraint each day at least during dinnertime, then they can live this way more easily throughout the rest of the day. So, the policy is a good entry point for teaching children to control themselves.

Finally, the policy works to dampen or even squelch bad feelings altogether. When kids (or adults, for that matter) must wait to argue, their tempers usually cool down anyway. To put off a quarrel is to move halfway toward peace. This family standard is tough to impose at first, but sooner or later it becomes routine custom. The resulting peace is worth the initial hard effort. Your investment handsomely pays off. Think about this: If you asked most adults (as I have) which scenes from childhood they most fondly remember, they would probably recall gatherings around their dinner table. Joining together around the table signifies important matters of the heart that your children should later look back on: Mom and Dad, brothers and sisters, all enjoying life together as a family in harmony. Later in life, years from now, will your children cherish these memories?

GOOD MANNERS

Courtesy is much more than a set of habits. It's basically an attitude. Good manners show others how much we respect their dignity, rights, and feelings. It is this attitude you are after when you teach manners to your kids—and keep at it until they behave well reflexively, habitually, scarcely even calling it to mind.

Healthy people rarely think of their health; in fact, this is one of the signs of good health, that we hardly think about it. It is the same thing with courtesy. We are courteous because, well, that's the way we are—that's the way we were brought up.

But this kind of "natural" courtesy does not blossom overnight. Dads and Moms hammer away for years to build it up inside their children's everyday conduct.

Practicing *respectful behavior* ramps up to forming *respectful attitudes*. Kids who say "thank you" often enough will eventually form the concept of gratitude. Kids will stop grabbing for things after they've learned to say "please." In any case, it's the underlying attitudes that a father tries to form. Mature adults think about others, and good manners show this.

Most lessons in courtesy are obvious, and you need to support your wife in her endless struggle to impose them. Table manners, saying *please* and *thank you* and *excuse me,* sending thank-you notes, holding doors for people, letting adults through a doorway first, and so on—all these courtesies need to be repeated, hammered away at countless times until they are inside your children like solid rock.

For your children's sake, don't give up on this. Look on it as a lifetime investment. What you're really doing is ramping your children up to a powerful conscience—the understanding that other people have rights and feelings, too, and because of this we have obligations to them. Other people's rights lead to our duties. The peace and stability of your children's future marriages will depend on their solid grasp of this others-centered attitude.

Let me now highlight a detail of courtesy that belongs in a special way to the father. In a sense it is Dad's specialty. I would guess that its decline in recent years stems from the father's diminished role in American families. I'm referring here to the handshake.

It is incredible how many young males, even well into high school, don't know how to shake hands and greet adults. They avert their eyes, mumble something quasi-coherent, and offer their right hand (if at all) as a limp mass of warm flesh. Shaking hands with them is like squeezing a lukewarm codfish.

When I worked as headmaster, I used to pay attention to how young applicants (aged twelve to fourteen) would shake hands and greet me during our interview. If a boy offered a limp hand, I certainly wouldn't hold this against him. Probably he never learned how to handle himself like a man, or in his nervousness he simply forgot.

But if a young boy, however nervous he was, extended me a firm handshake and a poised greeting, I saw this as a good sign. It told me that some sort of character formation was going on at home. This youngster's family was probably not of the picnic sort. Both parents—father as well as mother—were teaching adult-level standards: at the very least, good manners. Later, when the boy joined us, I saw plenty of other evidence that his parents were doing their job. Sure enough, this young fellow showed himself to be mature, self-disciplined, and considerate—a youngster who brought honor to his family.

Genuine courtesy really does say something about kids' character. What's more, it says a lot about their parents. *Well-mannered children bring honor to their parents.* So, when your children live good manners, praise them, show how proud you are that they honor their family.

HONOR AND INTEGRITY

Honor. The term isn't heard much these days but it lies at the core of children's conscience and sense of commitment. Personal honor is one of the most vital lessons a man must teach his children.

Let's say something here about lying.

Nearly all children will spontaneously fib—blurt out a falsehood—to wiggle out of blame and punishment. At least they will try. Lying is one of the two defenses kids rely on to thwart adult power; the other is weeping, bursting into tears.

You must never let your youngsters get away with lying, of course, but you should distinguish between a spontaneous, almost desperate on-the-spot fib and a cold-blooded, deliberate falsehood. A purposeful lie is much more serious. It's like the crime of perjury, and it is flatly unacceptable. Your children need to learn that it's one thing to *lie*—but it's another to *be a liar*.

To live as a liar is to lose personal honor, the trust people put in us, and this is an enormous loss. Every father needs to teach this to his children, and for keeps. It's one of his most crucial duties as a Dad.

Many great fathers rely on the following practice to drive the lesson home, starting when the kids are old enough to understand (age five or so): When they suspect their child is lying, especially in a fairly serious matter, they say this—"Go to your room and think this over seriously. When you come out, tell me the truth *on your honor*. Whatever you say then, I will believe it—because you're on your honor. . . . And heaven help you if you refuse, on your honor, to tell the truth!"

Children from families with this practice will nearly always tell the truth. Early on, the kids learn that their parents must be able to trust them; and that, if they lie while on their honor, they do immense damage to that bond between you and them. If they betray your trust by sticking with a lie under honor, and you find out about it later, then you should treat it as a felony (as we saw earlier) and punish severely—with strong, unforgettable explanation about the utter importance of personal trust. Kids will seldom, almost never, repeat the mistake.

On the other hand, if they admit on their honor that they fibbed before, then give them some minor, slap-on-the-wrist punishment—but praise them lavishly for having the courage to tell the truth. Welcome them quickly back into your good graces and complete trust. They've earned it, and they've learned a hugely important lesson.

If you live this policy when your kids are small, you'll have few problems with openness when they enter adolescence. You may even have no problems at all. By that time, your children will know what you mean when you tell them you trust their integrity. They'll know what the word means.

Integrity. You can cultivate your children's sense of personal honor and healthy self-respect by occasionally explaining what integrity entails.

In adult society, and especially in the workplace, personal integrity is more valued than almost any other virtue. Responsible, mature adults know this, but kids do not. Consistently, bosses rank integrity as the number-one characteristic they demand and expect of their workers; they see it as more important than talent or skills or credentials.

What's more, a lack of personal integrity seems to lie behind marital problems and break-ups. Spouses stop trusting each other, and in time they fall out of love.

Given this nearly universal agreement about integrity, it's puzzling why so many parents fail even to mention the word at home, much less teach what it means.

So, what does it mean? How can you explain integrity to your children?

Try this: The word is related to other terms we use—*integer, integrate, disintegrate*—all centering somehow on unity and wholeness. *Integrity means unity of someone's intention, word, and action.* A person with integrity says what he means, means what he says, and keeps his word. That is, he tells the truth and he keeps his promises. He takes his honesty and commitments seriously, sometimes to the point of courageous sacrifice. Integrity is honor put into action.

A moment ago, I explained a way to handle children's attempts to lie, reinforcing their concept of personal honor. Here are some other suggestions.

As much as possible, teach your children this life lesson: Don't make promises lightly, but if you make them, you're obligated to keep your word. If out-of-control circumstances keep you from honoring your promises, then you owe the offended party an immediate, sincere apology. People's respect for your word, your integrity, depends hugely on your *commitment to keep your commitments.*

This is the way honorable, responsible adults live. And this is what your children must learn and live by.

Also, try to turn some rules of the home into occasions where kids, older ones especially, obligate themselves through their given word. For instance, rather than simply imposing a set curfew to return from a dance, negotiate an agreement with them about a reasonable hour. (The word "reasonable" goes very far with teenagers.) Then exact from them a promise to return at that time. From that point on, their responsibility is not merely to obey your curfew but rather to *keep their word*, to hold up their end of the agreement.

As much as you can, try to treat your adolescent children as responsible adults. When you apply this tactic, exacting promises rather than obedience, you're giving them a taste of the way responsible adults do business. After all, outside of the military, an employee doesn't really "obey" his boss so much as he honors his business commitments. He makes certain promises to his company, spelled out in his job description and contract, and he labors to keep his word. This is the way professional life works.

Other approaches along this line, with younger kids: You ask them, "When will you start your chores this evening? Is that a promise?" "Will you call from the game if you're going to be late? You promise?" "Have you done your best on your homework? Do I have your word on that?"

If the kids fail to follow through, then they're committing two mistakes: the misdeed itself and their failure to keep their promises. Clearly it's breaking their word that's more serious to you, and this is what you come down hard on.

In the same way, you teach integrity in the areas of accepting invitations and keeping appointments. Spoiled children accept invitations swiftly and thoughtlessly, and then feel free to ignore them if something more alluring pops up. What's more, they see no reason to apologize for this neglect and will even give the offended party a phony excuse.

Don't let your kids get away with this. You can maintain a flat rule in the house: Don't accept any invitations until you've first checked with your parents. But once you've accepted, you're obligated to be there, period.

The same holds true for appointments—say, with music lessons, visits to the doctor or dentist, sports practices. Your children must show up every time, and on time, and with any equipment they need. An appointment is really a promise, and we keep our promises.

If your children want to undertake some long-term activity— music lessons, karate, Scouting, buying and caring for a pet, delivering newspapers, and the like—you first make them think the matter through carefully and then commit themselves for a reasonable trial period. They promise to stick with the activity for, say, a year or six months, and they may not quit before that time even if they tire of it. A promise is a promise. In this way, they learn that our given word is vastly more important than convenience or "feelings." This is the way we responsible adults live. Routinely we put commitment ahead of comfort, especially in the greatest of all commitments: marriage.

Finally, there should be no falsehood in your family. You should never lie to your children.

This doesn't mean the kids need to know everything that passes between you and your wife or any confidential matters between you and your other children. The "need to know" principle applies as much in family life as in business. As people of integrity, you and your wife never withhold any information to which someone has a clear right; but that doesn't mean you're obligated to share everything with the children. It's your call where to draw the line here. In any event, do not tell falsehoods. Whatever the kids hear from you must be the truth.

The one apparent exception to this is Santa Claus. The myth of Santa is false only in the sense that any fictional work is false. It's a game, a harmless make-believe, not a lie. Our Santa Claus fable serves the same purpose as the fairy tales we read at bedtime—to bring delight to children.

Your effort to teach integrity has long-term consequences for your children's later lives. Their success in business and social life will depend on it. And they'll be solidly prepared for life's greatest commitment—a happy, stable, permanent marriage.

RESPECT FOR CHILDREN'S RIGHTS

Effective fathers combine rightful authority with respect for their children's rights.

Children do have rights, of course. Not because they're children, but because they are people, and all people, even young ones, have certain basic rights. Here are the rights that great parents keep in mind as they exercise moral leadership in the family:

• *Right to privacy (up to a point).* Children need a certain security of privacy. For instance, they should have a place of their own to keep personal effects away from prying by other family members. And their normal, above-board dealings with friends should be respected as "personal," essentially no one's business but theirs.

Naturally, these privacy rights are not absolute, just as they're not absolute in adult society either. Sometimes privacy rights must give way to a higher necessity; for instance, the law can force testimony under oath about some personal affairs, and it makes allowances for "reasonable search" in criminal investigations.

So, too, in your family. Your children's privacy rights give way to your parental rights wherever some serious danger suggests itself—for instance, in possible involvement with drugs, or what you perceive as excessive intimacy with the opposite sex. But in normal circumstances, *parents who respect their children's privacy generally find that their children grow to be open and sincere with them.* If you respect their rights, they will respect your judgment, and then come to you with the truth. It is control-oriented, excessively prying parents who find their children close-mouthed, secretive, and sneaky.

• *Right to presumption of innocence.* Don't rush to judgment. Listen to your children's side of things, especially in dealing with your older children, and most especially when you did not personally witness the alleged misdeed. But by the same token, never undercut your wife if it was she who witnessed things. If you think she's mistaken or overreactive, then discuss things with her privately.

• *Right not to be publicly embarrassed.* Whenever you can, make corrections personally and privately, as you would in business. If you chew out your child in front of siblings or friends, the lesson is probably lost. Your child's resentment at public humiliation acts like static to cancel out your message. Corrections made privately—eyeball to eyeball—go straight to the point.

• *Right to just punishment.* An angry, overreactive punishment easily skyrockets way out of proportion to the original provocation. To be effective and long lasting—to get the lesson across for life—punishment has to be fair. It will be fair if it's rational, and it's rational if thought out carefully beforehand, as mentioned above. Sometimes, in fact, you can even ask your son or daughter to propose a suggestion of their own for reasonable punishment: "What do you think is fair? Make me an offer." More often than not, surprisingly, their proposals turn out to be reasonable and sometimes even tougher than what you had in mind.

• *Right to a second chance.* This means that, once apologies and restitution are forthcoming, the kids start with a clean slate. Children, like all the rest of us, resent grudge-bearing and long memories for past misdeeds that were supposedly forgiven and over with. We do not really forgive unless we also forget. When you truly forgive and forget, you show the kids that you disapprove of their faults, not them personally. Forgiveness like this is crucial, absolutely indispensable for family solidarity. The family is one place in the world where we can always count on a fresh start.

From time to time, through rage or oversight, you may blunder in doing justice to your children. Nobody's perfect. Whenever this happens, follow up with an apology.

If you imposed an excessive punishment, then retract it and scale back to whatever seems reasonable. Don't ever be afraid to say "I'm sorry" to your children, and to explain why. Never fear that you'll seem inconsistent in their eyes. You really are being consistent in what matters most—your heartfelt determination to treat them fairly. When you apologize, you teach them a valuable lesson: you put justice ahead of your ego.

What are we talking about here? In all of this we're really talking about the way responsible grown-ups try to treat each other. You, like anyone else, would expect other adults to respect your rights to privacy, presumption of innocence, personal dignity, just punishment, and so on. You'd expect this treatment from your wife, your employers, the law. So, *what you're really teaching your children is ethical conduct among responsible adults.* You are treating your children as adults-in-the-making, and you begin by respecting them as people.

SOME "NEGATIVE KNOW-HOW"

Sometimes negative guidelines are at least as helpful as positive ones, often more so. It's sometimes useful for a man to know what not to do—that is, what to avoid—in a complicated situation.

I used to ask veteran fathers (men whose children had grown and gone) what warnings or other "negative know-how" they'd pass on to younger dads. In paraphrase, here are some bits of hard-earned fatherly wisdom they shared with me:

• Don't neglect your wife. She needs what we all need: understanding, affection, gratitude, support, and appreciation. For sure, she doesn't get these from the kids when they're small. So if she doesn't get them from her husband either, then she doesn't get them at all. You can tell you're neglecting her if she starts complaining about small things around the house, one after another, circling around and around the central problem: your apparent unconcern for her. Wake up. Pay attention. Listen to her opinion, help her out, tell her she's great, hug and kiss her from time to time—all this goes a long way.

• Don't underestimate your children. Have high ambitions for their swift, step-by-step growth into maturity. We all tend to become what we think about, and kids tend to become what their parents expect of them. Even when they sometimes let you down and you have to correct them, make them understand that you see this as merely a blip along the way. You have no doubt, none whatsoever, that they'll someday grow into excellent men and women. You're proud of them, confident in them. Always will be.

• Don't treat teenagers like large children. Think of them, and treat them, as near-adults. Pull them up, fine-tune their consciences, welcome them to adult reality. Show them how to balance a checkbook, pursue a job, work professionally, please their bosses, deal respectfully with the opposite sex. Show them how to buy good clothes, take care of their wardrobe, and dress well. When they complain, "Why don't you trust me?" teach them that you distinguish between integrity and judgment. You trust their integrity and sense of family honor, their honesty and good intentions—always have, always will. But what you must have reservations about for now, in good conscience, is their inexperienced judgment; that is, you cannot let them hurt themselves through their naïve blunders. When they start thinking like responsible adults, then you'll trust them right across the board—in judgment as well as integrity.

• Don't ever tell your teens that the high school years are the best part of their lives. This isn't true. Adolescence, in fact, is one of life's toughest times: coping with blunders and glandular upheavals, surfing up and down learning curves. Tell your kids, and above all show them, that every stage of life is interesting, challenging, and enjoyable for anyone with a sporting, adventurous spirit. Teens who've been well brought up have a great life ahead of them, like the life they see in you. (Think about it: How many older teens and young adults commit suicide because they believe what they've been told: the best part of life is behind them?)

• Don't let your kids weasel out of commitments. Don't let them take back their word on a whim. Before they make promises or otherwise commit themselves to a course of action, press them to think consequences through and understand their terms, because you will hold them to their word. If they want to buy a pet, make them first commit themselves to feeding and caring for it—then hold them to that. If they accept an invitation to a party (after first checking with you and your wife), they're obligated to be there even if something more alluring turns up. If they want to take guitar lessons, make them promise to persevere, no matter what, for six months or a year or whatever seems reasonable.

• When you're correcting your kids and they ask "Why?"— don't argue with them. If they're looking for an explanation, give it once only. If they persist with "Why?" then they're looking for an argument, not an explanation. Close off the matter. In other words, they must take your "no" as an answer, but you don't take theirs. You can dialogue with your kids about many issues, but there's no "dialogue" about your rights as a father.

• Don't let your kids dress in such a way as to bring shame to the family. Nobody has a right to do this.

• Don't miss small opportunities to talk with your kids. Listen politely and respectfully. You can talk with them while driving, doing dishes and other chores together, walking and biking, working on hobbies you share, tucking them into bed. If you cut down on TV-watching, you'll find slivers and chunks of time here and there. Make the time, and never forget you haven't much of it left—your kids will grow up with incredible swiftness.

• Don't shout at your kids all the time. It's a waste of breath. If one of your kids needs a talking to, take him or her out for a walk or a soda—and say what you have to say in a calm, serious way. Don't forget to listen, either—for your kids' view of things, though wrong, may still have a point. A couple of heart-to-heart talks are better than a dozen explosions.

• Don't get trapped into blazing arguments, especially with your teens, and most especially if you have a temper. Words can wound and take a long time to heal. If tempers are flaring, put off the discussion till later—that evening or the next day—when you've both cooled down. If you go too far, be the first to apologize.

• Don't forget to praise your children, and be specific about it. Kids need a pat on the back from time to time. We all do. Give praise for effort, not merely for success. Teach the kids this adult-life lesson: because success depends on effort, then effort is more important than success. You always appreciate when your children try.

- Come down to your children's level, but don't stay there. Kids are kids, and you have to come down to their level to take them by the hand. But your long-term goal is to bring them up to your own level—to lead them, patiently over time, to think and act like mature grown-ups. So live like a grown-up. Enjoy being an adult on top of life, and let them see what this means. If they see you enjoy living as a confident, productive adult, they'll have a life to look forward to.

8 | *Treat Electronic Media as Your Rivals*

I hear it over and over again from busy fathers: "Where can I get the time to be with my children? I'm working longer hours than ever, and my kids are always on the go. How can I make more time?" No easy answers for this almost universal problem. But I will tell you something that other men have found for themselves: When you cut back the intrusion of electronic media in your house, it's incredible how much more time you create. Imposing sensible control over TV and other gadgets adds hours each week to a father's time with his kids. When a man makes up his mind, and acts, to shove the media's distractions out of his house—the noise, the blather, the hours and hours of useless staring—he gains time to be with his children and wins their respect for him as a leader.

It's like this. A smart father senses that television and other electronic doodads—VCR's, computer games and the Internet, radio, tapes and CD music—intrude in the home as *rivals* for his children's serious respect. When used to excess, they loom as competing authority figures that distract his children's minds and pull at their hearts. Kids don't pay much attention to Dad and scarcely hear or overhear what he says at home, when their gaze fixes for hours each day on a glimmering picture screen.

But note I use the term *rivals* here, not *enemies*. No question about it, the media can certainly benefit family life, add a lot to kids' minds. Smartly controlled, they can teach lessons about current affairs and life outside the family, helping to build children's judgment. They sometimes present good-quality entertainment, serving to shape the children's taste and leading people in the family to enjoy life together, as they should.

DISCRIMINATING CONTROL

For the sake of simplicity, let's use the term *tube-watching* to lump together all uses of electronic devices at home—commercial and cable television, video games and computer games, films via the VCR, sites on the Web.

An effective father teams with his wife to control the family's access to the TV. In practice this means he joins minds with her in three high-priority areas:

—which programs, films, games, and sites the kids will have access to;

—how much time will be allotted to this access;

—which programs, films, games, and sites the kids will *not* have access to at all.

What we're talking about here is the power of discernment—that is, evaluating what comes into the house and allocating time according to the parents' considered judgment. This discernment aims to teach the children over time to *accept what is good, reject what is harmful, and know the difference.*

In other words, parents work to form the children's character strengths of judgment and self-control. Both parents want to shape up significant lifelong habits: a habit of *not* watching the tube (there is such a thing), a habit of watching only worthwhile programs, and an adult-level habit of seeing time as a resource that should never be frittered away.

So, what standards do effective fathers use for selecting what their children see? The following are found in the healthiest families I've known:

• We will watch programs and use games that bring us together as a family: sports events, high-quality movies and entertainment, games that two or more can play.

• We will watch programs that teach us something and strengthen our judgment: news, documentaries, special programs about current events.

• We will not watch programs or use games or sites that treat human beings as objects. This means (a) no pornography (which treats women as objects), (b) no gratuitous violence (no practice in killing people for fun), and (c) no portrayals of characters, especially children, treating others with coarse language or disrespect.

• We will not permit children to watch the tube or play games alone to excess—to the extent that they're wasting precious hours that could otherwise go toward constructive activities like sports or reading. We won't let children use the tube in such a way that they draw themselves apart from family life.

In short, Dad and Mom assert that the tube will be used only when it promotes family life together or serves to build the children's judgment. Any use that strays outside these broad areas is probably harmful, or at best a waste of time, and so the screen stays blank.

How can you make a judgment call about a specific program's worth, or whether kids are spending too much time with a game or the computer?

The best rule of thumb is this: If you feel uneasy or begin to have reservations, then chances are the line has been crossed already. If a show or game strikes you as too violent, then it probably is. If your son seems to be putting in too much time with a video game, he probably is. Your uneasiness is a signal; it's time to act. Enough is enough. Turn the tube off and direct the kids to other recreations that firm up their growing bodies and minds.

This whole area of parental tube-control underscores an iron principle of parental leadership: *Don't let uncertainty lead to inaction.* In any given family-life situation, you may be unsure whether a given decision is right—but you should have no doubts about your right to make a decision in the first place, and to make it stick. Your rights come with the job. When you act as a father for your kids' welfare, your right to make and impose a decision should remain unquestioned.

Don't be too concerned about "mistakes" here. Years from now, your children will only dimly remember your mistakes. What they will hold in heartfelt memory all their lives is your fatherly leadership.

STRENGTHENING YOUR RESOLVE

When you, as a father, support your wife in controlling the tube, keeping its use to a discerning minimum, you'll find this requires time, effort, and sometimes an iron will. It's a tough task, which is why so many parents (the picnic-like consumerists) simply give in. You must spend more time with your children, if only to keep them from distracting your busy wife. This means you watch far less TV yourself. You have to struggle to master the kids' resistance to your decisions, grappling with their pleas and arguments. All this extra effort and vexing inconvenience can wear away at your will.

So, be smart about the media. Here are some ideas for you to weigh, some insights to help you steel your resolve for your children's sake:

• Countless psychological studies since about 1960 have shown what a powerful and convincing force television is to children (and to adults, as well.) Children deeply respect its sheer power. Consequently, if you control the television—if your power is greater than that of TV—then you loom even larger in your children's eyes. You show you have the power to shove aside your adversary. In your rivalry with the tube for your children's esteem, you win hands down.

• This respect for your moral authority (leadership in discerning right from wrong) grows especially urgent when your children enter adolescence. Teens with little respect for their parents, especially their father, are strongly attracted to the rock-drugs-sex culture. Their adulation for entertainment figures stems from a vacuum in their longing for leadership. These poor kids have no adults, not even their father, whom they respect enough to imitate. But on the other hand, those teens who deeply respect both parents remain virtually unmoved by the adolescent culture. Like other adolescents, they enjoy aspects of the music and follow after some of the fashions, but they don't *believe in* the culture—they're not sucked into it heart and soul—and sooner or later they outgrow it. In one way or another, they esteem and unconsciously imitate their powerfully confident parents and, as a result, internalize their values.

• Remember—for children, seeing is believing. Kids today have almost no exposure to the realities of grown-up life, and they don't come into the world with sound judgment. So, they naturally soak up what they see; they believe what adults set before them in a powerful way. Now think what your kids witness repeatedly on most tube programming. They spend hours in a frantic, glamorously attractive make-believe universe where entertainers substitute for heroes, where "problems" are resolved without effort and often violently, where commercials flatter them with pseudo-promises of joy, where people (adults and children) address each other with sass and coarse humor, where anything—anything at all—can be done for a laugh. What on earth does any of this have to do with grown-up reality, or with your family life, or what you want your kids to become?

• Think, too, what they do *not* witness on the tube. They see no form of work except entertainment and a grotesque caricature of law enforcement. They see no one actually working, praying, or reading. (Have you ever seen anyone on TV reading a book?) They see no old people or clergy or members of minorities except as clownish cartoon-like figures. They never see any *boring* activities either, such as patient labor, careful planning, steady learning through trial and error, quiet but meaningful discussions—the array of steady, substantial achievements that are the stuff of real grown-up life. In fact, television watching is itself so boring that we never see someone on TV actually watching TV! In TV sitcom homes, everyone is constantly talking and no one watches TV—the exact opposite of many, maybe most, American homes.

• To look at it another way: the media attractively portray—and therefore powerfully teach—the exact opposite of character strengths. Not levelheaded judgment, but emotionalism and bathos. Not real responsibility, but phony and effortless power-grabbing. Not courageous perseverance, but escapism and quick solutions. Not self-mastery, but "shop-till-you-drop" self-indulgence. Not serious, sacrificial concern for others, but a one-note booming message: Enjoy, enjoy, enjoy . . . for pleasure is what life is all about. . . .

• Think of time spent watching the tube as time away from the family. Remember that kids learn mostly by example at home: by what they witness, hear, and overhear in family life. None of this is happening—not at all—when your kids sit alone staring at a screen. You have a great deal to teach your children about life, love, work, family history, personal honor, integrity, conscience, healthy enjoyment, the greatness of their mother—the sprawling range of your experienced judgment and principles. You have only a few years to do this, only a tiny window of time. But tube-watching steals that time forever.

• Look closely at your children's bodies and facial expressions while they're watching the tube. Kids' bodies are programmed to be kept in motion; they grow lithe and sinewy through physical action. It's unnatural in a sense, and positively unhealthy, for kids to sit still for hours. Inertia builds flab, not coordinated muscles. And what about their minds? When kids' minds are active, their eyes flit about in constant sweeping motion. They reach out to reality—they scan, search, notice, question, appreciate beauty and courage, and make connections of cause and effect. But when kids fix their eyes on the tube, they only stare. Their minds float and drift along in a lazy glowing river of sensory stimulation. Is this what your kids need?

• Think what else your children could do with all that time, mastering activities they could enjoy all their lives. For instance, how many hours do they spend watching or listening to music? What if they spent that same time learning an instrument? If they took up the guitar as youngsters and put those same hours into serious practice, they could nearly master the instrument by the time they're in high school. They could empower themselves with a musical skill that would bring lifetime enjoyment, real recreation (re-creating their powers), and delight to the families they'll later form. But what good will hours of cartoons and reruns do for them twenty years from now—or next week, or even tomorrow?

• If two hours of daily tube-watching went instead into reading, what would happen? Consider this: suppose your children read thirty pages an hour and did this for two hours a day. If they did this every day, they could read seven books a month, about eighty books a year. Over a five-year stretch, this would amount to at least four hundred books! Even with only one hour a day—the time for two half-hour sitcoms or a few cartoons—this would add up to two hundred substantial books over five years. By any standards, this would be a great accomplishment.

One final thought that might help you stoke your fatherly ambition for your kids: If your children watch little TV, they may someday be on it. Think about it. Aside from professional entertainers, which normal people are most often interviewed on television? People of serious accomplishment, people who make things happen in serious adult affairs. Do you want your kids to become this sort of people? Here is a fact of life, then, that you should pass on to your kids: People who watch a lot of television almost never appear on television—whereas people who appear on television almost never watch it.

PRACTICAL TIPS

Here are some ideas for getting television and the other electronic media under reasonable control:
• Have only one television in the house. A single port of entry is much easier to monitor. If you think your family needs a second TV, it should not be in any child's bedroom. Some parents make the mistake of letting children's rooms gradually fill with a panoply of entertainment gadgets—then wonder why the kids are distracted from homework and pulled apart from family life. Effective fathers and mothers see kids' rooms as places exclusively for homework, reading, conversation, and sleep. Experienced parents will tell you: the more kids' bedrooms resemble yuppie apartments, the more the kids withdraw from the family.
• When children are small, parents pre-select which shows and films will be watched, and when. As the kids grow, they can offer suggestions, but the parents decide matters in final form.

Here, as elsewhere in family life, "input" is welcome, but it doesn't lead to children's control. The parents are in charge of the house, period. If one parent is unsure about a selection, he or she puts off a decision until consulting with the other.

• Parents establish a firm policy: If children are squabbling over a game or program, they get one warning to cease and desist. If wrangling continues, the tube is shut off at once. The kids will watch in peace or they won't watch at all.

• In cases where parents meet with strong resistance, they resort to more physical control of the tube. This can be done with a small padlock of the type used on suitcases. This little lock fits neatly through one of the holes on the prongs of the television's plug. When the lock is secure on the plug, its prongs can't fit into an electrical outlet; the TV is out of commission until Dad or Mom removes the lock. And they won't remove the lock until their terms are met.

• Sometimes more drastic action is called for—when use of the TV is out of control and the kids seem virtually addicted to it, or, worst of all, they're sneaking the TV in defiance of their parents. In these cases, parents need to reassert their authority by putting the television out of commission altogether for a set time. Six weeks seems to work best; most habits, it seems, can be formed or undone within six weeks' time. So, the parents put the TV or video games in a closet or seal up the plug with sticky tape, which is almost impossible to remove without cutting. For six weeks, the whole family goes "cold turkey," and during that time they all discover (or rediscover) reading, homework, conversation, games, sports. At the end of six weeks, the parents reintroduce the tube but strictly *on their own terms*. By that time, the kids know that Dad and Mom mean business. Parents who have resorted to this tactic will tell you it works.

▲ ▲

The flitting images and gadgets and "personalities" of the media are a big part of our culture. (See how many questions in your newspaper's daily crossword puzzle refer to shows, movies, and celebrities.) If your children don't watch much TV or dribble hours away in the latest computer games, they may feel a bit out of touch with kids their age, a little different from their neighbors. This is a problem, sort of.

But think of it this way. It's not a bad thing, all in all, for your kids to get used to living a little bit different from the crowd. Where could the crowd lead them if they're afraid to be different?

It is absolutely certain, have no doubt about it, that your children will one day be pressured by kids their age to try drugs, get wasted on beer, see sex as a naughty but normal teenage recreation—and all because "everybody else is doing it." Parents have to recognize that "no" is as much a loving word as "yes," often more so. And kids can't say "no" to themselves if they've almost never heard it from their parents. Loving parental control leads to self-control, and kids can't start forming this power from scratch at age thirteen. They are powerless to "say no to drugs" if they're used to having peer pressures whipsaw and dominate their moral choices. Bumper stickers are no substitute for a conscience.

So, there's a payoff later for your efforts. But you don't have to wait long for other benefits in your family. When you and your wife get the media under your control, some wonderful things start happening at home.

You have hours more time each week to learn the ins and outs of your children's minds, and let them know yours. Your kids pay much more attention to you.

Your authority is enhanced, and your kids respect you more deeply. This, as we've seen, is crucial to everything you have to teach them.

Family life centers on conversation, reading, sports, games, and work—the "natural" life in families for centuries.

Dinnertime becomes a prolonged get-together—nobody's in a hurry to go anywhere.

If you have lots of books around the house, the kids will read them. They'll turn into readers. (Young people who have read a lot since childhood consistently ace the verbal section of the SATs.)

The kids take up musical skills and hobbies that enrich them all their lives.

Increased activity sheds flab and puts the kids in better physical shape. Think ahead: If kids get in good shape by the time they're fifteen, they'll probably stay that way till their mid-forties. This can enhance their social lives, their marriages, and even their careers. No matter how you look at it, soft and pudgy couch potatoes are at a competitive disadvantage in the workplace. Unfair maybe, but true.

Kids have even been known to go off and do their homework out of sheer boredom. And since they have few choices but to work, they tend to stick with it till it's finished and done right. They earn better grades in school.

All in all, instead of bombarding themselves with carnival-like noise and jolting sensations, the kids cope by reading, talking, listening, and stretches of benign silence—and they begin to think.

9 | *Play with Your Children: Sports, Games, Hobbies*

If you win in keeping the tube under control, your family will find stretches of time for healthy, character-building pursuits. Every smart father knows that play is not merely pastime, a way to keep kids busy and out of mischief. Play has a serious side to it, a constructive set of effects. The roistering mayhem of kids—running, jumping, crawling, climbing—is nature's way of making children's muscles hard and limber. And tiny kids' endless curious exploration—tasting, looking, poking, building, pulling things apart—is how they learn to judge, imagine, link causes with effects, and ask themselves "What if . . . ?"

All this vigorous, natural empowerment of mind and body simpers to a halt, stops dead in its tracks, with the sloth and sauna-like sensations of tube watching. When kids bathe in television and computer nirvana, they stop playing; their sinews and brains grow flabby. Passive entertainment replaces real play and does practically nothing good for kids' bodies and minds.

So, when a smart father clicks off the tube, he liberates his kids to know once again, as in infancy, the joys and blessings of healthy play. He sets out to build his kids' character through their recreation.

Let's look at how this happens.

SPORTS

Heywood Broun, the great sports writer, said, "Sports do not build character; they *reveal* it."

He had a point. Playing sports can, in a broad sense, build character, but only under certain circumstances.

Every game of sports involves highly articulated rules and complex interpersonal relationships. (Try explaining a game of baseball to a foreigner and you'll see what I mean.) Though sports are played mostly by kids, they're invented by adults; and so kids need adults to help them benefit from sports. Excellent coaching can build kids' character, but this sort of leadership is uncommon. So many coaches, unfortunately, concentrate on skills and winning for its own sake and leave untouched the character-building dimension of athletics. If your sons and daughters belong to highly organized sports teams in school or neighborhood leagues, they typically have a great deal done for them. Maybe too much. Your children may not be learning as much about character—judgment, responsibility, perseverance, self-discipline, and heart—as you think.

Consider what neighborhood sports were like a few decades ago before eager (not to say manic) adults took charge of the games and organized everything. Typically when kids gathered to play pick-up games, there were no adults even in sight. So the kids did all the thinking and work of self-organization. They had to.

This led, of course, to bickering. Maybe as much as a third of the time was spent thrashing out points at issue: who was in charge, where foul lines would go, who would play where, whether someone was "safe" or "out." But eventually the kids got around to playing and enjoying their game. It was *their* game.

Today, a good many adults would lament this former state of affairs as messy, disorganized, and inefficient. What they don't understand, though, is the great value this adult-free play had for the kids. Because the children had to fend for themselves, they learned a great deal about adult life, much more than they learn today.

What did kids learn through their messy squabbling? They learned firsthand lessons about fairness, honest disagreement, working out compromises, sensible consensus, living by the rules (reasonable rules that everyone agreed upon), and keeping one's word.

They also learned about sizing people up, assessing others' strengths and limitations, avoiding past mistakes, coming to terms with one's own shortcomings, the difference between honorable and dishonest competition, collaboration with others, forgiving and forgetting and getting on with the game.

In short, the kids learned the whole gamut of moral judgments and interpersonal relations that are the stuff of life among grown-ups, especially in the workplace.

I'm not suggesting here that we need to eliminate adult-organized sports and revert to that era of free-for-all, laissez-faire athletics. That's impossible in any event. Like it or not, we run kids' sports programs today such that the children do little of the thinking, the really sound judgment-making that can build their character.

What I want to stress, rather, is that a smart father needs somehow to compensate for what we've all lost through this micromanagement of kids' athletics. If your children are active in highly organized team sports, you need to help them learn at least some of these sports-related lessons about character. Don't let their adult-driven activity serve only to keep them busy. All by itself, busy-ness does not build powers of mind and will. If their coach is dedicated to building his players' character—and the best coaches are—your kids can benefit a lot. Unfortunately, coaches like this are not numerous, especially in this age where talent is so often prized over moral uprightness and coaches pay more attention to the scoreboard than to their players' hearts. (How many of today's famous professional athletes could be described as technically skilled scoundrels, people who have dazzling natural talents but whose personal morals are scandalous and whose private lives are a mess?)

If your children are blessed to work under a dedicated, caring, character-building coach, you should give him or her all the support you can. You and the coach can teach your children a lot. But if the coach is so-so or worse, you may have to do most of the teaching yourself, before and after the games. Whatever you do, think of your children's futures and help them learn from their play.

LESSONS FROM ATHLETICS

Let's look more closely at the life lessons learnable from sports. Under your leadership, what can your children learn from athletics that can direct the course of their lives?

First, a physical lesson. They can learn to stay in shape. If your children get into good physical condition by the time they're in high school, they'll probably stay this way until early middle age or later. If they can form habits of regular exercise and see its important benefits, they can better cope with adult life's unavoidable stresses.

Second, they learn to cope with setbacks and mistakes. You teach them what we've seen earlier: that there's nothing wrong with mistakes as long as we learn from them. Moreover, setbacks and disappointments are part of life, inevitable. Responsible adults pick themselves up and keep on trying. This attitude—to keep trying, no matter what—is the common trait of every successful adult. This is true of professional matters, marriage, and the trials of family life. Great men and women refuse to quit.

Third, they learn to get along with people, all kinds of people. They're led to appreciate people's honest best efforts. With guidance, they can assess people's strengths and, in a sense, ignore their shortcomings—a lesson for business and professional life. A football quarterback, or a linebacker, has peculiar strengths of skill, and the two positions are not interchangeable. These players' different powers complement each other and, in a sense, each player compensates for the other's "weakness." All competent bosses, like smart coaches, build a team around people's strengths. Whether in work or play, team members need each other and know they are needed in turn. Somehow, mysteriously, the strength of any team, whether in sports or in business, is greater than the sum of its parts.

Fourth, kids learn to control their impulses and separate "feelings" from objective reality. Getting control of one's impulses, saying "no" to oneself, is vital to children's character. Later, in adolescence, the power of self-control is crucial in dealing with the more sordid and dangerous allurements of adolescent culture. Kids can't "say *no* to drugs" if they're out of practice in self-mastery. Moreover, kids need to learn that we can't always get what we want. If we're tagged out at second base, we're out, period, no matter how bad we feel about it. Our self-interested "feelings" are not a guide for action. The rules are our guide—and this includes our internal rules of conscience.

Fifth, and related to the above, kids learn *sportsmanship*. This is really adult-level ethics applied to athletic competition. Our opponents are opponents, not enemies. We bear no ill will to anyone; there's nothing personal in our competition. Win or lose, we are ourselves at our best. So we neither mope nor gloat, because a sore winner is as bad as a sore loser. In short, we respect the rights and sensibilities of everyone, even our opponents. This is what we mean by honorable competition.

Finally, the kids can learn that winning is not everything. The great Vince Lombardi is often misquoted here. It's true he said, "Winning is the only thing," but he said this to stress the importance of dedicated teamwork and all-out effort. People tend to forget that Lombardi devoted himself above all to his players' character. He dealt with his players' hearts and souls, driving them—leading them—to personal excellence. And this dedication to character is why he's honored as a great man.

Winning *honorably* is everything. What really counts is not the final score but rather what has grown inside the mind and will and heart of each player.

It's important to emphasize this point with your children. Athletics, with proper coaching, can teach children that perseverance is more important than short-term victory. A flat refusal to give up—or to quit, to escape whatever is unpleasant—is a moral victory. It is a form of courage, a mark of great character.

Look at it this way, and teach this to your children: If winning—that is, easy and early victory—were everything . . .

— The Romans would have surrendered to Hannibal after their disastrous defeat at Cannae.
— Columbus would have abandoned his exploration scheme after fifteen years of fruitless quest for financial support.
— Beethoven would have quit composing when he went deaf.
— The American Revolution would have collapsed after the defeat at Bunker Hill.
— George Washington would have resigned, or been fired, halfway through the War of Independence.
— After losing several elections, Abraham Lincoln would have quit politics for good.
— Robert E. Lee would have been reviled after Gettysburg and forgotten after Appomattox.
— After four hundred unsuccessful experiments, Edison would have quit his quest for an electric lightbulb.
— After Dunkirk, the British government would have surrendered to Hitler.
— Winston Churchill, who suffered from a serious speech defect, would have abandoned his ambitions for public life—and never gained fame as one of the great inspiring orators of the twentieth century.

Your children should learn this truth about life: that heroism comes in many forms, and courage is written on the human heart. One of its greatest forms is the steadfast refusal to admit defeat. If you lead your children to look around, you can draw their attention to ordinary people—in sports, in literature and history, in their own family lineage—whose lives were marked by quiet, heroic, sporting perseverance. And great parents are courageous mostly in this way: they never give up on their children.

I don't have to tell you, I'm sure, that you should go to watch your children's games as often as you can. This means a lot to them, to know that their parents are their greatest fans. But you should go to *observe* as well as watch. Look for details in your children's play that you can discuss with them later.

Your teaching can have greater effect, can form your children's character better, if you live by the guidelines of spectator sportsmanship. Here are some of them:

• Stay in the spectator area. That's where you belong. Don't let your own impulses get out of control.

• Give your children example of good sportsmanship: no negative personal remarks about opponents, coaches, or anyone else, especially umpires and referees.

• Don't try to do the coach's job for him. No matter how strongly you feel about something, mind your own business. If you want to make suggestions, save it for later; then do it personally and privately.

• Never go over a coach's head unless you've first consulted with him.

• Cheer all the players on your child's team, not only your son or daughter.

• Give praise for effort. Encourage kids to try again.

• If the team loses, help your child to shrug off disappointment. Life goes on; tomorrow is another day.

INDIVIDUAL SPORTS

For all the reasons mentioned so far, it's important for all your children to try playing team sports, regardless of their natural ability. No matter what they later do for a living, they have to learn to get along with other people, all kinds of people, to contribute in team enterprise. Nobody can get through life without some sort of team collaboration. To repeat, they must at least *try.*

But, let's face it, not all youngsters are athletically gifted, and kids like this can have a tough time enduring teammates' scornful criticism. This is especially true if their coach is a win-at-all-costs fanatic, unappreciative of kids' best efforts. Sad to say, a great many kids who receive this abusive treatment, through no fault of their own, become soured on sports for life.

So, if your children are middling athletes at best, and maybe a bit discouraged, you should lead them to try individual sports instead—golf, tennis, swimming, track, cross-country, squash, handball.

Once again, think of their future. No matter what their ability, almost certainly they will not play basketball much after their late thirties, and they could wind up in a hospital if they tried. But they can play individual sports all their lives. A practiced competence at golf or tennis can do great things later for their social and professional lives. In fact, if they've practiced these sports since childhood or their early teens, they can have a competitive edge (for a while at least) over people their age who take up the sports later in life, as most adults do.

All young people grow in self-confidence when they are competent at something physical, whatever it might be. So don't overlook other disciplined pursuits: gymnastics, martial arts, hiking and rock-climbing, camping and wilderness survival, biking, even gardening.

The point here is to help your children find some physical activity they can develop and enjoy all their lives. You may find, as many fathers do, that you gradually develop a keen interest in whatever pleases your children. And, just as this common pursuit can bond you to your sons and daughters, so it can later bond them to their own children. Who knows? You may be starting an athletic tradition in your family that will last several generations.

In sum, a smart father wants his kids to be active, not only now but also later in life, when they need physical exercise more than in childhood. He acts now to protect his children from the later scourges of adult inactivity—obesity, lassitude, and depression.

YOUR DAUGHTERS' SPORTS

Don't neglect your daughters' sports, either. All the advantages of athletics, whether team or individual sports, are as valuable to girls as to boys. In some ways, more so.

Someday your daughters may hold down a responsible job in the workplace both before and after marriage. Eventually they will need the same strong character and sense of team collaboration that their brothers have. Being able to play and enjoy sports will be a great recreation for them. They will need this.

I once knew a psychiatrist in New York who told me this (to paraphrase him): "If people today would only eat right and exercise properly, I would lose about half my patients. Women especially. Unfortunately, most women over forty today never really learned the great stress-relief of physical exercise. They were shortchanged in their youth. Their so-called 'physical education' classes were a watered-down version of what the boys received; so they were never really encouraged, or taught, to get hold of their emotions through sports. Women's endocrine systems are more powerful than men's; the glands cause stronger emotional reactions. So, in a sense, women need athletic outlets, strong habits of sheer physical exercise, even more than men do. Thank heaven that girls today are much more encouraged with athletics! This has been one of the healthiest breakthroughs in American education, long overdue."

There's another advantage, too, which I think is usually overlooked by fathers. The more your daughter knows about team sports, the more enthusiastic a fan she becomes, the more she will later have in common with her husband.

Someone wise once said, "Male and female is all the 'opposite' a marriage needs; the more a husband and wife have in common, the better." Your daughter will someday be some man's wife, and the more activities they enjoy together, the stronger will be the bond between them. Unity among husband, wife, and children is crucially important today and will be at least as important twenty years from now. The current rate of marriage break-up (more than 50 percent for new marriages) shows no sign of turning around in your children's lifetimes. So, for the sake of your daughters and the families they'll form, get your children into sports.

GAMES, PUZZLES, AND PROBLEM SOLVING

Let's look now at games and puzzles—and see how they, like athletics, can empower your children's minds.

You should stock your home with board games: Monopoly, Chutes-and-Ladders, chess and checker sets, and the like. Aside from these traditional standbys, there are dozens of other excellent board games on the market. For decades now, kids playing these games have matched wits with each other and with parents and grandparents.

If you have any doubt about the great value of chess or other board games, watch your children's faces while they play. See their concentration, alertness, planning, scheming. Watch how their eyes move. Contrast all this mental activity with the blank stares and passive postures your kids fall into when they sprawl before the television—or their manic glares and jerky stimulus-response with video games.

Think, too, what their emotions are like after extensive time with TV or video games.

Many parents have told me this: After an hour of chess or some other non-electronic game, kids are typically both alert and rested at the same time. Their energies are "re-created." They're ready to move on to some other activity, especially sports, or simply to retire for the night.

But after an hour or more of tube-centered stupor, children are typically wound up, irritable, restless, and hard to control. In some ways, they look and act like addicts afflicted with a hangover, desperately craving another fix. Tube-watching does something to the brain, but whatever it is, it's not recreational. Your kids don't need this problem; neither do you and your wife.

If you make the time to compete with your children in chess and other games, you'll probably discover what so many other dads have told me. You reawaken interest in pastimes from your childhood. Or, if the game is new to you, you share the discovery along with your children. With most games you even find time to chat together. You come down to your children's level, and in subtle ways you bring them up to your own.

Years from now, your kids will only dimly remember what they stared at on television. But they'll never forget those evenings looking across the chessboard, matching wits with Dad.

Puzzles, too, have great merit for kids beyond simple fun. Word games, crosswords, jigsaw puzzles, logic problems—all these, with practice, help develop children's character. What could happen to your children's powers of judgment and will if they formed a lifelong delight in solving puzzles?

Think about it. Solving problems is a universal, absolutely unavoidable part of responsible adult life. No matter what we do for a living, we have to solve problems. Or at least try our best. Some, of course, are insoluble or nearly so; these we live with as best we can. Nonetheless, we eventually solve most professional problems through our efforts, patience, ingenuity, and know-how.

Here's the point: Much of professional people's success in problem solving seems to depend on their *attitude*—the way they approach problems in the first place, and the way they stick with them.

Weak-willed adults tend to see problems as hardships, bothersome hassles that complicate life, distractions from the really important pursuits of comfort, pleasure, leisure, and amusement. Young people with this attitude have generally been raised as consumers. They've been apprenticed at enjoying things, not producing them; they're habituated to avoid problems, not solve them. When they eventually meet with really serious, challenging problems—in college, or starting out in careers, or in the first few years of marriage—they lack patience and realistic self-confidence. Consequently, they confront these problems with dread, rapidly mounting frustration, and a reflexive reaction to escape. Unfortunately many quick-escape expedients today are addictive and dangerous.

Other young people, though, have internalized a much healthier attitude. *They see problems as interesting challenges.* Strengthened by a lifetime habit of solving problems, at home and in school, they view them as tests for their powers of ingenuity and healthy stubbornness. Certainly many of their problems remain tough or even insoluble; but these young people don't give up until they've expended a serious try.

In short, these healthy, self-confident young people tend to approach problems as though they were puzzles. Pushing to solve them becomes a delight in itself, a kind of serious play. As you'd expect, people with this attitude—seeing problems as puzzles—usually succeed in business. They are self-confident, and this confidence moves others to respect them.

Most of this practice in problem solving takes place, or should take place, in school. For centuries, competent teachers put challenging problems before their students, especially in mathematics. Generations of kids have groaned their way through so-called "word problems" in math, but in the long run this exercise was healthy for them. Thinking through word problems helps kids build certain attitudes and powers: patience, hunting for patterns in messy situations, discernment of means and ends, and tenacious perseverance.

Moreover, really dedicated teachers aimed to show children a fact of adult life: some drudge work is inherent, absolutely unavoidable, in any long-term serious achievement. Sustained mental and physical effort is not always "fun" but, with the right attitude, it can be enjoyably rewarding. Happiness in life can come from work as well as play. This is what happens when we see problems as puzzles.

You can encourage your kids to form these healthy attitudes

by putting puzzles into your family life, especially if you sometimes join the kids in solving them. If you do this when they're young, you form a natural lead-in to helping them later with their homework and school projects. What you're really teaching here is an attitude toward work: "If we stick with this thing long enough, we can lick it!"

While we're on the subject, let's give special credit to crossword puzzles and other word games.

Words are the building blocks for effective reading, writing, and spoken communication. Adults who've mastered these skills seem to have one thing in common: they love words. They enjoy learning words, distinguishing words, using words accurately. In their writing and speaking, they have the skill to employ thousands of them, picking the right word or phrase to express precise meaning and subtle emotional associations. This power (for that's what it is) builds up over a lifetime's practice with words, the building blocks of clear thought.

When your children work their way through crossword puzzles and other word games, they build a database of vocabulary, at least for their reading. They train their memory—a precious exercise in itself—and form a habit of thumbing through the dictionary. What's more, they practice what all children need: paying attention to detail.

If you work with your kids to solve word puzzles, you also show them a side of you that they may not otherwise appreciate: the vast extent of your *reading* vocabulary. You know many more words—that is, have a greater power of language—than what you display in normal family conversation. (Typically we speak with only a fraction of the words we know.) Indirectly, that is, you show your children yet another dimension of your intellectual strength. This, in turn, gives them even more reason to respect you, and pattern their lives after you.

READING

No doubt you and your wife already try to promote recreational reading at home. Like most parents, even those over-involved with TV, you already know that a lifetime habit of reading—for learning and recreation—is a solid foundations for good judgment and later success in life. It's obvious that this habit best begins in childhood.

Sometimes, though, we tend to overlook the obvious. That is, we don't think often enough or deeply enough about important matters we take for granted. This being the case, let's look at some ideas about forming your children's reading habits, some concepts to help you lead your children as their father.

• It seems to be a fact: When the tube and computer are kept under control at home, *everyone* in the family reads much more, parents as well as children.

• Your children already respect you as a "smart man," someone who exercises impressive powers of experienced judgment. You know a lot. If your children see you read a great deal, they unconsciously put together a cause-and-effect connection—you know a lot because you read a lot. This alone is incentive for them to read; you're teaching by example.

• When your children are under age ten or eleven, lead them to read widely and in quantity. Even if they read a lot of light fiction, they're still forming a habit of being at ease with books. Later, when they meet really high-quality literature, they'll more easily recognize its superior quality, especially if you draw it to their attention. Their wide reading in childhood will form a framework for comparison; quality work will stand out from the mediocre. In high school, when young people first meet great literature, those kids who never read much in childhood find it a pointless chore, pure drudgery. Kids need to ramp up to worthwhile reading; but if a ramp is too steep, it turns into a wall.

• After age eleven, the children should begin to read with some discernment. They should be steered toward the best books in different *genres*, including mysteries and science fiction if they like works of this type. Ask your librarian or some respected teachers for specific titles.

• Boys, it seems, do not always take easily to serious fictional literature. But they're attracted to narrative history (especially military history) and biography. Even if they never acquire a taste for novels and poetry, they can read and enjoy history all their lives. Don't forget, most schools today stress only fiction as outside reading for kids; almost never do they push history and biography. (Why this is, I don't know, but it's a pity.) You can take up the slack, especially with your sons. In fact, many adult men "discover" the pleasures of narrative history long after leaving school. The same holds true for biographies of prominent men and women, past and present. Give it a try.

• No matter what your kids are reading, you can talk with them about it. Quality fiction, history, and biography teach us a lot about people's character. Down through the centuries, it seems, nearly all cultures used stories to put examples of heroism and virtue before youngsters' eyes. Heroes appear as ordinary folks, like us, who rise to great heights by struggling to carry out their responsibilities. Lead your children to appreciate the virtues of these people, their motivations and courageous perseverance. In other words, use your children's reading to help form their judgment and shrewdness about people as well as their personal ideals. Culture is not a decoration, an external adornment like jewelry. It is a cordial familiarity with the finest achievements of the human spirit. The humanities teach us how to be human.

• There's one type of fiction you should steer your daughters away from. This is the collection of supposedly true-to-life romances for pre-teen and young adolescent girls. Critics of these pulp works complain (correctly, I think) that they're essentially narcissistic. They lead girls to dwell too much on their feelings, to grow excessively and prematurely preoccupied with boy–girl complications. After age eleven, your daughters will have to contend with the normal emotional ups and downs of adolescence, and they don't need pressure to exaggerate these. Lead your daughters instead to high-quality fiction and healthy engagement with hobbies and athletics. At such an emotional time of life, they need confident direction toward reality—and away from the mirror. You, as the number-one man in their lives, should encourage them to grow in realistic, confident womanhood.

• A practical consideration here: Young people who read a lot manage to succeed well in post-secondary education. After all, college life is mostly experience with ideas and people, books and friends. If your children build a habit of extensive reading through childhood, they will do well—probably very well—on their college-admissions examinations. The verbal sections of the SAT and similar tests are designed to find the most competent readers. An ability to read quickly and accurately leads to high scores. In fact, even the mathematics part of these tests requires skills in rapid, careful reading.

• Finally, if your children develop a love for discriminating reading, they will continue to educate themselves all their lives. This is what a real education aims to accomplish, and it begins mostly at home.

HOBBIES

Hobbies are not merely pleasant pastimes for children. They're healthy recreational pursuits for people of all ages. In most ways, they're even more valuable for adults than for children. Hobbies are a way for adults to recapture, for short spurts of time, the sheer delight they knew as children—concentrating all their intelligence, will, and imagination on some activity that's unimportant to anyone but themselves. This occasional absorption with the unimportant is healthy for grown-ups, especially if their normal workday lives are full of stress.

So, it makes sense for you to help your children find hobbies they can enjoy throughout life. If you can join them in these pastimes, maybe even rekindling an interest you had as a boy, so much the better. Who knows? Some thirty years from now, you and your grown children and grandchildren could work on some hobby together. Once you've retired, wouldn't you enjoy joining your grandchildren in gardening, building models, woodworking, stamp collecting—some constructive play activity that's a family tradition?

While I'm on the subject of retirement, consider this: One big problem in retirement communities is that many retirees, particularly men, have practically nothing to do. Along their paths of life they never took up any serious hobby interests. Unfortunately, out of sheer crushing boredom many of these retirees turn to alcohol. When hands have nothing to do, it seems, they often reach for the bottle.

On the other hand, older adults with several serious hobbies can't wait to retire; they look forward to having lots of time for their interests. Typically these retirees remain young in outlook, happy with life, recapturing (so to speak) the delights they knew in childhood. (Winston Churchill took up oil painting and became highly proficient at it when in his sixties.)

Finally, let's note something here that you may have noticed yourself. Some of the happiest, most confident people we meet are those who've managed somehow to turn their hobby into their life's work. Typically they enjoyed several hobbies while growing up, and one of these later grew into their profession. Every day, these people wake up looking forward to their day's work. Please remember this when you lead your children to pursue hobby interests. You may be steering your kids toward satisfying, successful careers. (An important related question: How many adults *un*happy with their work today squandered their childhood in endless television watching?)

Anyway, whether your children's hobbies lead to a career or not, they can still help form character. Let's look at some examples.

Learning to play a musical instrument competently is superb for children, for reasons parents scarcely seem to think about.

As in the study of a foreign language, youngsters start off at ground zero; they know nothing about the subject. Therefore, through practice the kids derive a strong sense of progress, a steadily increasing mastery of some power. This is excellent for their self-confidence. And this confidence grows even stronger if they can play the guitar or piano by the time they're in high school, for they can enjoy a richer social life. What's more, as adolescents and young adults—indeed, all their lives—they can use music to express emotions, or to cope with them. Later still, they can have fun with their children as well as their friends. Making music brings people together.

Countless adults today were pressed by their parents to learn an instrument, and often through times when they wanted to quit. Today they're grateful that their parents led them to persevere, pushed them past the threshold where mastery sets in and the instrument becomes enjoyable. Think about it: Have you ever met someone who mastered a musical instrument and now regrets it?

If your children sing well, they'd benefit from joining a choir or choral club. Singing in harmony teaches a lot about disciplined drive toward perfection. This type of singing has most of the advantages of team sports, plus the added incentive to perfect performance; a singer must hit every single note perfectly, along with everyone else. This kind of "stress" is healthy. It channels anxious nervousness into high-quality performance —a great preparation for real life in the world of work.

Moreover, group singing has another long-term benefit. Youngsters and teens learn a repertoire of songs that later enrich their later lives with family and friends.

Woodworking and home repairs form skills in hand-eye coordination—as well as planning, time management, and attention to detail. In addition, these hobbies give young people something they need: a chance to *produce something,* to *earn* some reward through personal effort. (Children today seldom even have to *wait* for anything, much less earn it.)

Consider, too, that your sons and daughters will someday want, or even financially need, to do significant repairs around the house themselves. Learning to use their hands skillfully is especially helpful for children who lack natural athletic skill;

everyone needs to do *some* physical activity well, even if only to feel the kind of confidence that comes with competence.

Gardening is another hugely valuable hobby. It teaches children some significant lessons about life, truths not found on television: Some things require time and cannot be hurried. Some steps (like seeding and watering) must be taken on time, for the results of slipshod neglect are fatal. Some things don't turn out as well as we expected, but life is like that. Some things, like the growth of plants, are mysterious and ultimately out of anyone's control, but we do the best we can anyway.

There are countless other pastimes your children can empower themselves with, and you, as a father, can help your youngsters shop around for what appeals to them: photography, assembling a scrapbook of family photos, keeping a diary or journal, fishing, making lures and flies for fishing, collecting stamps or coins, making maps, helping to plan family trips, making birthday cards for family members, drawing and painting, building models, following the stock market, cooking (for boys as well as girls).

I have to forewarn you here about something many parents have experienced. When your children later plunge into the busy social swirl of high school, they'll probably lose interest in their childhood hobbies, except maybe for music. Be patient. If you pursued the same hobbies they did, be sure to stay active. Hold onto their collections and handiworks. Later, when they have children of their own, they'll have incentive to return to their childhood interests and pass them along to your grandchildren.

How about you? Are there interests from your boyhood that you'd like to take up again? Or are there hobbies you've always found appealing but thought you never had the time for? Maybe now is the time. Let your children see that you, like them, enjoy life to its fullest. Let your children see you play.

10 | *Lead Children to Take Work Seriously*

Here's something for any smart father to think about.

Pre-teen and adolescent boys often deeply admire their athletics coaches, even to the point of hero-worship. Sometimes, in fact, they have greater respect for their basketball coach than for their own father. Why is this?

Maybe it's because their coach is the only adult male whom kids see up close, over an extended time, actually working.

The children see their coach's strengths of character in action on the job in a powerful, manly, and attractive way. They see him really work: planning ahead, laying out strategy, paying attention to detail, concentrating his effort and that of others, shrewdly assessing people's strengths and shortcomings, overcoming disappointment, starting from scratch, dealing with difficult people and problems, controlling his temper, abiding by rules, giving direction and encouragement to people he works with—the whole wide-ranging array of active masculine endeavor and manly accomplishment.

Moreover, any outstanding coach acts like a father in another important way. He concerns himself with his athletes' growth in character. A great coach, like Knute Rockne or Vince Lombardi, devotes himself to his players' inner strengths of mind, will, and heart. Coaches like this—fathers like this—win lifelong devotion from young people.

DAD'S WORK

In former centuries, boys saw their fathers live this way literally every day. Without being really conscious about it, Dad gave this sort of example to his children as he went about his business at home, on the farm or in his shop, dealing with clients, customers, and hired hands. But as we've seen, this is history.

As I explained on an earlier page, one of the banes of family life today is that most kids never see their father work. They do not witness their dad putting his powers up against problems to solve them for some serious business purpose. Their father's daily exercise of his character strengths—his judgment, responsibility, perseverance, self-control, considerateness, and teamwork—lies beyond their field of vision. And what kids do not see, they do not grasp.

What do the kids see instead? Typically they see Dad go off somewhere in the morning and disappear until dinnertime or later. They then see him spend evenings mostly at leisure, including (lamentably) passive TV watching. As a result, most children underestimate their father's powers. To their eyes he appears mostly as a passive, even dispirited figure, someone wholly given over to amusement and rest.

This narrow, blurry vision of Dad's life has consequences. Because we respect people mostly by judging their strength—physical, intellectual, spiritual, moral—then a weak perception leads to weak respect, sometimes none at all. A man routinely exercises great strength of judgment and will and action on his job, but how do his children know this? His world of work is like the other side of the moon.

What's more, if children fail to witness or to hear about their dad's life of work, they are left with a flaccid, unfocused concept of real-life adult responsibilities. Their only picture of adult life outside the family is what they see on television and in the movies. No wonder so many young people are fearful or totally unrealistic about their professional futures. Normal adult life in the world of work is, for them, unknown territory, something vaguely threatening in the future. So . . . why grow up? What does it mean to grow up? Why not put off the hassle as long as possible?

What can you do to help your children understand and respect that side of your life they seldom see? Here are some approaches that smart fathers have pulled off successfully:

• If you can, take your kids to your workplace, even for a couple of hours. Let them witness you work for a while. Let them see another important part of your life—how your fellow workers, in subtle and friendly ways, show you their respect. Your kids will pick up on this: how other grown-ups enjoy working with you, show confidence in you and your judgment, and consider you valuable.

• If you cannot have your children around when you work, then take a day off and visit the workplace with them anyway. Even though you're only visiting for an hour or so, they will see your place of work, the people you work with, and the way they greet you. Almost without exception, this experience delights and impresses children. In a quiet way, they grow proud of you.

• If you can't take them on workdays, then take them on a

Saturday. Let them get a tactile sense of your workplace, which to them will appear large, serious, cluttered with papers and machines that convey serious, powerful responsibility. Give them a tour, explaining what happens every day and how you fit into the teamwork.

• From time to time, take work home with you. I know this runs counter to prevailing wisdom about family life, but in moderation—if not overdone—it's an eye-opener to your children. Kids are impressed when they see Dad's judgment, concentration, and will at work, even for an hour or two a couple of nights a week.

• Let your children join you in work around the house. Even if they're so clumsy they get mostly in the way, your confidence in them builds their own self-confidence. You show them how to use their powers and stamina to serve the family—which is what every father does every day in his workplace. Praise them for their efforts, their patient concentration, and their good results. Let them see your pride in their guts and workmanship. As the historian Thomas Carlyle put it: "Tell a man he is brave, and you help him become so." Remember, a huge part of the father's job is to teach his children competence.

• Talk from time to time about your job, especially around the dinner table: your current tasks, your obstacles and problems, your plans, your teamwork with your staff. It's enough to chat with your wife in the children's presence. Your children will learn a lot from what they pick up in your conversation. Remember, kids learn a great deal about their parents from what they *overhear* in family life. Very often they learn more from snatches of conversation than from lectures aimed directly at them.

CHILDREN'S WORK AROUND THE HOUSE

Your children should have chores around the house. That is, you should entrust them with areas of responsibility where their efforts benefit the family. For two basic reasons, this does an enormous amount for their growth in character.

First, they feel genuinely needed. Like all people of any age, children grow in confidence from being needed. We all need to be needed. One of the sad by-products of our society's material abundance is that children's effort—their hard work—is no longer really needed at home. Children who perform responsible work at home grow up to be *producers,* not simply *spenders.*

Children who pitch in to *serve* in family life learn to give as well as receive.

They learn early that normal life isn't simply a round of amusement, leisure, and entertainment. They learn the satisfaction, the real joy, of serving one's family with a job well done. This is a great preparation for married life and their later careers.

Second, children grow in confidence from solving problems. It seems to be a fact of life that kids who work seriously at home grow to know their strengths and shortcomings more clearly and realistically. They know who they are and what they can do. Consequently, they are much more willing to take risks. Over the course of time, they learn to see apparent obstacles as challenges—chances to test and build their powers.

But those kids who are never pressed to work at home remain unsure of themselves, reluctant to take risks, fearful of new situations. As teens and young adults, when finally faced with real-life work problems, they are prone to react in dysfunctional ways. Some of them drastically overwork, put in too many hours on the job, and then see their marriages suffer or even fly apart. Others underreact: they perform sloppily on the job, or see their jobs as merely drudgery to be endured for the sake of "spending money." Like adolescents or perennial bachelors, they work only for the cash to live it up on weekends and collect expensive toys: new cars, closet-bulging wardrobes, and mammoth electronic gadgets for wall-to-wall entertainment.

No smart, conscientious man will let these inner weaknesses cripple his kids.

So, what sort of jobs should your children do? Just ask your wife. The kids can do dishes and put them away, clean the kitchen floor regularly, make their beds and clean their rooms, vacuum carpets, take care of pets, wash windows, rake leaves, sort the laundry . . . whatever needs upkeep around the house.

And don't think there's such a thing as "men's work" versus "women's work," either. Your sons and daughters should be equally competent to tackle any job in the home that needs doing.

There's nothing new about this. In former centuries, it seems, men and women often overlapped in their domestic duties, especially when they had to. Men did cooking and cleaning when their wives were ill or busy nursing or otherwise indisposed. When men went off on business or to war, their wives competently managed the farm and business. Each parent had a dual competence up until the mid-nineteenth century, at the onset of the industrial revolution—when most men, for the first time, worked apart from the home at a factory or mine or office. So, leading your sons and daughters to do the same kinds of work is, as it were, a natural training in overall competence, something done routinely through most of Western history.

When giving a job to your children, try to put the task slightly above their level of natural competence. That is, set things so they must put in persevering effort. Initially you may have to show them how to approach the job, to define what you mean by success. For instance, as we saw earlier, clean their room with them a few times—call it a "Ten-Minute Drill"—until they have a clear idea what you and your wife mean by a "clean room."

In any event, make sure your children understand that you care most about their *personal best effort*. And praise them for this effort. The real "results" you care about, what you are really aiming at, is their growth in character.

DIRECTION VERSUS MANAGEMENT

An important distinction here: As a father, you should *direct* your children but not *manage* them. What's the difference?

You direct your children when you show them what to do, then explain how they might do it, and then step back to let them try for themselves. If at first they're unsuccessful and return to you for help, you point out how to tackle the problem and then send them back to try again.

In other words, you give intelligent direction to their efforts. You teach them how to shift for themselves. This direction— where we're headed, how to get there—seems to be a hugely important part of fatherhood, the job a man undertakes with his children: building confident competence.

Encouragement is crucial to direction. You keep saying to them: "You can do it . . . keep at it . . . don't quit yet, you're almost there . . . you're stronger than you think . . . if you stick with the problem, you can lick it." You show your children your confidence in them. You press them to outdo themselves, to exert their powers of initiative and ingenuity, to go the limit. (Doesn't every good coach do the same?) If after all-out effort and several tries, they cannot do the job, then you step in and finish the job with them—all while praising them for trying their best. All this is fatherly direction.

On the other hand, those consumerist parents who manage, rather than direct, their children fall easily into micromanagement. They're too result-oriented. They're concerned more with getting the job done than teaching children to tackle it themselves. If the kids have a project to do for school, these parents will do it for them. If the kids forget to complete a chore, they'll do it themselves, thinking that this is easier, more efficient. If the kids have left a mess around, they'd rather clean it up than undergo the hassle of correction. They will busy themselves with tasks around the house while their kids spend hours sprawled before the TV or slouching in front of the computer. They hover over every task the kids have to do, but they'll intervene immediately at the first sign of trouble. They won't let their children make mistakes or learn from them.

Micromanaging parents don't see it yet, but they are asking for trouble.

Which teenagers most often rebel against their parents? It's the ones who have been micromanaged and oversupervised since childhood. They want to get out from under their parents' thumbs. They say, "Let me do it for myself!" and they're vehemently disinclined, to say the least, to heed their parents' advice.

But those teens that have been affectionately *directed* since childhood—whose parents' confidence in them has engendered their own self-confidence—turn willingly to their parents for advice, as they've done all their lives. And they do it long into adulthood, as long as Dad and Mom still live.

TIME MANAGEMENT

A smart father helps his children to budget and manage their time. He's aware of several truths about life that his kids need to learn and live by.

• "Time management" is another term for self-control. It's all about the power to sit down and get to work on top-priority tasks at will, to put off leisure until after duties are done, and to shove aside temptations to slack off or quit.

• One of the signs of maturity is the ability to foresee future events—including consequences of present situations—and set out to control them way ahead of time. The more effectively someone can do this, the more he or she receives respect from colleagues. Long-term planning is one of the most powerful traits of professional leadership.

• Habitual punctuality is not merely a courtesy. It's an absolute necessity for business and social life. Punctual people show themselves to be considerate, self-disciplined, and faithful to their word. For these reasons they are respected.

• Planning ahead and acting now to control future events are habits that build up through years of repeated practice. Young people should be able to live this way before they're out of high school.

A father and mother teach their children, especially after age ten or so, that time is not an elusive dimension of life, an environment we lazily drift through. On the contrary, it's an irreplaceable resource. If we waste it, it's gone.

Moreover, at some point before adolescence, children need to learn that neglect, like big blunders, leads to unpleasant consequences. Spoiled children, as I mentioned before, have little sense of time and almost no concept of *deadline*. For them a deadline is merely a spongy target date, something they can keep kicking ahead like a beach ball. Nothing unpleasant happens if they fail to do something on time, so why bother? They're accustomed to having parents intervene and rescue them from the unpleasant outcomes of their own careless neglect.

Effective parents insist that their children, starting in junior high school, keep their own personal calendars to stay on top of upcoming responsibilities. This includes dental appointments, homework, long-term projects, sports practices and games, social events, getting out early (in February or March) to hunt summer employment, and the like. Moreover, by the time kids are juniors in high school, they should be able to manage most details of their college application process by themselves.

Of course, children's calendars need coordination with the general family calendar, especially if the kids need transportation. But a smart father's overall strategy is to teach his children the importance of foresight, initiative, realistic planning, attention to detail, coordination of resources (for instance, arranging car rides and permission slips), and meeting deadlines. Over the course of time, the children internalize, through directed practice, one of the most crucial powers of grown-up life: the ability to set up and then meet our own deadlines.

ALLOWANCES

How can you and your wife best handle children's management of money? For some reason, this is a controversial question, one that both husband and wife need to agree on as family policy.

Some parents give their children (after age nine or so) a weekly sum of cash to cover basic expenses, plus a bit extra for unforeseeable emergencies. Their aim here is to let the kids budget their own expenses and, like responsible adults, live with any unpleasant consequences of over-spending.

Other parents decline to give a set allowance of some fixed figure. Instead they simply give the kids sufficient funds whenever needed on a case-by-case basis. They think that budgetary self-direction can wait until later, when the children are spending their own money earned in part-time jobs. When the children ask for cash, these parents want to know what it's for. They prefer to keep closer tabs on their children's expenses and the judgment involved. This they see as more important than lessons in budgeting.

So, which of these two approaches is better?

Actually, both seem to work well. Some healthy families give allowances; others rely on the case-by-case method. In the long run, it doesn't seem to matter. From what I can see, both types of families turn out young adults who use money responsibly. So, it's your call. You and your wife can follow either approach as long as you both agree on it. After all, whatever you're comfortable with, you're more confident about—and confidence is half the secret of effective parenting.

Whatever you do, though, do not give your children too much cash. Keep them fairly poor. Excess money, like too much of nearly anything else, is unhealthy for children. One rule of thumb is this: give them enough to cover basic expenses (lunch money, for instance) plus 10 to 15 percent for extras like a snack or soda after school. There's nothing wrong with being occasionally broke; most of the human race lives this way. And besides, being cash-poor tends to prompt ingenuity. Flannery O'Connor, the great American novelist, said of one of her characters: "He was so well adjusted, he never had to think. . . ."

Another thing to avoid: Don't link money as a reward for performance of duties such as chores or schoolwork. Separate cash entirely from what they're expected to do anyway as their contribution to the family. Your policy is to give the kids money for two reasons only—they need it, and you love them. On their part, they should fulfill their duties because this is one way, among others, they can pitch in to serve the family. Family life, for them as well as for you and your wife, is all about people serving each other without looking for any payback. Cash has nothing to do with this.

One final note of experience: When children are old enough to profit from part-time or summer jobs, some parents impose this policy—half of what the kids earn goes in the bank for later expenses: college tuition, car insurance, clothes, prom, and other hefty expenses. Because the teens have earned the money, they can spend the other half as they see fit. If the kids spend some of their earnings unwisely (and most do, at least initially), then they're stuck with the consequences. They learn the hard way what the term "rip off" means in teen marketing: bogus man-made fads, overpriced posters and CDs, inflated prices for junk entertainment, clothes that quickly fall out of fashion. As P. T. Barnum put it, "There's a sucker born every minute."

Sooner or later, they see their pocket cash swiftly disappear without leaving much to show for it. But the banked-away money stays put and even gains interest. Valuable lesson. Here you can help them learn from their mistakes, but please try not to say, "I told you so. . . ." Let them learn for themselves.

I I | *Watch Over Your Children's Education*

Your children's experience in school is immensely important to their growth in character. Education isn't a matter of data-transfer (from teachers to kids) or skill acquisition or feeling good about themselves. It is really all about character.

What areas of knowledge your children learn, how they learn, the people they work and mix with every day—all these will either reinforce what you and your wife teach at home or work against it. The worst schooling can undermine your children's character development. The best schooling will support it, or at least do nothing to unravel it.

Given how important this is, and given the skyrocketing costs of education today, it's surprising how few parents give serious thought to their children's character formation in school, the second most important influence in the kids' lives.

Choosing or Sizing Up a School

Many parents are unsure how to evaluate a school in these terms: how it builds, or even tries to build, children's character. They don't know what sort of questions to ask school personnel or how to assess what a school claims about itself. All parents will say they want a "good school" for their children, but they seem to have only a vague idea what this means. (Ask any group of parents this question: "What is a good school?" Watch how the answers will wander all over the map.)

Here I want to help you firm up your own understanding of a "good school" and suggest ways of sizing up and selecting one, if you have such a choice.

If, like most other Americans, you change address often, you find yourself shopping for schools frequently, especially if you are weighing private-school alternatives. Like many parents, you might move into a certain community because of the schools' reputation for quality. In this chapter, I want to help you choose schools for your children wisely. A lot is riding on this choice.

You, as a smart and responsible father, should think as much about school matters as your wife. Don't fall into the temptation, epidemic among so many men today, of letting your wife handle most school issues alone. This is unfair to her and to your children. Besides, experience shows that children take education most seriously when *both parents* take it seriously. Your attitude toward your children's schooling is crucial to shaping theirs.

FEATURES OF A GOOD SCHOOL

Like an excellent family, a high-quality school shows three outstanding features: a long-term *vision*, a sense of *mission*, and a *unifying spirit of service*. By contrast, a bad or mediocre school is missing one or more of these features, usually all three.

A high-quality school is energized by administrators and teachers who have a clear concept (an ideal, really) about *what kind of men and women the children should be as adults, ten or more years after graduation*. And people who work in the school share this vision with the children's parents. That is, school and parents try to work together toward the same goal—the children's later life as adults.

This ideal might be (as it was in public schools early in the twentieth century) to turn out a responsible, literate group of citizens. Or the concept might be to form children into competent, responsible, respected professionals. For religious schools, it might be all of the above plus forming lifelong commitment to the family's religious principles.

No matter what form it takes, a good school's strategic goal extends well into the children's future lives. If you asked the school's administrator at a graduation ceremony, "Well, do you think you've succeeded with these children?"—the response would be something like, "It's too soon to tell. Come back in ten years and then we'll know. . . ."

What follows from this strategic vision is a sense of mission.

A first-rate school has an active, dynamic ambiance to it, with high morale among the teaching staff. Every aspect of the school—classroom instruction, athletics, extracurriculars, discipline—serves a clear purpose. Everything works toward forming the children's lifetime judgment, realistic self-confidence, and sense of responsibility. In a healthy school, as in a healthy family, a sense of idealistic mission turns hard work, even drudgery, into purposeful achievement.

Moreover, a high-quality school, like any other high-quality business, fosters a spirit of service. It does not turn in on itself and become entangled with bureaucratic process—for bureaucracies tend to emphasize process rather than results. People in a quality school dedicate themselves above all to service. In other words, they're professionals.

The best schools see themselves serving the whole family, parents as well as children. Teachers and administrators treat parents as partners and take their needs and expectations seriously. This attitude leads, in turn, to ongoing mutual trust and open communication. Parents sense that, outside their own family, these teachers and administrators care most about their children's welfare, not only now but also later in life.

If you are blessed to have your children in a school like this, you should do all in your power to support it, financially and otherwise.

This being said, let me outline the outstanding features of a high-quality school. What are they? What should you look for?

• The school's written mission statement spells out the institution's commitment to collaborate with parents in leading children toward some ideal of responsible adulthood. That is, the children's later life as adults is absolutely central to the school's overall strategic mission. Though its wording may vary a lot, this statement should say something like: "to educate the children such that they grow up to become competent, responsible, considerate, learned men and women who are committed to live by principles of integrity." No matter how it's phrased, the school's statement of its reason for being should show, at least implicitly, a serious ideal for the children's lives long after graduation. Beware a school that seems more concerned with process than results—it talks a lot about curriculum and course-sequences, but says nothing about students' distant future lives.

• This mission statement is much more than a rhetorical flourish or shapeless abstraction in a brochure. It's a reality in the life of the institution, something the school's director often spells out to the faculty, the parents, and the students—all three. So, if you were to ask anyone in the school community, including the older students, what is the school's purpose, you'd hear roughly the same response. In other words, everyone in the school community knows what the school stands for. Beware the school that lacks this unity of outlook.

• The school's principal or headmaster can articulate the school's mission readily and without resort to jargon. If you, as a parent, were to press the administrator for details about *how* the school delivers on its stated ideals—"How do you teach the children to act responsibly?"—you should receive specific answers in clear, confident, vernacular prose.

• Ideally, all teachers, no matter what their subject specialty, insist that students perform written work with good spelling and correct English usage. Throughout the school, English is treated as a set of standards, not merely another "subject."

• Homework involves writing in sentences and paragraphs. Work is returned promptly and with some sign that the teacher has critically examined it. In other words, teachers take the students' work seriously. If homework is obviously not important to the teachers, it will not be important to the children either.

• Children work hard but are also happy with the school. In a bad or mediocre school, children *either* work hard *or* are happy. In a good school, serious work and personal satisfaction go together. Children are like us adults in this respect: they do not mind hard work as long as two conditions are being met— (a) they sense they're accomplishing something, and (b) they like the people they're working with.

• Administrators and teachers can readily explain how they handle "problem" students. That is, they show a willingness to control or even exclude students whose non-cooperation threatens the school's service to everyone else—in other words, the common good. The school's disciplinary procedures are both fair and compassionate, but they center principally on the community's common good.

• The faculty is a mix of mostly experienced teachers and some relatively new ones. The veterans are concentrated in the youngest and oldest grade levels, where their know-how is most needed. That is, the younger children need mastery of serious basic skills, while the older need confident, savvy class leadership.

• Students in the *middle* ability-grouping receive as much of a challenge as the top track and the slowest learners. Most schools, unfortunately, attend to the needs of the brightest and slowest students but tend to neglect the broad middle grouping. A good school challenges everyone.

• Parents willingly support the school with volunteer help and financial aid. Supportive parents are, after all, "satisfied clients." In concrete ways, they show appreciation to the school for its dedication to their children's welfare.

• The school's physical plant shows professional attention to detail. It is clean, orderly, lively—a pleasant place for working and learning, like any other well-run business.

- The sports program for younger children is reasonably competitive but not overly so. Not-so-talented kids are encouraged to take part, and their personal best efforts are appreciated. The school tries to foster the best ideals of athletics—bodily conditioning, a lifetime habit of exercise, sportsmanship, team collaboration, and a healthy spirit of honorable competition.
- In all its academic, athletic, and extracurricular aspects, the school clearly tries to build certain lifetime attitudes and habits in the children, certain *powers* that the children internalize over time—problem-solving ability, respect for intellectual achievement, powers of concentration, high-quality technical competence in math and sciences, habits of clarity and precision in spoken and written English, competence in at least one foreign language, appreciation for artistic excellence, understanding of historical development and trends, sense of responsibility in good citizenship, respect for rule of law, and ethical uprightness.

In short, a good school seems to operate according to the maxim: "An education is what you have left over after you've forgotten the material." It's dedicated to turning out competent, learned, responsible producers.

To look at it another way, a good school seeks to produce the sort of capable, levelheaded adults who serve so generously on its own school board (or board of trustees).

Of course, the description outlined above is an ideal of near-perfection. All schools, like all other human institutions (including the family), fall short of perfection. But *the best schools never stop trying*.

THE PRINCIPAL

Probably the most critical force for an excellent school, one often underestimated by parents of young children, is the leadership ability of the principal. A school's quality will rise or fall depending on the vision and professionalism of this one person, the school's chief executive officer.

Any school, large or small, is an immensely complex operation. It's far more complicated than most parents understand, because countless centrifugal forces constantly strain to pull the operation apart. Consequently, a school principal needs relentless energy and iron will to unite the operation and give it purposeful direction. A school's head works hard to keep reminding everyone—faculty, parents, students, even the school-board members—what all their sacrifices are really for.

A real professional in this field needs both strategic vision and attention to detail, reflection and action, justice and compassion, courteous and tactful assertiveness, idealism without illusions. It is a tough, demanding job.

So, when you set out to scrutinize a school, you should start at the top. Look for signs of esteem toward the principal by teachers and older students and other parents like yourself. Make a point to ask other parents some key questions:

• What is the principal's reputation for able administration, communication with parents, and availability for conferences?

• If parents come to a principal with a complaint, they have a right to either corrective action or at least a reasonable explanation. So, do they receive either of these actions, and quickly, or does a problem persist unchanged and unexplained? After all, a principal is the school's executive, and an executive's job is to execute, to make things happen.

• Is the principal sincerely open to parents' suggestions, but without bending to undue influence from pressure groups? Does the principal know, when appropriate, how to say *no*?

• Do the children (and therefore their parents) perceive the principal as kind and understanding, but at the same time fair in administering justice? Children put great weight on *fairness*.

• In short, does everyone in the school like and respect the principal as a competent, confident leader?

If your children spend several years in the same school, it's no exaggeration to say that this leader will have, directly or indirectly, one of the most long-lasting influences on the course of their lives.

VISITING THE SCHOOL

How do you go about evaluating a prospective school for your children? What should you look for in the physical plant? Which questions should you ask, and of whom?

Like many other parents today, you and your wife may consider a private school alternative. Because the private option means substantial cash outlay (an investment, really), what follows here will pertain mostly to schools of this type. But the point here is to give you some basis for comparison. A great many public schools are excellent, and many private schools are dismal.

In any event, whatever type of school you choose—or even if you have little or no choice—you still need a framework for overseeing your children's education outside the home. The kind of scrutiny you'd give to an expensive private school serves just as well to evaluate any public school. Whether public or private, a school should offer you top-quality service, and you need some way to judge this before settling on your choice.

Let's begin with this: You and your wife should plan to visit the school on a normal school day. So-called "open house" days are fine as far as they go, but they don't reveal nearly as much as inspecting firsthand the day-to-day environment your children will live in. It's worth your while to take a day off from work so the two of you can observe as a team. This is especially important if you're applying to a competitive private school. You make a good impression to the school's authorities, because competitive schools like dealing with a family where the father takes serious interest in his children's education.

Call ahead and arrange an appointment to meet with the principal and ask if you can also meet with two or three of the teachers as convenient, just for a few minutes each. Also ask if your son or daughter can spend the day in class with the group he or she would be joining next year; your children's impressions of the day should be quite telling. (Kids sense immediately, in less than a half-hour, how well they fit in with a group.)

If possible, plan to visit between 10:00 A.M. and lunchtime. This is when any school is most active and "typical." (For the same reason, most standardized tests are administered to kids in mid-morning.) The best times of the year to visit are early October to late November and early March to late April. Other times of the year would probably present problems that could skew your perspective; even the best schools experience untypical incidents of kids' unruliness during winter months and at the very end of the school year. (For that matter, so do most families.) You want to see the school when it's operating most efficiently, and the time slots mentioned here are best for this purpose.

As with any other professional interview, you should prepare with some homework. So, when you set up the appointment, ask for the school's promotional literature (if any) and read it carefully. Pay special attention to the school's mission statement and the experience of the faculty. You will want to query the principal about the school's mission (see below) and find out which of the most experienced teachers will be working with your child over the next few years. Naturally, as in any other interview, you shouldn't ask questions that are already answered in the literature: "How many book are in your school library?" or "Where did your teachers earn their degrees?" This is a waste of time.

PHYSICAL APPEARANCE

On the appointed day, you and your wife should arrive a half-hour ahead of time and walk around the grounds. What do you see?

If you're looking into a high school, walk over to the outer limits of the students' parking area. There should be trash receptacles in place, and the ground should have little or no litter scattered around. After all, the students who drive are the oldest in the school and should have internalized by now some of the school's rules about order and cleanliness. Don't be harsh, though, for even conscientious teenagers can be messy. (Adults as well.) The point is this: There should be much more trash discarded in receptacles than littering the ground. This is a small matter, but it says something about the students' sense of collaboration.

If you can, travel to the back of the school building and see whether there's a spot littered with cigarette butts. If so, then students are sneaking smokes there. If the smoking doesn't bother you, the sneakiness should. What does it say about the school's supervision? If you and your wife could spot this obvious puffing-place, why hasn't the school noticed and done something about it? Questions for later, when you meet the principal.

Finally, as you approach the building and enter, do you see signs posted to show visitors where to go? A set of clear directional signs means that the school is accustomed to receiving visitors and welcomes them. On the other hand, a confusing lack of signs may mean (though not necessarily) that the school's administration is looking inward, more concerned with internal operations than with public service. Or it may mean that signs, damaged or removed through vandalism, remain unreplaced. This, in turn, generally means mediocre or poor management.

These are small details, certainly, and you should withhold critical judgment until you've probed more thoroughly. But, for good or for ill, they may form part of a pattern. Wait and see.

As soon as you enter the building, you should check in at the school office. If you have time before your interview with the principal, you should spend a little while looking over the premises. Or you can do this later in the morning. In any event, you ought to inspect the physical environment where your children may spend the next several years. What should you look for?

Look for evidence that the place is well maintained: neat, clean, safe, pleasant, like any other professional workplace. Attention to physical detail nearly always signifies good management—which in turn suggests that instructional matters are well run, supervised with a sense of quality control. On the other hand, any evidence of neglect—excessive dirt and litter, graffiti, burned-out lights, unrepaired damage, and the like—points to a sub-satisfactory level of supervision, a negligence that probably affects the whole school operation.

Look inside some classrooms. These ought to have students' work on display. Look the work over. Do you see misspellings and obvious usage mistakes in the children's writings, especially if they're marked with "A" or other high grades? On these papers, you're looking at what the teacher considers commendable work. Does it look commendable to you? If possible, look inside some children's desks. Do you see food wrappers—a sign perhaps of poor supervision? (If kids eat snacks in the classroom, then all food wrappers should be in wastebaskets and nowhere else.) Do you see doodling on desktops? This may mean boring instruction or inattention to children's responsibility for keeping the room clean.

If you can, take a peek in the washrooms. Are there graffiti on walls? Food wrappers or cigarette butts in the wastebasket or on the floor? These messes speak for themselves about supervision of the students and thoroughness of clean-up. Washrooms are the part of a school least likely to receive attention. So, if they're very clean, this is usually a sign that the school is well managed: the principal pays attention to detail.

Stand in the hallway and listen. You should hear the low hum of children engaged in interesting work punctuated from time to time with healthy laughter. What you should *not* hear is raucous, clearly out-of-control boisterousness—or long spells of pure silence surrounding a boring teacher's steady drone. If a teacher is talking to a fairly quiet class, have a glance inside the room; you can tell whether the students are actively listening or just sitting there in a glassy-eyed, daydreaming trance.

Observe how the children change classes or go outside for recess. How do they act and react to each other? Do they seem to enjoy each other's company? When teachers call to them or give direction, how do the kids respond? Are they attentive, or do they ignore what's being said? Do you see some of the students linger a bit and make pleasant small talk with teachers? These many subtle signs between teachers and students—that these people like and respect each other—say a great deal about the school's unity and spirit of collaboration. Your wife, as a woman, may be more sensitive to this interplay than you are, but both of you can form an overall impression: If I were a child, would I enjoy working in this environment? Would I like living with these people every day?

INTERVIEW WITH THE PRINCIPAL

When you and your wife are seated comfortably with the principal, you should ask questions you've prepared beforehand. Remember, you're trying mostly to determine the *attitudes* and *philosophy* behind the school's operations, to see how well the school's vision of your children's education squares with your own. Do you and the school's personnel share the same expectations for your children's future, so that you can work together? Or, on the other hand, does it seem that you and the school might be working at cross-purposes?

Your first question gets right to the heart of the matter and should be phrased something like this: *What is your long-term vision (ideal) of your students' later lives as adults—say, ten or fifteen years after they graduate? How would you describe your students as adults? In what ways would you hope your students would be different from, or better than, their contemporaries as a result of the years they spent with you?*

Watch out for any hesitation or stumbling over words to come up with an answer, or any other signs that the principal is taken aback by this line of questioning. After all, these questions probe to the very core of the principal's job, the concerns he or she should hold uppermost in mind and reflect about constantly. The CEO of any organization deals mostly with *why* things are done, not merely *how*.

A first-rate administrator should have no hesitation coming up with clearly articulated answers to these questions. Listen carefully and judge whether, or to what extent, the school's institutional vision coincides with your own. You can now probe more deeply by asking *how* the school's different elements—courses of studies, homework requirements, athletics, extracurriculars, and disciplinary system—work together toward the school's claimed mission. If you're satisfied so far, you can move on to other matters.

QUESTION: *What do you do to oversee your teachers' quality of instruction?*
You are looking for facts here, not merely intentions. Look for evidence of ongoing quality control: clear syllabus devised by teachers and administration working together, supervision of new teachers (very important), frequency of faculty workshops and personal meetings, regular performance review, policy for dealing with parents' inquiries or complaints about teachers. The school should have an institutionalized process for directing, correcting, encouraging, and otherwise shoring up the faculty's professional performance. The principal should know this process inside out and be able to explain it thoroughly, with facts.

QUESTION (especially for private schools): *For what reasons is a student expelled from this school, or at least dropped from the rolls at the end of a school year? Without naming names, of course, could you cite a couple of examples from recent years?*
A private school with high standards and sense of mission will drop students who refuse to perform or who pose a danger—through drug use, for example—to the school's common good. Beware of the school that does not act swiftly and effectively along these lines and can't cite specific instances to prove it.

QUESTION: *What percentage of your parents support your school financially or with volunteer help?*
The higher the figure, the greater is the level of satisfaction and gratitude among parents like yourselves. The principal should have no trouble coming up with the figure. Remember the old axiom in fund-raising: People give most generously to *success*, not need; it is successful, efficiently run non-profit organizations that raise the most money.

QUESTION: *If we were to ask other parents what they thought were the school's strongest points and shortcomings, what do you think they'd probably say?*
Putting your question this way ("If we were to ask others . . .") nearly always prompts a fairly candid assessment of the school's features, plus and minus. Once the principal explains, you and your wife can then probe for specifics. If the

principal thinks that people's perceptions of school problems are out of line somehow, you have a right to know why.

At this point, you may want to ask for some references; ask if you could have the names of two or three parents who'd be willing to talk with you about their experience with the school. As a courtesy, of course, you should offer the principal a day or so to come up with names and phone numbers; explain that you'll call back later for the information. (It is a sound principle in any business, of course: always check references.)

QUESTION: *What would you expect from us, as parents, to collaborate with the school?*

A good school wants and expects close communication with parents. Therefore it holds periodic meetings with parents as a group or in private consultation. A good school would want you to oversee assignments and projects done at home and otherwise take serious interest in your children's schoolwork. Moreover, the school should show that it welcomes phone calls and visits by parents. Finally, don't be surprised to be told that the school expects a certain measure of parental support, financial and otherwise. If administrators and teachers are confident they provide a highly valuable service, over and above minimal professional requirements, they're certainly justified in expecting an equally generous response—and the best schools get exactly that.

Don't be concerned about putting the principal on the spot with probing questions like these. Real professionals (in any field) enjoy talking about their work, and they like questions that prompt them to do so.

What's more, your question would make a good impression. Any conscientious principal, someone with high expectations for the students' future lives, is delighted to work with parents who share those ideals. Your questions reveal a lot about your own efforts at home to raise your children well. To the principal, then, your line of questioning means your children would probably work out well as students. All this means that your family and the school would make a good match.

INTERVIEWS WITH TEACHERS

After you've met with the principal, you should chat briefly with a couple of teachers, especially those who teach English and mathematics. You should have set up appointments with these people earlier. Because teachers in a good school are extremely busy people, you should keep your meeting short and to the point. Here, as with the head of the school, you're looking more for *why* things are done, not simply how.

QUESTION: *What skills, attitudes, and work habits do you try to impart to your students that should last them for years?*

Though teachers must work with "material" in a course, the best of them know that sound teaching goes far beyond this. Excellent teachers see themselves building habits of thinking and approaches to work in their students—powers of mind and will that long outlast "material." So, you should look for a teacher's sincere concern about long-lasting benefits of mind and will: respect for learning, powers of clear and critical thinking, concentration and attention to detail, holding children responsible to high standards of performance. The best teachers love their intellectual pursuits (English, math, language) as well as their students—and delight in bringing them together. They are both disciplined and enthusiastic. Like other competent professionals, they enjoy explaining their work. Look for signs of these attitudes.

QUESTION: *May we please see copies of some past exams, especially final examinations, in your course?*

A good teacher should be able to produce blank copies of past exams easily from his or her files, and would be happy to explain the contents to you. Real professionals are dedicated to learning, not simply instruction, and so they see their tests—feedback from the kids—as crucial to their work.

You can tell a great deal about a course's content and method of teaching from its final exam. Are exams devised by the teacher, or are they run-of-the-mill tests provided by textbook publishers? Do the tests have clear instructions telling the students what to do? (Clear instructions on tests usually points to clear teaching in the classroom; that is, the teacher habitually focuses on what the students need to know.) Do the tests rely mostly on "fill-in-the-blank" responses or do they require written answers, even one or two sentences? Do the tests seem to go after mostly factual data (one-word responses, matching items, multiple choice) or do they also have short essay questions requiring some reflective thought and written expression?

QUESTION: *How does homework fit into your teaching; how do you grade it; and how soon do you return it to the children?*

The best teachers use home assignments as an important part of the students' learning. They keep homework moderate in length (twenty to thirty minutes for each hour of instruction in high school, less in lower grades) and assign it regularly. They require students to keep an assignment notebook. They use homework in class, collect it, and grade it. The teacher's standards for grading should be clear and reasonable. Finally, the teacher returns homework promptly, no more than two or three working days after submission. Prompt return shows that the teacher considers the work important, and so students are pressed to take it seriously.

QUESTION: *What books in your subject would you recommend to parents or to gifted students who would like to learn more?*
Excellent teachers read a great deal. What you're looking for here is evidence that this teacher enjoys reading in the field and stays current with developments. When teachers work with gifted students, they are eager to encourage additional reading; they're never at a loss for titles to recommend.

QUESTION: *In what ways do you stay in touch with parents of children who need help?*
Many teachers will take initiative to call parents periodically, especially if their children need extra help in some way. At the very least, they send home regular written reports. In the best schools, teachers provide parents with a phone number and time when they can be reached for parent inquiries. Look for signs that this teacher wants to maintain open communication with parents. There should be no hesitation in the response, nothing theoretical; the teacher should tell what he or she habitually does *in fact* to keep parents informed.

Finally, if you have been impressed with what you have seen and heard, by all means say so. Thank the teacher and express your appreciation for his or her evident professionalism. Teachers, even the best of them, scarcely receive as many expressions of gratitude as they deserve. Sincere appreciation means a lot to them.

Working with the School

So, you enroll your children in a school. What comes next? Let's begin with some basics:

• Remember that teachers, like parents, take on a hugely challenging job. They are trying to develop permanent strengths of mind, heart, and will among a *group* of diverse young people during the most unstable years of life. Though teachers must grapple with an essentially spiritual entity (the children's minds), something inherently out of control, they're held responsible for short-term results. It's hard to work under these circumstances—that is, to be held answerable for a situation that's, at best, barely controllable. So, try always to understand the teachers' situation and be patient; look for *conscientious efforts* rather than *results*. Remember, too, that nobody is perfect, and anyone—teacher or parent—can sometimes have a bad day.

• From your kids' point of view, your attitude of *serious interest* in their education is more important than specific details of what you do. It's your active interest in their performance that your children will notice and respect, not merely the number of hours you work with them. Children, like us adults, work more seriously when someone in authority takes interest and gives encouragement. You show interest mostly in the kind of *questions* you ask your children and how often you do this. In schoolwork, as in the rest of life, absence of questions nearly always means lack of interest.

• Your children's later success in life will depend on two personal traits (among others, of course): (a) an ability to concentrate on tasks, to stick with problems until they have done the best they can; and (b) an ability to get along well with other people, especially those in authority. When you look for your children's progress in school, you should put priority on these two broad areas. Are the kids growing in powers of self-control and concentration? How well do they get along with teachers and other students?

• Getting television and electronic games under control is more than half the battle for empowering your children's minds and wills. Challenging schoolwork builds competence, but mindless entertainment builds nothing. Your children need to learn through practice that life consists of both work and play in healthy balance, but—for them as well as for you and your wife—work has to come first. We don't really enjoy leisure unless we have earned it.

• Paying a lot of attention to your children's home assignments is your principal responsibility. It's also one of your most effective ways as a father to teach standards of work well done.

Indirectly, you also show your solid support for the teachers' efforts in school.

• Never undercut teachers' authority by speaking critically of them in front of your children. This is unethical. Save all critical comments for personal, private conversation with the teachers.

• *Direct* your children's work, but don't *manage* it. That is, show them how to do a better job but don't do their work for them. It's not important that they always get good grades; it's important that they honestly earn whatever they get. Look for *personal best effort.*

• Consider your time going over your children's homework with them as a serious and valuable investment, for that's what it is. Even though you may be dead tired at night and longing for some quiet rest, invest the time and effort into checking your children's work, giving your kids correction and encouragement and specific praise. Get inside your children's minds and hearts. Years from now, they will fondly remember these nightly sessions with you going over their work, when they learned so much about your judgment and standards, your mind and heart—how you lovingly led them to responsible competence. That's what a father does.

Choosing Teachers and Courses

When choosing teachers and courses, be realistic. If your children are in junior high or high school, and they rotate among several teachers each day, you can generally count on some variation of teaching quality. That is, some teachers will be excellent, some mediocre, and one or two (especially beginners) will show room for improvement. This is true among practically all large schools, even the best. Think back to your own experience at this age. If you're like most people, your teachers each year had this range of competence.

If you want to maximize your children's contact with the school's best teachers, though, there is something you can do about it, or at least try.

First, you should ask around among other parents and find out which teachers are most experienced and most respected. Your wife may try yet another tack: ask the school's secretary. The principal's secretary is usually one of the shrewdest and best-informed people on the staff. She knows everything that goes on, sometimes even more than her boss. As a professional, of course, she certainly won't speak negatively about any of the faculty, but she knows who the best teachers are. Have your wife make a couple of discreet inquiries.

Once you have this information, get in touch with the principal or director of studies and make your preference known. Be nice about it, of course, but be assertive too. Naturally, if you have a track record of strong support for the school and faculty, you stand a greater chance of getting your way.

As matters go, you may have no choice but to accept someone else. At least you tried. Make the most of the situation.

This general approach, seeking out the best teachers, applies as well to your children's choice of electives in high school. Guide your children with some sound advice they can take with them later to college. Tell them this: Never pick courses from a catalogue. Rather, ask around to find out who are the best teachers or professors—that is, the people most challenging, interesting, stimulating, dedicated to their field and their students. Within limits of your pre-professional interests, sign up for whatever courses they teach, even if you have (for now) only marginal interest in their specialties. At the very least, you'll learn a lot and probably enjoy the experience. You may even acquire an interest—in history, art, Russian literature, whatever—that could last for years and maybe even point to a career. A good teacher's enthusiasm is contagious. Moreover, in school as in business life, it's enjoyable to work with really competent, confident professionals.

It's a life-lesson for your kids: Excellence lies with people, not "subject matter."

TEAMWORK WITH TEACHERS

Here are some pointers about dealing effectively with your children's teachers.

• Early in the year, either you or your wife should contact each teacher and ask for a phone number and optimal time for calling in case you later have a question or concern. On your part, give each teacher the time of day when you or your wife can be reached; if you're willing and able to be phoned at work, give your workplace number. You and your children's teachers need this information from each other to stay in touch.

• Find out if the teacher requires students to keep an assignment notebook, a pad for listing home assignments. Teachers should do this routinely, but if they don't, you should have your children keep one anyway. This you should check nightly. An assignment notebook is critical to children's management of their time and responsibilities. In a real sense, it's a preparation for their later use of a calendar to manage their own affairs. Think ahead: At what age should my children start to jot down tasks with a deadline and stay on top of their upcoming responsibilities?

• Keep phone conversations with teachers brief and to the point. If a conversation seems to require more than ten minutes, then you should arrange a sit-down meeting for later.

• If your son or daughter has an emotional complaint about some teacher's alleged misconduct, do not make the big mistake of forming a quick, one-sided judgment. Children are highly prone to misjudgments; after all, this is one reason they're in school. Even if your child's version of events seems factual, bear in mind that he or she may not know all the relevant facts. So, keep an open mind and respect the teacher's right to presumption of innocence. When you call the teacher, maintain a tone of courteous respect and simply ask for the facts of the matter—what the problem (if there is one) seems to be. Remember, when two good-willed people are at odds, the cause is nearly always some sort of misunderstanding.

• Related to the above, never go to the principal with a complaint about a teacher's alleged misconduct unless you have *first* discussed it with the teacher. This is a sound and fair principle. It applies as much to schools as to any business: Do not go over someone's head except for appeal. Dealing with a perceived problem directly and personally is in everyone's best interest.

• If a teacher comments on some problem he or she has with your child, listen politely and take the judgment seriously. A veteran teacher has plenty of experience with kids your children's age and knows what's normal and acceptable in kids' behavior. If the teacher has trouble with your child's behavior, he or she is probably right—not always, but most likely. A child benefits when both his teacher and his parents disapprove his misconduct and support each other's efforts to correct it. Sometimes misbehaving kids need to be put in a "box" of disapproval from all sides, at home and in school—and the only way out is to apologize and reform.

• Remember, too, that teaching is often a lonely and thankless job. Teachers work on their feet for hours a day, cut off from other adults. Children, as we've seen, are normally ungrateful;

sad to say, so are many parents. So, if you see your children's teachers doing a commendable job, then have the thoughtfulness to commend them. Even in those touchy situations where you'd like to give constructive criticism, try to sandwich your remarks with appreciation for what's done well. If you do this with your children's teachers, your judgment will be taken seriously, even gratefully.

Homework

As mentioned in an earlier section, your kids are more likely to take their studies seriously if they see that you take them seriously. Psychologists have noticed that when parents, husband and wife together, share the same high expectations and make the same demands, then the children fall readily into line. This dynamic is badly weakened, though, when the mother shows interest but the father remains distant or apparently indifferent.

In other words, *the father's serious, active interest seems to be critical for shaping children's attitudes toward work responsibilities outside the family.*

The first detail you should check, therefore, is your children's assignment notebook. What are they responsible for doing and turning in? Have your kids clearly jotted down their assignments? Children, like all of us, need to know what's expected of them. If you're going to direct their efforts intelligently, you need to know this, too.

Let your children learn the satisfaction of checking off, one by one, tasks on a "to do" list. There's a certain healthy enjoyment in crossing out jobs as we complete them. It's a fact of adult life: Completing work is pleasurable, like play itself. Only after we've finished our duties can we then turn to leisure and really enjoy it.

When your children show you their completed homework, look at it with your experienced "professional eye." Is written work obviously done with care, or does it appear slapdash? Do sentences and paragraphs (if required) make sense?

Your children should learn, both at home and in school, that the first obligation of writing is *clarity*. Read their writing aloud to them, so they can *hear* their thoughts—and thereby spot faults of clarity and sentence structure. (Unfortunately, many schools today don't lead children to read their own work aloud; this neglect leads to sloppy, careless writing.) Because the craft of writing lies mostly in *re*writing, you shouldn't hesitate to send your kids back to redo their work until it meets your standards.

Your children must learn early in life to consider the rights and sensibilities of the so-called "reader"—the person to whom the writing is directed, someone who has a right to clear, virtually effortless understanding of our thoughts. It's discourteous and ultimately self-damaging, whether in school or in professional life, to present this reader with work that's carelessly muddled. Artfulness in writing is to be hoped for and aimed at, certainly, but clarity is always a must. Quintilian, the Roman rhetorician, said, "Write not so that you can be understood; rather, write so you cannot be misunderstood."

Because the "reader" for most schoolchildren is generally only the teacher, and since both the kids' writing and the teacher's reading are done silently, then kids are slow to grasp this all-important lesson: we always write for people.

You can drive this lesson home by being your child's critical reader. If you keep up this habit for years, then gradually and subtly your children come to write for you—to win your approval. Through this approach, your standards for clear writing become their own. In many ways, you are really teaching adult-level standards of job performance, along with their importance. This is a big part of a father's overall role in shaping his children's competence.

Related to this, form a habit of checking your kids' mastery of material they're required to memorize. When they think they know, say, their spelling or vocabulary words or dates for historical events, have them come to you to check how well they've mastered everything. This exercise is a kind of rehearsal for their performance on quizzes and tests the following day. Likewise, if they don't understand a problem in math, be available to help them think matters through. Don't do their work for them, of course, but show them how to approach it logically, stubbornly, confidently—the way we adults approach problems at work.

All this collaboration with your children is certainly time consuming; it interrupts your own time of well-earned leisure in the evening. But it pays off, both now and later. Children deeply sense their father's interest and availability. A strong bond forms between father and children when the kids know one thing for sure: *no matter how busy Dad is, he's always available if I need him.*

Moreover, this habit you form in family life—that the kids come to you for directional advice—will be important for them later. In adolescence and young adulthood, indeed all their lives, they can turn to you confidently for sound advice and sensible direction. You know what you're talking about; you're a wise man, a smart father.

By all means, praise your children for their efforts and attitudes and steady progress. Be specific in your praise, too. Children respond well to praise when it's clearly deserved and when it comes from someone they respect. We all do.

What I'm saying here is that your close attention to your children's work is vitally important to their growth in character. You use their schoolwork to teach them an enormous amount—by example, directed practice, and word—about sound judgment, responsibility, perseverance, and self-mastery. Recall the maxim—we really don't know someone until we see him or her at work. So, you can learn a lot about your children's growth in maturity by overseeing their work. This is worth any sacrifice.

Extracurriculars

Even if your children are still young, you should start thinking about their future involvement in high school extracurricular activities.

Unfortunately, in our athletics-centered society, the high value and even lifetime worth of extracurriculars is underrated, especially by fathers. Though men look forward to their kids' involvement with sports in high school, they seldom think seriously about how clubs can benefit their children as well—often more than sports.

If your children are better-than-average athletes, they should play for school teams, assuming they make the cuts. But if they are less than first rate, or if they are headed toward a large high school with tight competition for first-string places, maybe you should study some alternatives. Instead of warming a bench as second-stringers, maybe your children could be learning to excel in some individual sport (as mentioned before) and in one or more extracurriculars. Give some thought to this way ahead of time.

Extracurricular activities have many advantages that fathers seldom consider. For instance . . .

• A debating club or newspaper operates more like a real-life professional enterprise than anything else in school. Classroom activities bear little resemblance to life in a business office, but a school newspaper or yearbook is run very much like a real business. It has division of labor, team collaboration, standards of performance, the give-and-take of working with others under pressures of time and budgets. High schoolers learn much more here about professional performance than they do in class. (In many ways, a classroom setting is artificial and unrealistic, not at all like a typical adult workplace.)

• Clubs are the only place in school where adolescents work together with people of different ages. Seniors teach freshmen and sophomores; younger students befriend older ones. Remember that a two-year age difference is nothing to adults but a huge gap to teens. In the eyes of a freshman, a senior is light-years older, practically an adult. This collaboration leads to a kind of ongoing apprenticeship, a handing on of experience and a preparation for taking on responsibility. Because these young people all share a common interest—in debating, writing, computer graphics, photography, whatever—they readily become friends, sometimes for life. (One of my close friends today was a fellow debater, two years older than I, in high school. That was forty years ago.)

• Clubs develop talents and competence. Quiet intellectuals can shine in debate and public speaking; their shyness transforms into real self-confidence. Kids who like to write can exercise their self-expression far better than in routine classroom assignments, and they can receive more effective constructive criticism. Socially awkward kids can benefit from dramatics; a combination of disciplined performance and peer support, rewarded by audience applause, gives them poise and self-assurance.

• Students can work their way up to directive positions in a club by the time they're upperclassmen. They then exercise responsible management and learn lessons of leadership, including its burdens. This is valuable experience. (And for this reason, competitive colleges seek out students who've earned top positions in club activities.)

• It's no exaggeration to say that countless careers have been launched with extracurriculars. Many professionals found their niche—and in a sense, themselves—through the work they learned to love in high school clubs. This is especially true of the sciences, journalism, and debating. Many a successful lawyer and business executive started out on a high school debate team.

One added word of advice here: It would be better for your

children to join one or two clubs at most and work on these seriously. They should specialize, as it were, and not spread themselves too thin. Debating and newspaper work are most valuable. After all, the ability to speak and write well, especially under pressure, will be important to your children's later careers no matter what they do for a living. So, too, will their skill at dealing with people.

Career Guidance

How soon should you start leading your children to think about college and career choices? Freshman year of high school is not too soon.

A word of caution here. You cannot choose your children's career for them; they have to do this eventually for themselves. It's their life. But you can help them find a direction, a general line of work that seems to suit them best.

One help here, generally overlooked by parents, is the array of career aptitude tests available in high school guidance departments. Arrange to have your children take these tests early in high school. Even if you are in a private school that lacks this service, you can still arrange for testing in your local public school; after all, you pay for the service with your taxes.

These tests serve a couple of useful purposes. First, broadly speaking, they show which areas of work your children seem best suited for. Just as valuable, they show which professions are probably *un*suitable. Many college pre-med students find out halfway through their studies that they are really unsuited for rigorous scientific work, something prerequisite for medical careers. Their desires to "help people" are not enough to earn an M.D. Their altruism needs another outlet, they come to see, but by then they are halfway through college. Shouldn't they have learned this earlier on in life, while they were still in high school?

The other advantage of these tests is indirect. Taking the tests and then discussing results with you serves to prod your young teens to start thinking seriously about their futures. This is something fathers have done with their teenage children from time immemorial. You can steer this thinking, urge it along, open avenues of planning and action. In short, you can begin to deal seriously with your teenagers as young adults. As a good father, you've always seen them as adults-in-the-making, and now they're almost there, needing your experienced advice as they approach true independence.

Your direct intervention in this kind of career-directed thinking grows especially important when your children enter high school. Why is this?

Unless the school is an outstanding one, truly committed to your children's future as responsible adults, then chances are you won't receive much help initiated by the school. You have to step in and make things happen.

Very many high schools, unfortunately, operate as self-contained, ultimately directionless centers of busy-ness. Teens have access to countless amusements and distractions, an endless swirl of social and athletic events such that they give little serious thought to their futures—unless you intervene to direct them. Your leadership here is crucially necessary. Put the time and effort in now, while your children are still young, and you will avoid the agony facing so many older parents today: having a son or daughter about to graduate from college with absolutely no idea what to do for a living.

So, what can you do? Take the results of the career tests and discuss the most promising avenues they reveal. Then help your sons and daughters start to network—to meet and talk with people who work in these fields. There is no substitute for personal advice from knowledgeable people.

Is your son apparently suited for engineering? Line him up to talk with some acquaintances of yours who are engineers. Teach him how to handle himself in an interview. Go over the kinds of questions he should ask: What does your work involve? What sort of problems do you solve each day? How do growth prospects look twenty years out? If you were in my position, what would you study, and where would you go to college? Important: What do you know now that you wish you had known at age sixteen?

Is your daughter interested in journalism? Ask around and see if you can set her up for some interviews with professional reporters. Better still, show her how to conduct the networking herself: Call people, set up an interview, show up on time, keep to the point, write a follow-up thank-you note, and the like. If she does eventually enter journalism, she will do this sort of interview work every day. Let her start now.

If you direct your children to cultivate professionals this way, you teach them a lot about the way things work in the world. You teach them to be shrewd self-starters. Now, as always in history, success comes from knowing how to deal courteously with people, especially people of influence.

Besides, there's another practical boon for your adolescents. This sort of networking often leads to a substantial summer job. Adults are always impressed with teens who display personal poise and mature interest in their fields. Professionals are often able to offer a slot in their firm for a job the following summer. This might be nothing but grunt work, like emptying wastebaskets, but it teaches a lot about the professional workplace—what goes on in an engineering or architectural office, for example—and, in any event, it beats flipping hamburgers at a fast-food joint.

Whatever you do, act to help your teens think of themselves as adults in everything but experience. For ages past, this is the way responsible fathers directed and encouraged their adolescent children. As the kids were on the verge of leaving home to start their own lives, Dad helped them—with his wisdom, experienced know-how, and encouragement—to take those first steps.

Finally, if your children form some fairly clear ideas about their career options, they can focus more sensibly on their high school studies. Their work has a unifying principle, a reason for being, and a direction forward to some distant goal. What's more, it helps them plan more clearly for college and start acting now to give themselves a competitive edge by the time they are high school seniors.

ON TRACK FOR COLLEGE

When your children enter freshman year of high school, you should help them start planning for their applications, three years down the road, to colleges and universities that are best for them, personally and professionally. This section will show you how to do this effectively.

But before we look at the steps involved, let's step back and see why your fatherly help is important here and how it fits into your overall responsibility as a father—*that your sons and daughters live as responsible, competent, self-directed adults by the time they're eighteen.*

As I have shown throughout this book, a smart father guides his children to think ahead, to treat time as a resource, to set clear goals, and then to act smartly to control events leading to their goals. A good father presses his children to grow out of childish *now*-centeredness and start giving purposeful direction to their later lives. Drawing on his powerful urge to protect, he strengthens his children for their future welfare.

What I'm proposing here is that you take advantage of your children's whole college-application process, starting in freshman year of high school, to teach them how to handle themselves and their professional responsibilities. You teach them the meaning of *professionalism*.

Look at it this way. We humans are goal-driven creatures. We work most efficiently when we focus on distant goals and work hard to attain them. If your teenage children, with your guidance, set a goal of being accepted later to a competitive college or university (as part of their overall career strategy discussed above), then everything they do in high school falls into a purposeful pattern. They will enjoy a competitive edge over their undirected fellow students who drift passively, almost randomly, through grades nine to twelve and then arrive at senior year without a clue about what to do next.

But here's the main point: The real goal you set and work toward for your kids is not simply that they have maximum options for college choice and get accepted into a competitive college. What you really want is that, by the time they're seniors, *they have become the kind of young men and women for whom the better colleges are looking.* By the fall of senior year, they should be mature self-starters, well educated, self-confident, at least reasonably career-oriented, and respected by all who know them.

In other words, regardless where they eventually enroll, you use the college-track process to strengthen your children's character.

As a smart father, you know—and teach your children—that their application to competitive colleges and universities is the first real professional challenge they will face. For the first time, your children will experience a competitive situation similar to what they'll meet later in their careers—a professional challenge calling for long-term preparation, shrewd use of resources, and savvy. Think about it . . .

• For the first time, your children will face adults outside their narrow home/school universe who will critically assess their competence and personal character, and compare them with other people their age. This will happen to them several times in life, with every change of job or career.

• As part of this assessment, these adults will ask some tough questions, the sort of questions commonly posed in professional situations: Who are you, really? What do you know? What can you contribute to our endeavors here? How well do people respect you, and why? What is the direction of your life? Are you self-centered or other-centered? What have you accomplished in your life up to now?

• These people's underlying assumption is the same that prevails in normal professional life: namely, *the best predictor of future success is past success.* "Potential" is only for children. By the time someone is eighteen, adults want to know one thing: What have you done with your time?

• To pass this scrutiny successfully, a college applicant needs a history of accomplishment. That is, a documentable case that he or she is a young adult who has won people's respect through solid accomplishment. This personal dossier must include:

—a transcript of high grades achieved in challenging courses of study;

—two or more recommendations, factually detailed, from teachers who know and respect the applicant and his or her work;

—a recommendation from the principal or guidance counselor attesting to the applicant's character, accomplishments, and contributions to the life of the school;

—a history of leadership and service in one or more extracurricular activities, including athletics;

—a proven record of using summer and after-school time productively: jobs, tutoring, courses, research, and the like;

—a list of details showing serious intellectual interests: books and periodicals read, papers written, films and plays enjoyed, projects undertaken on the applicant's initiative;

—one or more carefully composed essays that reveal the applicant's writing skills as well as his or her individual character: interests, ideals, heroes, accomplishments, experiences.

I'm sure you see what I'm driving at here. Over the years your children spend in high school, you can direct them intelligently, professionally, toward meeting this challenge they will face as seniors. For you and them, this goal-oriented college-application process is a means to an end, not an end in itself. You show them how to direct their experience in high school, every aspect of what they study and do, as an exercise in professional achievement. By the time they are seniors, they will know where they're headed and how to get there, and—above all—how to manage their affairs professionally.

How do you go about directing your children's thinking, planning, and action during their years of high school? Other fathers have worked along the following broad lines.

Early in freshman year, sit down with your children and select with them some three or four colleges to examine. Direct them to come up with four names. These can include, of course, the colleges you and your wife attended (if appropriate) plus a couple of well-known ones and your state university for good measure. It really doesn't matter which ones you look into at this point. You simply want to open your young teens' eyes to what awaits them a couple of years down the road.

Be sure, though, to include at least two institutions with competitive admission—that is, schools that have two or more applicants for every place. You may be surprised to learn that this comprises only about a hundred colleges and universities in the United States. You and your children are exploring what these selective institutions expect from qualified applicants. What sort of young men and women are they looking for?

Have your children secure the addresses of these institutions by asking at the reference desk of your local public library (a hugely valuable but underused resource). They should then write for catalogues and application forms. A simple postcard will do, but you may prefer to show them how to write a business letter. (At some point, somebody has to do this; it's seldom taught in school anymore.) Alternatively, your children can study these items in the guidance office or school library, but obviously it's better to have your own catalogues to study at home.

Once you secure the catalogues, study what sort of courses the colleges like to see on applicants' transcripts. Clearly they do not want fluff courses, mental bubble gum, easy busy-work with little substance. They want to see rigorous, challenging studies, especially in English, math, sciences, and foreign language. They like and expect to see several honors and advanced-placement courses. Knowing this in advance can help you direct your children's high school studies starting in sophomore year.

Turn to the application form, a bulky and formidable-looking mass of paperwork. Teens are unaccustomed to handling bulky paperwork and therefore they are intimidated by it. Show them that it's less scary than it appears; and besides, plowing through complicated forms is a normal part of adult life. Better they start getting used to it.

Look at the section that an applicant needs to turn in to the principal or guidance counselor for the school's official assessment of character and academic performance. For most high school seniors, this is an eye-opener. Someone officially representing the school needs to evaluate the applicant's overall character *in comparison with that of other students*. Some categories are "intellectual motivation," "reaction to setbacks," "sense of humor," "leadership qualities," and "respect accorded by faculty." In addition, the school official needs to write a letter describing, in factual detail, the quality and maturity of the applicants' work and his or her contribution to the life of the school.

What does this mean for your freshman? Among other things, it means he or she has three years to turn in conspicuously high-quality work and become well known in the school as a leader. Your teen can't afford to be merely a face in the crowd, a passive follower, a mediocrity. When the school's principal or guidance officer sits down to compose the school's evaluation, he or she and the other teachers should know your teen so well that this task is easy—and the recommendation is sincerely enthusiastic. Working over three years to make this happen is your teen's goal.

Look also at the two recommendations required, as well, from your children's teachers. These also need to be detailed, specific, and, if possible, enthusiastic. So, what's needed here? Earlier on, I noted that you and your children should find out who the best teachers are and then enroll in their courses. Your son or daughter would be smart, then, to choose which two teachers among these could later write the best recommendations. Once this is decided, the rest is obvious: do your very best work for these people, and make sure they know who you are. That is the way things work in the world. Smart teens, like smart fathers, think ahead.

Now turn to the "student" section of the application, the parts your children fill out about themselves. Note the data required: Which books have you read *on your own*?

Which newspapers and magazines do you read regularly? What jobs and other activities have you had in the summer and during the school year? What *offices* have you held in extracurricular activities? Which awards have you won, if any?

Right now, your freshman is looking at blank spaces next to each of these questions. So, what needs to be done over the next three years to fill them in? Who can recommend worthwhile books to read? (Start with your best teachers, of course, and other adults whose judgment you respect.) Why not form a habit, starting now, of reading the whole newspaper every day, not only the comics and sports? Why not shoot to be class president next year, or president of your extracurriculars by junior year? If you're interested in law, why not get moving now to line up summer jobs in a law office?

Your teen should see the point: the blank spaces need filling in, and this means thoughtful planning and action from now until senior year.

Note that this strategic overview of the college-application process is not intended as a cosmetic exercise, merely assembling details to look good on the application. What we're aiming for is that your son or daughter really and truly works to become a well-read, well-informed, well-respected young person. The application form's blank spaces serve as an incentive for real-life professional development.

The last part of the application form is the most interesting. Here each applicant needs to write two or more brief and exceptionally well-written essays. These should demonstrate high-quality writing and original, imaginative thought. Pity the poor senior who sees these essay topics for the first time in November of senior year and has only four weeks to write his responses: two or more essays for each college, and this on top of all the work required in school!

What you can shrewdly point out to your freshman is that colleges seldom change these essay topics from year to year. And even if they do change them, the topics are still remarkably alike. So, in junior year, secure an application form and check out the essay topics required. Then spend the summer before senior year thinking, composing, securing advice, writing and rewriting, until the final drafts are the best work your teen has ever done. Once again, your son or daughter learns a lesson about life: we get ahead by thinking ahead.

One smart father I knew in Chicago sat down one day with John, his sophomore son, and explained some financial facts of life to him. He showed his son that the family, which had six children, couldn't afford the projected annual outlay of $35,000 for the son's college tuition. If John wanted to get ahead, he would have to earn substantial aid through his performance in high school. Alternatively, since the son liked the idea of a military career, then enrolling at one of the service academies (at zero tuition) was an attractive option. The boy and his dad decided to go all out for West Point.

This they did. The father arranged for John to meet with West Point alumni, and he showed his son how to handle himself courteously and professionally in these interviews. John gleaned a lot of useful advice from these meetings and acted on it with his father's guidance.

Now highly motivated, John put in extra time and effort with his schoolwork so as to earn a number-one position in his class ranking; he moved from the middle of the class to the top slot in less than a year. He took the initiative to found a literary magazine at the school. He secured a volunteer summer job tutoring and coaching disadvantaged city kids, something he enjoyed immensely. He studied and practiced Spanish to the point of near-fluency. Also over the summer, he undertook an extra-credit history research paper about journalistic reporting during the Vietnam War. He spent hours practicing tests for the Scholastic Achievement Tests. He was elected captain of the school's soccer team. He read dozens of books about American history, including biographies. He worked for weeks writing his required college essays.

In short, John became a self-starter, a serious scholar, a leader and contributor to the life of his school. Every step of the way, he grew from his dad's encouragement and savvy advice.

John studied at West Point. Today he's a successful young executive in the Midwest. Though he learned a lot about heroes and heroism in his military education, his greatest hero is his dad.

Aside from this exercise with the application forms, you can lead your children to think ahead in other ways—not merely for college but also for professional life.

Encourage your kids to study at least one foreign language thoroughly, to the point of near-fluency. This means four full years of a language before college. Being fluent in a foreign language is not simply a cultural adornment; it's really a *power*. In their future professional lives, they'll be glad they possess this power, especially if their professional colleagues (competitors) do not. Because Spanish is the second language of the United States, and since we will increasingly do business with Latin America, this widely spoken and interesting language is a sound choice.

Consider athletics, too. Most young people prefer the standard team sports: basketball, soccer, football, baseball. But they shouldn't overlook other athletic options. Larger schools often field teams in lacrosse, gymnastics, wrestling, track, cross-country, tennis, squash, and other somewhat unusual sports. How do these fit into a college application strategy?

They fit in this way: Colleges don't look for a well-rounded applicant—they want a well-rounded *class*. They put together such a class by combining applicants who have specialized skills. Consequently, many colleges will offer a place and even scholarship aid to applicants who excel in these sports. They have multitudes of applicants who play basketball, but few who are expert in squash or wrestling or gymnastics. All these smaller teams at the colleges lose seniors each year, so they need to replace them with qualified incoming freshmen. Maybe your son or daughter can be one of them.

By extension, don't forget that the college orchestra needs incoming students who play the oboe, bassoon, and cello. The university newspaper needs staffers who can make computer graphics.

The life lesson for your children? Specialization goes a long way toward success, especially these days. Give it some thought.

More practical details:

Sometime early in your children's high school education, you and they should start a little collection of books that coach for the SATs and similar tests, along with works that explain the college application process in canny detail. Books published by *The Princeton Review* are among the best in the business. Read them and use them.

There's no question that your children can do better on their SATs and similar tests by frequent practice. These exams require certain skills, especially time management, that greatly improve with repetition. What you, as a father, want to avoid is that your kids' performance on these exams is *artificially lowered through unfamiliarity*. If your children practice taking these tests a dozen or more times before the real thing, they will almost certainly perform at their very best, whatever that turns out to be.

Certainly, you make clear to your kids that what they score on the SATs is, in itself, immaterial to you—as long as that's the best they can do. All you expect is that they try their best, and this they do by practicing tests beforehand. Here, as in other aspects of family life, you expect them to try.

Besides, as you can explain to them, the tests are a one-shot deal, not particularly important in later life. Once they've taken the SATs in high school and enrolled in college, nobody will ever again ask them what scores they earned. Plenty of successful professionals did so-so at best on their SATs. After you've enrolled in college, nobody cares.

Serious studies, challenging extracurriculars, and athletics—these make for a busy experience in high school. But don't press your teen children to the point where they're overloaded. We all work best under reasonable pressure, but only when it's reasonable. Aim for what's reasonable, and you won't be far off.

Your children's experience in school should be, by all means, enjoyable. As Aristotle put it, a person finds happiness in "the full use of one's powers along lines of excellence." It's healthy for your children to sense themselves growing in powers of competence. This is a solid preparation for their later success in handling family and work responsibilities.

Never forget that this is what you're really after. What counts to you, a loving dad, is that your children meet with every success and happiness in life.

I2 | *Your Teens and the Workplace*

When your children enter high school, they will want to work in part-time and summer jobs. Potentially this is a great experience for them, their first real-life exposure to serious, money-making work.

If you have always seen your children as adults-in-the-making, you should be pleased to see your children enter adolescence. You have always wanted them to grow up, have always tried to deal with them as near-adults. Now you and they are coming down the home stretch, almost there. Your job now is to fine-tune their conscience and judgment and workplace savvy. Show them how to be truly self-starters, responsible workers, honorable young men and women—adults in everything but experience.

It's your job as a father to provide this experience. Take advantage of their burning desire to work (which is really their ambition to be needed, to test their powers) to teach them the ins and outs of professionalism. If you treat your teens like adults this way, you will bond more closely to them than ever. You will do what great fathers have done for centuries with their adolescents: pass on to them your workplace wisdom, and launch them out successfully into the world.

Start with some principles:

First, make them understand that *schoolwork comes first*. A part-time job during the school year can help your children use their time wisely. Kids with a part-time job often do better in school simply because they have less time for homework and therefore, remarkably, are forced to concentrate harder and work more efficiently. (Don't forget the old maxim: Work expands or contracts to fit the time allotted to it.) But if you see that the after-school job is eating into productive schoolwork—kids have far too little time or are too tired to tackle their homework—then the job has to go. You make this agreement with them, and make clear that you intend to enforce it.

Second, as you did with their sports and games and hobbies, use their experience with job-hunting and day-to-day work to build their character. Finish the task you started in their childhood. Flesh out and give depth to all your former lessons to them about honorable, active grown-up life: good manners, sustained hard work, honesty, integrity, initiative, foresight, risk-taking, respecting the rights of others.

Third, when planning what to advise them, start with these questions: *What do I know now about the world of work that I didn't know at fifteen?* What do I wish I had known before I started my first serious job? What mistakes have I seen young employees make, errors that my children should avoid? Remember, most men underestimate how much they've learned about life and work. Whatever you know now is much, much more than your children know. So, teach them what you've learned.

▲ ▲

What sort of know-how and savvy can you pass along to them? How can you steer them to handle themselves maturely in applying for a job and carrying it out professionally?

What follows below is an outline of the best advice I've ever seen smart fathers pass on to their children. When clueing in your teens (speaking to them as "you"), this is what you can teach them:

One of the questions that competitive universities ask of applicants for admission is this: "How have you used your summer vacations?"

There's a good reason for this question. College officers know that, all other things being equal, the best predictor of future success is past success. "Potential" is only for children; as you grow older, people increasingly judge your maturity and sense of responsibility by asking one key question: "How have you used your time?"

People in their mid to late teens can be placed in two groups.

(i) Some are more like children than adults. They are passive and shortsighted. They center their lives on present-day diversion and fail to plan more than a few days or weeks ahead. They see life as mostly play, and view time the way children see it, as a passive environment. They depend on adults to direct their lives and have little or no sense of self-directed action toward goals of personal accomplishment. If they have a job, they use it purely as a source of "spending money"—with no regard for its fitting into a long-term career strategy. At age fifteen or sixteen, they still view the summer months the way they did in childhood: as an entitlement for mostly fun and games.

(ii) Other teens are more like young adults. They see time as a non-renewable resource, something either *used productively* or simply *wasted*. They set long-term goals (months and years ahead) and work now to accomplish them. They see their summer months as an opportunity to grow in learning, achievement, and practiced maturity. What they produce over the summer fits into an overall strategy for their life years from now, especially their later careers. They know that time management is simply another term for self-control, which is one sign of real maturity. They learn by practice how to get along effectively with responsible adults, and most especially those adults who can help them later in their careers. They are savvy young grown-ups, men and women of action, people who will amount to something in life, starting now.

You can belong to this second group if you set your mind to it. Sooner or later you will have to compete with them anyway, so you might as well begin right now. You can start by using your summer months productively.

So, when you later must answer the question posed by colleges, you can have something substantial to report. Your answer will say a lot about your own maturity.

SUMMER JOB WITH A FIRM

Secure yourself a paying summer job, one that will teach you how to work well and manage your time effectively—and that may lead you to later (even better) summer employment and maybe even a career. If you can work for a firm in a field you're aiming toward as a career (engineering, medicine, law, architecture), so much the better. But even work in a fast-food restaurant or supermarket can profit your growth in character and professionalism.

Bear some important matters in mind, facts of life often overlooked by people your age:

• Imagine a bull's-eye target with you at the center. Surrounding you is the circle of your friends and acquaintances. The next circle out is that of *their* friends, that is, people whom they know but you don't. That's where the jobs are. To land a good job, or build a good career, you have to work through people. The greater the number of people who esteem you, the better you will do. That's the way the world works.

• In order to get ahead, you've got to plan ahead and act ahead. This means you should think and act to get a job months before the summer falls upon you. People with savvy and initiative start to line up a job in February and work at it for weeks.

They beat out the competition—those passive, immature high schoolers who wait until May or June to get moving, when it's too late. It's a law of life: people first in line get the best seats; people later in line get the worst seats; people at the end of the line don't get in at all.

• The ideal situation would be to work for a firm related to your professional interests and return to work with them, at increasing levels of responsibility, each summer through college. This may not be possible with your first summer job, but it's a goal to shoot for later. In any event, it would be a big plus if you could count on an employer who would like to rehire you each summer when you're in college, especially if you live away; it's hard to line up a fresh summer job back in your hometown when you're studying hundreds of miles away. So, think about long-term repeat summer employment.

• For this to happen, you need to favorably impress your boss during your first summer job. Remember, too, that even if you want to work elsewhere in the future, your future employers will want a reference from your present boss. So, work for your present employer in such a way that he'd be glad to recommend you later.

• What do bosses want most from teenage employees? It's *reliability*. Many young employees are notoriously unreliable. They show up late for work. They call in "sick" when something else comes up. They slack off when nobody's supervising them. In other words, they don't keep their end of the employment agreement—conscientious work in exchange for pay. None of these faults should be found in you, for you are a mature and reliable worker. Your boss should notice that you keep your word, you have a spirit of service, you're pleasant and well mannered to everyone, and you work diligently whether you're being supervised or not. If you're this kind of worker, your boss will notice and appreciate you. You've earned his respect. "Reliability" is another term for integrity.

• When you're nearing the end of the summer, give your boss ample notice and tell him the exact date for your last day. On the day you leave, thank him personally. Ask him if he'd like to rehire you next year; tell him you'll contact him in February. If you plan to work elsewhere, ask him if you can use him as a reference later.

How do you go about lining up your first job? Here's what experience teaches:

• Keep a file someplace where you store all papers related to your job search: notes about leads and references, gist of phone calls, addresses of people, copies of letters you send, and the like. It's a good idea to date these items. Also, of course, keep a calendar where you note deadlines and call-backs (see below).

• Before you start looking, ask three or four people who know you well if you may use them as references for your job search. That is, would they agree to recommend you to any prospective employer who calls them? (Everyone who knows you and your work would be glad to agree.) Then ask them for their title (e.g., English teacher, school principal, clergy), address, and phone number. Type up a sheet with this at the top: "References for . . . (your name, address, phone number, e-mail)"— then your references' names, titles, etc. Make photocopies of this; be prepared to give the sheet to a prospective employer when he asks you for references. Or, even better, offer the sheet yourself during your first meeting with whoever interviews you. Your prospective boss will probably be impressed that you handle yourself so maturely and professionally—a sign that you'd make a good worker.

• Sometime before February, ask among friends and acquaintances for leads. Get names and phone numbers of leads, and ask your friends if they can make an introduction.

• Call prospects and politely introduce yourself. Explain *briefly* what you want. Ask if you can drop by to discuss. If prospects say it's too early to hire summer people, say you understand but want to get things moving early. Ask when would be a good time to call back—mid-March, early April? (Already you've impressed your prospective boss.) Note what he says on your calendar. Call back at that time, and offer to come in for an interview.

• Do whatever it takes to show up for the interview on time and fully prepared. This means dress your best; pay special attention to shirt, tie, and shined shoes. Have a pen with you to fill out any required application form; also have your Social Security number. Be prepared to tell him the exact date when you can start work, and offer him your sheet of references. Ask how soon you may expect to hear from him, or whether he'd prefer that you call back later. Writing him a personal thank-you note the next day is a nice professional touch.

• If you secure another job elsewhere, make sure you call your interviewer back promptly to tell him, so he's free to hire

someone else. Thank him for his time and interest. This is an important professional courtesy.
• When you get a job, call or drop a note to the people you used as references. Thank them for their help. They'll be happy for your good fortune and pleased with your thoughtful, mature courtesy.

If you're too young or too busy to get a full-time job with a firm, you can go into business for yourself. People in your neighborhood probably need help for gardening, lawn mowing, cleaning, and fix-up. You can perform these services for cash. Here are some tips:
• Sometime in March, have a stack of business cards printed professionally. It should give your name, address, phone number, and kind of work you're willing to do.
• Set your rates ahead of time. It's a good idea to begin with hourly rates for new customers. Once you know each other, and you know enough to estimate time needed for each kind of task, you can then charge a flat rate. In any case, have your rates set when you approach prospective clients; one of their first questions will be how much you charge.
• Dress well and go door to door in your neighborhood. Introduce yourself politely, and explain the kind of work you're seeking. Count on the fact that most people will initially decline or demur; they have other plans, or they'll say they want to think it over. No problem. Just thank them and leave your business card; say you'd be pleased to hear from them later. Your goal here is simply to leave the people with your card and a good impression of you. The calls will come in later. If you leave cards with three hundred people and 5 percent of them later hire you, that's fifteen jobs you've lined up. And if you do a good job for each of them, they'll spread the word among friends—which will lead to more jobs.
• Show up on time, every time. If you're unavoidably late, call ahead, then render an explanation and a sincere apology.
• Do the very best work you can. Work quickly but thoroughly. If you must enter the house for some reason, don't track in a mess and don't dawdle there. If you're on an hourly rate and take a few minutes for a break, don't count this break time in your billing.
• If you accept payment by check, have a copy of your

business card ready so your client will spell your name right on the check. If you foresee that your client will prefer to pay in cash, carry sufficient change.

• Respect your clients' privacy. If you're inside someone's home, don't even appear to be snooping around. If you see or overhear anything that's none of your business, ignore it entirely and don't talk about it with anyone afterwards. In other words, never gossip about your clients. Professionals know how to respect people's confidentiality, and they mind their own business.

• Keep records of your income and expenses. Save receipts in a file.

• At the end of the summer, thank each of your clients. Offer to be available for any odd jobs they may have during the school year, such as shoveling snow. Bear in mind that one or more of your clients may later help you find leads for a summer job with a firm, maybe even their own. Don't forget, people aren't only judging your work—they're also judging *you*. Get used to it; this is the way things work in the world.

13 | *Workplace Etiquette and Savvy*

To return to the central idea here: It is the father's role to protect his children by strengthening their judgment and will-power so they can later protect themselves.

One part of this teaching, hugely important, is to teach teens how to comport themselves honorably and competently in the workplace, no matter what they might later do for a living.

Experienced professionals in the workplace (maybe including yourself) have noticed that many young people starting their careers—say, in their first job after college or grad school—were apparently never taught the basics of professional etiquette or how to handle themselves in social relations at work. Though well-meaning and technically skilled, they seem uninformed, not to say naïve and even "clueless," about standard professional courtesy and savvy dealings with others—bosses, co-workers, and clients or customers. This lack of preparation for the world of work causes problems for them and others they must deal with, and it can hurt their careers.

Where do young people usually learn about these basics? They're not written down anyplace, and business schools seldom mention them. So, how are young people "clued in" on what to do, what not to do, and what to watch out for in the world of work they will soon enter?

It would seem that such learning traditionally came from the home, and especially from the father. As we've seen, throughout history the father has prepared his nearly grown children on how to handle themselves competently as they set out on their careers. We have copies of letters written by famous men—such as those of John Adams and Lord Chesterfield to their grown children—filled with savvy advice about work and honorable dealings with others. These fathers drew from their experience and passed on their knowledge in order to guide their children to honorable, successful careers. This loving fatherly guidance built confidence and competence among young people, and it protected them from harm.

In a sense, this fine-tuning of young people's conscience and judgment served to round out everything that had been taught at home in the years of childhood. It led the young people to a great career and marriage—and it bonded the young people to their dad for life.

Etiquette: General Guidelines

I have listed below some of the words of advice that fathers traditionally pass on to their grown (or nearly grown) children about life in the workplace. The points deal with etiquette and with savvy comportment. All these are meant to prompt your thinking and action, both now and later, to guide your children's progress in the world of work. Please use them as you see fit and as the occasion arises in your conversations with your children. I can assure you that your children will be listening, and they will grow more and more to value your wisdom and your loving leadership.

• Courtesy is not simply a matter of polite practices. It is a set of attitudes, a genuine thoughtfulness for the rights and feelings and needs of others. This attitude shows itself in deeds, in the way we live good manners. A courteous man or woman—that is, a gentleman or a lady—is one who does no harm and gives no offense to anyone on purpose, who is open to friendship and cherishes friends, who sees work as mostly service, who has the grace to disagree without being disagreeable, and who has eyes for the needs of others. Strive to become this kind of person.

• Say "please" and "thank you" a lot. Be known as a person who appreciates other people's dignity, rights, feelings, and earnest best efforts. Show appreciation; it's the greatest human need.

• "Thank you" is always an appropriate response to any kind of praise or favor. When you're at a loss for words to respond to praise, simply say "thank you" and let it go at that.

• Keep on hand a supply of good-quality thank-you note cards or "monarch" stationery—that is, good-quality stationery (7-1/4 x 10-1/2 inches), preferably personalized with your name, address, etc. Use these to send a personal handwritten thank-you note immediately (within 24 hours) for gifts, job interviews, and substantial favors.

• Whenever you are meeting people after some absence, give your name. Do this even if you've met the person sometime before, as he or she may not recall your name.

• If you're meeting someone for the first time and you didn't understand the name, ask the person to repeat it. ("Please forgive me, I didn't quite catch your name.") This isn't awkward. You show you are sincerely interested in getting the name right and in making the person's acquaintance.

- When speaking with someone, make eye contact. Show that you're interested in that person and what he or she has to say.
- Be patient with slow talkers. Don't interrupt to finish other people's sentences for them, especially your boss.
- Whether in the office or on social occasions, you should stay away from certain topics in conversation because they may lead to awkwardness, boredom, embarrassment, or resentment. These topics are (a) your own health or others' health, (b) controversial issues, (c) the cost of items, (d) topics of a sexual nature, (e) personal misfortunes, (f) gossip, (g) stories of questionable taste or dirty jokes, and (h) politics.
- Never use humor that offends: no racist, sexist, ethnic, or crude jokes.
- In conversation, don't shake your finger or point at anyone.
- Don't open conversation by asking people what they do for a living. Though Americans are inclined to do this, for many people the question is awkward, especially if they're currently unemployed. And for foreigners especially, the question seems personally intrusive and therefore rude. Wait and let the person's occupation come up naturally during the conversation.
- Whenever you must send a letter or memo to someone, make sure you spell the person's whole name correctly. Do whatever it takes to get the right spelling: look it up in a directory or make a phone call to someone who knows. People get annoyed when you misspell their name; they tend to attribute it to unprofessionalism on your part, and they're inclined to discount what you have to say in the rest of your message.
- Don't use the term "Mister" when referring to yourself, either on your stationery or on the phone. Just use your name. The word "Mister" is an honorific term; we use it of others to show our respect for them. So, we don't use it when referring to ourselves.

ETIQUETTE AT SOCIAL EVENTS

- When inviting someone to a social occasion, don't preface your invitation by asking, "What are you doing this Friday night?" or "Are you busy this Saturday evening?" or anything of the sort.

This puts people on the spot. Leave your friends a way, if they prefer, to decline your invitation gently and diplomatically.

• If you receive an invitation that says "RSVP" be aware that it means to let your host know whether you will attend or not. Do this without fail, and promptly. Your host needs this information to plan the event's food, seating arrangements, etc., and your negligence here is a real disservice, exceptionally ill-mannered.

• Arrive on time. Always be punctual in keeping appointments—even with light social occasions, even with good friends. If you're unavoidably late, try to call ahead; in any case, offer an apology.

• When you're invited to someone's home, try to arrive on the dot, no more than five minutes late. Don't arrive early, though, for your hosts may not yet be ready to receive you.

• Mingle with other guests, not only with your friends. Seek out people who seem to be standing alone.

• Don't linger too long in conversation with your host. Be aware that he or she needs to circulate among the other guests.

• Limit alcohol: one or two drinks maximum. Stick with wine or some non-alcoholic drink rather than hard liquor and learn to nurse one drink throughout the party. Beware imbibing alcohol on an empty stomach: before you drink, eat some "finger food" so the alcohol will take longer to enter your system and thus keep you in good shape. And of course, never, ever, drink to the point of inebriation.

• Never press an alcoholic drink on someone who declines it. He or she may be unable to drink for religious or medical reasons or may be trying to recover from an alcohol problem.

• Don't eat too much food. The purpose of a social event is to mingle with people and make friends, not to overindulge with food and drink. In other words, the people come first and the food and drink are incidental. Don't give people the impression that your priorities are reversed.

• If you're having a business lunch, don't start talking business until everyone has ordered food. Make small talk until the waiter has taken everyone's order.

• If you're having a meal with fellow workers, avoid shoptalk. That is, unless the meal is clearly for business, don't discuss work. A social occasion is supposed to be a break from work routine.

• When you meet with professional people socially (especially physicians, accountants, and attorneys), don't put them on the spot by asking for professional advice. If you think those professionals can be of help to you, ask if you can call their office sometime later to make an appointment.

• When you attend social occasions, always carry a couple of your business cards. But don't offer your card to someone until the very end of a conversation, when you're parting, and then only if it's clear that the new acquaintance might like to meet with you again sometime. Passing out cards gratuitously looks pushy and amateurish.

• Don't be the last to leave, but stay at least one hour.

• Before leaving, be sure to thank the sponsor or host. If you leave along with several other people, it's courteous to call the next day and thank the host personally. If you received a written invitation to the affair, it's courteous to write a thank-you note. (The protocol is this: an informal phoned invitation should lead to a phone-call thanks, and a written invitation to a written thanks.)

TELEPHONE MANNERS

• Speak with a normal, pleasant, courteous voice, especially when answering. Get into a habit of smiling when you speak.

• When you phone someone you don't know well, you should identify yourself to whoever answers the call.

• Very important: Before launching into a phone conversation, first ask if this is a good time to talk.

• Try to answer before three rings. Don't ever slam the receiver.

• If you foresee that you might have to leave a message on voice mail, have a brief, clear message rehearsed, one that doesn't sound nervously improvised. Always leave your number, even with people who probably know it; you save them the trouble of looking it up. Say it slowly at the beginning and end of the message.

• Return all phone calls promptly.

• Don't waste people's time with phone tag. Let people know when you'll be available.

• Give people on the phone your undivided attention. Don't make side remarks to someone else in the room or otherwise convey that you're doing other tasks while on the phone.

• In the office, limit personal calls to important matters only, and be brief.

• Don't make collect calls, even if callers offer this to you as a courtesy. Long-distance calls are cheap these days, and you don't want to look cheap.

• Unless you want people to call you at home or on your cell phone after hours, don't give out your home or cell phone number.

OFFICE ETIQUETTE

• When guests enter your office or cubicle, stand to receive them, make eye contact and give a warm handshake, gesture to where they may sit. Unless you are both going to look at papers, arrange your seating so you don't have a desk or table between you and them. Give them your undivided attention; don't glance at your watch or otherwise convey that you're impatient for them to leave. When they're leaving, walk them to the reception area.

• The top of someone's desk isn't a bulletin board. Don't read what's on other people's desks or computer monitors. (Above all, don't do this with your boss.)

• Unless you have explicit permission, don't enter your boss's office when he's not there.

• Avoid standing directly behind people when they are sitting at their computers.

• Never take something from someone's desk without asking.

• Don't hang out in the doorway of someone's office or cubicle while he or she is on the phone.

• When you walk into an office or cubicle, remain standing unless invited to sit. Then sit down gracefully and maintain an attentive posture.

• If you're in someone else's office or cubicle and that person receives a phone call, exit gracefully without interrupting the call. That is, stand up and silently gesture that you'll wait outside.

• Keep office visits businesslike and brief. Be pleasant–but get to the point, get what you need, and then leave.

• If a fax comes to your office and it's not addressed to you, don't read it.

• Business people these days are deluged with e-mails. An executive typically receives at least sixty a day. So, try to avoid sending unnecessary or multiple e-mails to someone you know is busy. Before you e-mail, pause to ask yourself: Is this message necessary? Can I hold off a while and combine several points of information into one message? (In order to cut back on e-mail traffic, some offices have a policy to hold off on perfunctory thanks and routine acknowledgments. Find out the policy in your office and stick to it.)

Professional Savvy—How Things Work in the World

CAREER CONSIDERATIONS

- Success in one's career doesn't necessarily mean great fame and big money. Real success in work and life means several things:
  —being able to support yourself and your family comfortably;
  —waking up in the morning and looking forward to the day's work;
  —earning the respect of everyone who knows you;
  —seeing your powers and skills work toward the betterment of others;
  —enjoying leisure pursuits thoroughly because you've *earned* them.
- There's such a thing as a professional vocation. It's some passionate love that directs your powers to the welfare of others and earns you a living. While growing up, you should search far and wide to find some line of work that appeals to your heart— some labor that gives you the joy you knew in childhood, when work and play were one. Few pleasures in life are more delightful than a job we really enjoy.
- One word of caution, though. You may love music or drama or sports so much that you think of these fields as potential careers. Fine, but anchor yourself in reality. The worlds of entertainment and sports bring delight to millions, so a few hundred thousand youngsters aspire to work in them— and everyone in this vast throng is competing against you. To succeed, you need to be exceptionally talented, extremely hard-working, single-mindedly ambitious, well connected with influential people, and (to be frank about it) very, very lucky. No matter how you look at it, the odds are hugely against you. Remember, no matter what you later do for a living, you can always enjoy these pursuits as recreational pastimes.
- Looking for a career? Look hard and keep looking. The world's inventions and discoveries came about (like Goodyear's vulcanized rubber) by people who were looking for *something*. To stimulate your thinking, read, and carefully do the exercises

in, *The Princeton Review Guide to Your Career* (latest edition) by Alan B. Bernstein and Nicholas R. Schaffzin.

• When leaning toward a career, ask yourself: "What can I be an expert in?" Then work to become that expert.

• Rely on family and friends to tell you what you're really good at. When we're good at something, we're usually among the last to know it. Others notice our talent before we do, because to us the gift seems natural, easy, almost effortless. So, pay attention when people close to you all say the same thing: You have some talent that you should develop.

• Throughout human history, finding a good job has always been a matter of whom you know. Credentials, experience, cold calls, mass mailings of résumés—none of these things beats *connections through friends.* Your friends won't have a job for you, but *their* friends might. We get a job most quickly and effectively through the friends of our friends. For this reason alone, it pays to have many friends and acquaintances. (Related piece of advice: Maintain contact with your closest friends from high school and college. Work at making them friends for life.)

• Know the difference between a referral and a reference. A referral is simply an introduction; that is, someone you know introduces you to a friend or acquaintance who might be interested in hiring you. It's basically a vouching of your character without comment or judgment about your technical competence, which your friend may not be in a position to know anyway. A reference, on the other hand, is an assessment of both your character and your professional competence based on the assessing person's familiarity with your work.

• Before you use anyone's name for a reference, be sure to get that person's permission. Because good professionals always check references, your failure to secure prior permission makes your reference worse than useless.

• Every few months, take a couple of hours to think deeply about your career and your future. How are things going? Where am I headed? What opportunities might I be overlooking? Where do I want to be five years down the road? Have a file where you keep notes on accomplishments to update your résumé, and do this at least twice a year. An updated résumé is like a first-aid kit: if you need it at all, you need it in a hurry.

• As you move along Plan A of your career, maintain a Plan B, as well—an alternative career course to rely on if you suddenly must. If you lose a job, you need to undertake thinking, planning, networking, and action quickly. Maintaining a Plan B means doing your thinking, planning, and networking ahead of time, long before the emergency, so you can move swiftly into action. Be prepared for anything.

- Always remember that the secret of success is passion. So, think big. We tend to become what we think about. If you have high ambitions of *service* to people, start with your family, and someday you'll be honored as an outstanding man or woman and a great professional.

DEALING WITH BOSSES

- In your first couple of jobs, try to work for a good boss, someone who'll challenge your powers, correct you, and help you learn from your mistakes. A good boss will teach you more in one year than you'll learn in four years of college.
- Notice that successful bosses have effective communication skills: they're attentive listeners and clear explainers. They learn from people, including their employees. They lead their people to understand what's important. They help their people to form the same picture, especially of where everyone is headed and how each person's effort contributes to reaching the goal. Learn from your boss how to deal effectively with people, how to be a leader. (Notice that an effective leader has joiners, not followers—and his exercise of authority is really a form of service.)
- Your boss is your key customer. Your aim is to keep him pleased with your work and pleased with you as a person. One of the great secrets in business is that bosses tend to hire and retain competent people whom they personally like and respect—people of integrity, hard work, and good humor.
- Work in such a way that you make your boss look good.
- Keep your boss in the loop. No surprises. Bosses generally hate surprises.
- Ask for a raise when you think you've earned it.
- Don't take problems to your boss unless you also propose some considered solutions. Bosses don't need additional problems; they have enough as it is. What they need and want are solutions.
- When your boss gives you a project, you should reach an understanding with him about how much time it should take. Try to deliver it ahead of time and done to the best of your ability.
- Personal integrity is crucially important in business. Tell nothing but the truth, and always keep your word. Bosses and

clients can forgive isolated, well-intentioned mistakes and even blunders—but if you lie, you're through.

• Unless you're the boss, it's not your job to change company policies. If you find policies or ongoing practices very hard to live with, don't complain. Just look for another job and try to leave on good terms. During your next job interview, or when you get another job, don't badmouth your previous company or its management. Remember, bosses tend to sympathize with each other as a class. Your perceived disloyalty to former employers would leave a bad taste and arouse mistrust.

PROFESSIONAL AND BUSINESS SAVVY

• The right thing to do is also the *smart* thing to do. In business, as in the family, the most important thing is trust. Your integrity is your most important asset. So, be honest, keep your word, treat your work as service to others, and mind your own business.

• Take care of the company's resources—money, cars, office supplies, travel accommodations, computers—as if they were your own. Never pilfer anything or pad your expenses.

• Read the company newsletter to stay on top of what's happening in your organization and what your bosses are thinking. Also, when people you respect recommend certain books, read them.

• Dress for the job you want, not the one you have. Let your dress and grooming reflect your self-respect and professionalism. Pay special attention to your shoes and shirts or blouses. Your bosses will notice.

• Get in good physical shape and work to stay that way. Generally speaking, noticeably overweight people suffer a competitive disadvantage in the workplace. Unless they're highly skilled in some technical area, they get passed over in favor of healthier looking competitors, especially if their jobs involve contact with the public. This is often unfair, certainly—but much of life is unfair, and we have to come to terms with reality.

• Similarly, don't make critical comments about matters that lie outside your areas of responsibility. Stick to your own job. Don't get a reputation as a busybody. Every responsible professional knows that loose-talking meddlers are also either slackers or control freaks. In either case, nobody trusts them.

• Don't talk about people behind their backs. If you gossip, people won't confide in you. Besides, office gossip has a way, mysteriously, of making its way back to the one being gossiped about. Here, as in so many other areas, keep your mouth shut and you'll stay out of trouble.

- If there's a lot of badmouth gossip in your office, especially about management, then start looking for another job. Poor morale nearly always arises from crummy management, and a company rife with gossip is on the verge of business collapse.

- Don't take things personally. If some coworkers are ill-tempered or rub you the wrong way, that's their problem, usually something in their private lives, outside of work. Don't let their problem become yours. Just shrug it off and stick to your job.

- Related to this, if you must correct someone, don't get personal about it. Correct the fault, not the person. Make the correction privately, never in front of others.

- Don't be rushed into important decisions. Just say, "I'd like a little more time to think it over." Indicate when you expect to arrive at a decision and then keep your word.

- Friday afternoon is the worst time to talk with anybody about anything important.

- Think of the intensity and concentration you put into your work on the last two days before you leave for vacation. Ideally that's the way you should work every day.

- Never send a letter or memo that you've written in anger. If you do, you'll probably regret it. Hold it for a day or two, look it over calmly, then either revise it or throw it away.

- Don't ever put anything in writing that could, in the wrong hands, be damaging or embarrassing to you. Documents tend to take on a life of their own; their destiny is difficult, sometimes impossible, to control.

- Never put your signature to anything without first reading it carefully. If you sign something hastily and carelessly, you may wind up needing a lawyer.

- Never tell racist, ethnic, or sexist jokes. They're hurtful to people and therefore dishonorable. Besides, they can land you in trouble.

- Be nice to people who wait on you or clean up after you: janitors, salespeople, waiters, bus drivers, people behind a counter. Look them in the eye, smile, say "please" and "thank you." They're human beings like you, with dignity and feelings, but seldom do they receive the courtesy and kindness they deserve.

- Don't whisper with people in hallways or other public

places. This looks sneaky and conspiratorial. Step into a room or out of people's earshot and then talk in a normal voice.

• No matter what it takes, be on time for all business appointments. If possible, arrive a few minutes early. No matter how late you work, get to your job on time.

• Strive your best to keep a deadline, especially one you've promised. If you clearly cannot meet it, then apologize and ask for an extension. (People won't remember that work was a little late, but they'll remember if it was crummy.) Once you've gotten an extension, then that's it. Do whatever is necessary— stay up late, call in outside help—to turn in good work on time.

• Don't use coarse language in the workplace. If you do, people lose respect for you. Consciously or otherwise, people associate habitual foul-mouthed speech with childish self-centeredness or basic lack of self-control.

• Admit your mistakes. Forgive those of others.

• Show appreciation. It's the greatest human need.

• Conduct yourself all your life with the standards of right and wrong that your mother and I have taught you since childhood.

James Thurber, the American humorist, said, "It is better to know some of the questions than all of the answers."

Like life itself, raising kids well is essentially a mystery, and nobody knows all the answers. But a smart father knows how to ask smart questions.

He reflects on what he's doing, where he's going, what he wants most for his children now and later in life: What is my job? Where are we headed as a family? What are the trends I see, and what do they imply about the future? What am I overlooking? What needs changing in family life, starting with me? What outcomes do I expect from my children as grown men and women? What does "success" really mean to me?

As I said in the beginning, I wrote this book to help you think deeply and realistically about your job as a father. I aimed to give you a clearer grasp of your job description, a firmer fix on what it means to be a successful dad, and an understanding of how other men like you have won victory in raising their children right.

In short, I sought to present you with a lot to think about, reflect upon, and put intelligently into action. A "successful" father thinks and then acts. He knows his children's lifelong happiness depends enormously on his intelligent, active leadership. I sincerely hope you understand all of this more clearly than you did when you first opened this book. You should take confidence from the fact of life that so many fathers before you have discovered: *Success as a father, as in any other great responsibility, comes mainly from long-term strategic planning and careful attention to detail. The rest, the execution of our thoughts, is a matter of heart.*

Here, toward the conclusion, I want to summarize the sort of critical questions a good father asks himself from time to time in order to keep himself and his efforts focused. In the midst of your busy life, pause every once in a while and think each of them through. Your answers and conclusions, of course, will be entirely your own.

• Do my children know how much I love and honor their mother? What do they witness and hear from me in family life that drives this lesson home?

- Am I careful to respect my wife's judgment and take her opinions seriously, especially in matters about our children's welfare?
- What do I need to do, or change, to live more united with my wife in our dealings with the children? Am I careful to check with her before giving an okay to our children's requests? Do the kids recognize that I will never let them come between her and me?
- Am I careful never to undercut my wife's authority in front of the kids? Do I hold up my end of our agreement never to quarrel heatedly in the children's presence? Do the kids see us reconcile after any impulsive argument that comes between us?
- How often do my wife and I talk about the children's growth in character, and what we need to do together about it?
- What do I do to give my wife a rest, a break, a chance for well-earned recreation? What gets in the way of making this happen more often?
- Do I maintain a clear strategic vision of my children's growth into responsible, competent, confident adulthood? Do I see my children as adults-in-the-making? Am I working to turn them into competent *other-directed* adults?
- Do I often think of my children as married men and women with family responsibilities of their own? Do I see my job as fundamentally preparing them to enjoy stable, happy marriages and to raise their children right?
- What strengths of character should my sons have developed in order to become successful husbands, fathers, and professionals—whatever they do for a living? What character strengths should my daughters have acquired in order to manage family and career responsibilities well, so they're as great as their mother?
- What strengths of judgment and conscience should my children have about dealings with the opposite sex when they're adolescents and young adults? What should they look for in a potential spouse, and what should they be warned to avoid?
- What misfortunes, and even tragedies, could assail my children if I fail to empower their judgment, conscience, sense of responsibility, personal toughness, and self-control? What could happen to them and their marriages and careers if they remain exactly as they are now, with all their immature faults and childish selfishness?
- If my kids must face a severe economic downturn in their

lifetimes, will they have the guts and savvy and religious strength to provide for themselves and their families?

• Am I working to acquaint my children with a fact of life: that we must *work* as well as play—that a life of productive work is normal, enriching, and deeply satisfying? Am I raising my children to see work as a challenging, sport-like adventure, a direction for our powers that brings out the best in us?

• How much do my children know about my life of work? What do I tell them? How can I better teach them what I do for a living? Can I take some work home with me, or bring them to the workplace more often, even on weekends?

• Do I give the kids responsibilities at home, jobs by which they can serve the family even in small ways? Do I *direct* and *encourage* them in their efforts and show how proud I am when they try their best?

• Do I make my older children *wait* for consumer things they want, and if possible *earn* them?

• Am I striving to teach my older children the value of money—how responsible adults earn it honestly, save it prudently, spend it wisely, and give it generously to people in need?

• When I must correct my children strongly, am I careful to practice "affectionate assertiveness"? That is, do I make sure the kids understand that I'm correcting the fault, not the person—that I correct them because I love them?

• Am I careful to correct my children privately whenever possible? And am I quick to accept their apologies affectionately, to give them a fresh start?

• Do I make my children apologize when they have offended anyone, and to accept the apologies of others?

• Do my children understand the meanings of the terms *integrity, honor, commitment, competence, deadline, courage, forgiveness, compassionate understanding,* and *reliance on God's help*?

• Do I teach my children how much *courage* it takes to live rightly—to stick with a tough job, to control impulses, to bounce back from setbacks and disappointments, to tell the truth, to keep promises, and to apologize? Do I show how proud I am as a father when they live this way?

• Do I make sure that rules in our home begin with the word "We . . ."? That is, do I strive as a leader to live by the same standards that I set for my children, so they'll never think of me as a hypocrite?

• Do I enforce a solid rule of the house: no squabbling at the table?

- Do I insist that the children practice good manners? Do they habitually say *please, thank you, excuse me, I'm sorry* in family life, especially with their mother? Am I giving a good example here?
- Who are my children's heroes? Whom do they admire? If they talk too much about entertainment figures, is this a sign of too much TV and entertainment in their lives?
- How much time do my children waste staring at useless programs? What constructive activities could they be doing instead?
- Are my kids forming a habit of *not* watching TV?
- At what age should each of my children start (a) getting themselves up in the morning with their own alarm clock, (b) making their own beds, and (c) working an eight-hour day (that is, *class work* plus *sports* plus *homework* equals eight hours of work)?
- Do I make the time to chat with each of my children personally, listening to them carefully, learning what's going on in their growing minds? Do they recognize how much I care about them and their thinking?
- Do I help them to think problems through, leading them to learn from their mistakes and to think ahead next time?
- Do I try to make eye contact with them and otherwise show my affection—patting them on the head, squeezing their shoulders and arms, giving them a quick kiss good-bye, or tucking them into bed?
- Are my children showing signs of physical softness? Are they in good shape? And do they have good eating and exercise habits that will keep them that way for years?
- If my children are overweight by the time they're in college, how can this adversely affect their self-esteem and social lives? How could obesity damage their careers?
- Do I make the time to play sports and games with the kids, and to watch them play team sports? Do I help them *enjoy* sports and avoid the "win at all costs" mentality?
- Do I encourage the children to take up hobbies and to read worthwhile books? Do I talk with them about what they're doing and learning?
- Do I check the children's homework as often as possible? Do I use this time to teach lessons of perseverance in work and high standards of performance? Do I help them learn from mistakes? Do I show my pride in their growing *competence*?
- When I think about their schoolwork and home chores, do

I pay special attention to *how* they work—their promptness and concentration, their thoroughness, their time management (self-control), their attitudes of healthy pride in accomplishment?

• As my children approach and enter adolescence—when they increasingly pay attention to their father—do I make myself more available than ever before? Do I think of them, and treat them, as near-adults? Do I talk more with them about courtship, marriage, career choice, standards of professionalism, and business savvy? Do I recognize I'm coming down the home stretch, that I have only a few more years with them at home to finish their growth into maturity?

• Do I remind myself from time to time that I have only one chance to raise my children right—and that this mission is my greatest accomplishment in life, the measure by which I stand or fall as a man?

• Do I rely confidently on God's help to make up for my faults and shortcomings, for my children belong ultimately to Him?

15 | *Draw Strength from Your Fatherly Heart*

One Sunday afternoon, some years ago, I dropped by the house of a friend of mine. Jack was a computer engineer who lived in suburban Washington, D.C., and the father of six children, teenagers down to infants. One of his sons was a student of mine at The Heights School, an outstanding young man already at age fourteen. Jack and I had hit it off as friends, and we were getting together for some small talk.

Jack welcomed me at the front door and led me into his living room. As we walked in, I saw him glance at something on the floor that made him pause in his tracks, give out a soft sigh, and slowly shake his head. He pointed to the floor and showed me a pair of dirty sneakers and socks lying smack in the middle of his otherwise immaculate living room.

He sat me down, got me a drink, and then said, "Please excuse me, Jim. I'll be back in a minute. I've got to take care of something first."

Off he went for a couple of minutes. Shortly he reappeared with one of his boys, Frankie, about eight years old, who looked a little embarrassed. Jack pointed to the filthy shoes, whereupon Frankie quickly reached down and scooped them up in his arms. Averting his eyes from me, the boy tried to hasten from the room, but his father stopped him with his arm. Holding his son affectionately by the shoulder, he pointed me out and said, "What do you say to Mr. Stenson?" The boy looked me in the eye and murmured, "Pleased to meet you, Mr. Stenson, . . . and I'm sorry for the mess I made." I accepted his apology, so he then turned to his father, who said, "You're excused, Frankie," and the boy made a hasty exit with his dirty bundle.

Jack sat down and then explained.

"Kids are messy, I know, and thoughtless too. They're always doing this sort of thing—leaving messes behind them. I can't get them to pick up their own messes every single time, but I try to whenever I can.

"The way I see it is this. When one of my kids makes a mess, there are two problems. One is the mess itself, and the other is the kid's attitude of carelessness. For sure, it would be a lot easier for me to simply pick up the sneakers and socks myself and let the matter go. This would take care of the first problem, . . . but not the second one, the slipshod attitude. I see it as my job to shape my kids' attitudes. I figure that the more I keep at this—making them clean up after themselves—the sooner they'll grow up. Sometimes I get worn out with this approach, at least for a while, but I'll never give up. There's too much at stake."

I asked him, "What keeps you going?"

He said, "Well, my wife depends on me, and I can't let her down. Besides that, the oldest ones show signs that they've finally gotten the message. All things considered, most of the time they're pretty responsible kids. By and large, they pitch in around here, and—thank God—they're self-starters."

They certainly are. I've followed Jack's family for more than twenty years now, and I've seen every one of his children grow to be an outstanding, successful adult. Jack is now a grandfather, beloved by his grown children, busy as ever, but in far less frantic ways. On Sunday afternoons he spends his time (as he puts it) "having a ball with my grandchildren."

I tell you Jack's story here to show what it takes to be a great father, a man who finally triumphs with his children.

I assure you, Jack is no charismatic superman. He's a perfectly normal engineer and married man, quiet spoken and even a little shy. He passionately loves football, enjoys getting together with friends occasionally. Like nearly everyone else, he's concerned about his job and struggles to pay his bills. When people compliment him on his children, he quickly and sincerely gives most of the credit to his wonderful wife. But if you spoke with her (as I have), you'd hear her warmly praise Jack as a great father.

Throughout his life as a father, Jack held a clear sense of mission about his fatherly leadership. He'd be the first to admit he fell into mistakes and suffered setbacks along the way, grew troubled at times by patches of doubt and discouragement. All the same, he never lost sight of his job as a father—to lead his children to responsible adulthood—and he never let up in this mission, regardless of the personal cost.

Jack was and is a courageous man, a father with a great heart. The secret of his success through the years is his relentless, self-sacrificing love.

Regardless of his faults and doubts and shortcomings, when a man is moved by this kind of love, he overcomes every obstacle—he becomes a great father.

Throughout this book, I've tried to help you in several ways. I showed you how other men, successful fathers all, maintained a clear, smart, far-seeing vision of their children's growth in character and what this means. I described the common family problems and social obstacles today that these men managed to overcome. I explained the many different approaches and tactics these men undertook to guide their children's thinking, conscience, willpower, and habits of right living. As much as I could, I outlined the kind of intelligent thought and practical actions I witnessed over and over again among the most successful fathers I've known.

I hope you've learned much from these men's hard-won fatherly experience—so that you live as a confident, active, effective leader to your children. I want you, like them, to enjoy the triumph of seeing your kids grow up to be great men and women.

As you can see from this book's many details, living as a competent father takes dedicated work. The mission is sometimes difficult, always challenging. A dad's responsibility calls forth all of his manly powers, the very best that is in him. He must surpass himself for years without letup. Being a great father-leader has always been hard and always will be. But no man anywhere has ever achieved great things without some passionate, self-sacrificing love.

Your love for your children is what will keep you going. Your great heart will drive you to persevere, no matter what, until you know the sweet victory of fatherhood—grown children who honor you with the conscience and conduct of their lives.

So, I close this book with some thoughts about heart. I want to leave you with some matters to mull over from time to time. I hope they will strengthen your resolve in those tough situations and moments of dejection that occasionally afflict all fathers, even the best of them.

Love has often been compared to a blazing fire, and so it is. Like fire, love brings energy, warmth, and light to a man's life. Love throws light on a man's duties, and conveys the power to carry them out. But love, like fire, needs nourishment to live. It needs stoking, kindling, and care.

Here are some thoughts that will keep your love alive and burning . . . and give you the courage to persevere, no matter what, through your years of service to your wife and children.

One man I knew in Chicago, a father of four children, told me this: "I read in the paper about teenagers and young people who get in serious trouble. High school kids are killed in car accidents through bad judgment, wild speeding, and beer parties. Girls are out on the street at 2:00 A.M. and hitch rides with men who are complete strangers—then get violated. College freshmen drink too much at a party, then get into serious trouble. Bright and promising college seniors suddenly take their lives because they see nothing to live for after graduation. . . . I ask myself: *Where were the fathers of these poor kids?* When I read about disasters like this among apparently normal young people, I vow to myself that, so help me God, *my* children will *never* have these things happen to them—not if I can help it! I will do anything, make any sacrifice, to keep tragedies like this from destroying my children."

So, let's revisit the basics.

Any normal man carries within himself a powerful instinct to protect his children. When any danger threatens his young ones, a man will swiftly surge into action, heedless of hazard to himself, to shield his children from harm. If his tiny son wanders into the street, a father will leap into traffic to snatch him from danger. If his young daughter runs to him screaming in fright, chased by a snarling dog, he will swoop her up to safety, then turn to drive the beast away with physical force. If his daughter cuts herself badly while playing at home, he will drop whatever he's doing and rush her to the hospital. If he senses that his teenage daughter's new boyfriend is a threat to her, he will step in assertively to break them apart. If his son needs an expensive operation, he will take on an extra job and borrow to the hilt to pay for it.

A man's primal instinct to protect his family leads him to surpass himself. It leads him to direct his powerful male aggressiveness against anything that threatens his loved ones.

As we've seen, a smart, conscientious father moves beyond this. He thinks ahead, twenty years into the future, and acts now to protect his children later in life. *He labors now to strengthen his children so they can later protect themselves.* The thought of his children's future happiness is what keeps him going, gives him the power and patience to act relentlessly, sacrificially, as a father-leader who empowers his children for life.

So, think deeply about these things your children's sake . . .

If you do not teach your kids to tackle problems self-confidently, they could be crushed with anxiety from life's normal burdens—paralyzed by self-doubt or driven to escape through drugs.

If you fail to give your children fatherly advice and direction, they may later seek it desperately from psychiatrists and marriage counselors.

If you do not teach your sons to control their impulses and respect the rights of others, they could injure or kill themselves in a car accident or destroy their marriages.

If you let your kids form habits of self-indulgence—instant gratification, slavery to their feelings—they can destroy themselves with substance abuse.

If you fail to teach your children to work competently and professionally, they could drift through life as permanent adolescents, without a stable marriage or career.

If you don't give your daughters an example of manly virtue, they could wind up marrying lightweights and jerks—and your grandchildren, if you have any, could grow up in a fatherless home.

If you do not work with your wife to establish a happy and stable family, your children will not know how to form one themselves.

The male mind is wired to project into the future, to exercise his imagination in foreseeing future events, especially problems that might lie ahead. Let your own mind work this way about your children's futures. Picture your little children as grown men and women, and imagine them afflicted with tragedy, tears, broken marriages—their happiness destroyed, their lives out of control.

Like so many other good fathers, you will feel the surge of protective manly strength arise within you. With your powerful love, you will steel yourself now, deny yourself anything, make any sacrifice, to keep these sorrows from your children's lives.

FIRST THINGS FIRST

A good father always puts his family first. Everything else takes second place, and this includes his job, his life's work.

A man, any man, performs his job well for any number of reasons. Through his labor, he earns his living, his means of paying his bills, or he piles up hefty wealth. He finds satisfaction in productive action, tackling problems and solving them, thus earning self-respect and the esteem of his professional peers. He treasures work as a healthy outlet for his driving masculine ambitions, his creative forces, his desire to make his imprint on the world, to make some difference for the better in human affairs. These are all good attitudes, to be sure, commonly found among seriously productive men.

But never forget, no matter how well you succeed at work, no matter how much you gain in fame and riches and personal achievement, your family must come first. *A great father applies himself to his work, but he dedicates his work to his family. The main purpose of his life's work, by far, is the welfare of his wife and children.*

Let me tell you about a friend of mine named John, a courageous man in his mid-forties who works as a lawyer in New York City. He lives with his wife, Karen, and four children in suburban New Jersey.

John married at age twenty-four, as he graduated from law school and began working at a powerhouse New York law firm. He and Karen quickly had a son and then a daughter; they had both grown up in large families and wanted one of their own. Meanwhile, like so many young associates in meat-grinder law firms, John was working seventy to eighty hours a week. (He told me at the time, "I have two forty-hour-a-week jobs, back to back!") In a fairly short time, he made partner and began earning a high six-figure annual income.

But John was a classic workaholic. He retained the habit, fiercely driven by who knows what, to put in twelve to fourteen hours a day. He would leave for New York around dawn and return, worn out, between 8:00 and 10:00 o'clock at night. Saturdays, too, were eaten up at the office. This went on for years, through two more births in the family and his wife's growing exasperation.

John's older children entered school, played on neighborhood teams, grew up quickly toward the age of middle school, and the oldest boy showed (at age eleven) some of the normal feistiness of early adolescence. John saw none of this. He couldn't. When he left home in the morning, his kids were asleep. At night, when he returned, they had gone to bed. He and they were virtual strangers to each other. At last, miraculously, he began to notice this.

One night when he returned late, his wife Karen, upset and close to tears, told him that David, the oldest son, had taken a nosedive in his most recent school grades. The teacher had asked for an afternoon conference the following week. Over the phone this teacher had warned Karen that David had recently been sullen in class, listless and irritable, and she thought it important to get to the bottom of things. Karen pleaded with John to make the meeting and to have a word in the meantime with David. John demurred about the meeting, but said he'd talk with David on Sunday morning—one of the few times that father and son had, so to speak, a hole in their schedules.

As John relates it, he and David sat down on Sunday after breakfast. The boy was withdrawn, sullen, and seething with unspoken resentment. John prodded with questions, but David answered only with shrugs and glances out the window.

John was impatient by nature and unaccustomed to frustration. Finally, in rising anger, he insisted, "What's the matter? Why won't you answer me? Don't you know I care about these problems of yours?"

But John was taken aback, shocked really, at what happened next. His son suddenly turned on him, his eyes blazing with wrath and filling with tears, and exploded, "No, I don't know that you care. You don't care at all what happens to me! You live your own life and I live mine!" Then, with his hands covering his eyes, fighting back sobs, David told his stupefied father the long litany of wrongs in his memory—soccer games played when his father was absent, awards brought home from school to be seen only by Mom, promises Dad made that he broke because "something came up," notes passed between father and son on the refrigerator, school problems consulted with Mom, going places only with Mom, talking only with Mom, *everything* only with Mom.

Shaken by this outpouring of grief, John left David alone and went off by himself to think. He walked into the bathroom and looked at himself in the mirror. He saw a thirty-seven-year-old man who looked ten years older: financially successful but strung out—and thoroughly, justly, chastised by his near-grown son. Over and over again, he asked himself, "What am I doing with my life? What's going to happen with my kids?"

He made the teacher's meeting that week and noticed something that drove home his son's words. He sat next to Karen as David's teacher prodded both of them with questions about the boy. He couldn't answer them. He sat there silently, almost helplessly, as a virtual outsider. His wife and the teacher carried on a dialogue about David, and he didn't have a clue what they were talking about.

I'm happy to say this story turned out well. John finally recognized that he was winning a lucrative career but losing his children. And, as he put it, "The trade-off wasn't worth it. David's tears and words gnawed at my conscience for weeks." Finally he acted. He left his partnership in the law firm and took a job as a company lawyer, working only fifty hours a week. He took a salary cut and swallowed his pride, but he won his wife and children for keeps.

And David? He spends hours sitting or strolling, talking with his father. He quietly sees his dad as a kind of hero, a man who turns love into action. And he wants to grow up to be a lawyer.

Please learn from John's experience, and that of other men.

One of the great surprises men encounter when they retire is how quickly their life's work is undone behind them, as if they had never existed, had never done what they did. A Polish proverb says, "We pass through life like a knife through water, leaving scarcely a ripple behind us, and then nothing."

A doctor or lawyer will work all his life to build a successful practice. When he retires, what does he have to show for his work? A couple of file cabinets full of papers, that's all. And someday, absolutely for sure, someone will throw the files out as useless junk.

A man will work steadily in a company to set up a productive division, stamp it with his personality, enjoy people's esteem for his creative leadership. But when he steps down or retires, someone else comes along and abolishes the division—scuttles the structure in reorganization. After a while, no one remembers what was there before.

An ambitious entrepreneur works all his life to build a thriving business. He puts up a building or factory of his design and crowns it with his name. When he retires, he sells it to someone or to some conglomerate. What happens next? The new owners send the work overseas, tear the name down, and sell the shell of the building to others—who use it to set up boutiques peddling scented candles, leather sandals, and knick-knacks.

It's a fact of life: Hardly anyone on earth leaves behind him any work of truly lasting value. Among all the billions of people who've made up mankind's history, those who've made a permanent imprint could probably fit comfortably in a small room.

Work has to be a means to an end—the welfare of our loved ones—otherwise it has little meaning at all. In the final analysis, only love endures. It is the family that lives on, and this is where a man's work finds its greatest meaning.

I learned a lesson about this truth some years ago in rural Massachusetts.

One glorious autumn day, I was out hiking with some men, all good friends of mine, and their children. We were enjoying the crisp air, cloudless blue skies, and spectacular foliage so special to October in New England. Our little group trekked off a trail into some thick nearby woods, our feet swooshing through the fallen leaves, sharing the kids' delight at running freely through the forest.

We hadn't gone far into the trees before we came upon an intriguing sight. There in front of us, stretching in a straight line through the thick stand of trees, ran an ancient, moss-covered stone wall. The sight of such a wall—large stones heaped upon each other—is common in rural New England. What struck us, though, was to find this wall, perhaps two hundred years old or more, coursing through the middle of a hardwood forest.

One of the older children asked the question that some of us adults, I'm sure, were thinking: "Why is this wall here? What's a wall doing in the woods?"

One of the fathers, an amateur historian, explained. A couple of centuries ago, this forest wasn't here. Where we now see trees, there was open farmland or pasture cleared over by a colonial family. Through several generations, the farmers, with their sons and workmen, picked up heavy stones from the rocky soil and stacked them to form this wall, probably as a boundary marker, maybe to keep livestock away from the crops. After many generations, the family moved on, the farmhouse fell apart, and the forest slowly returned to cover the land again. All that's left is this wall, covered with moss.

This little history lesson struck me. And it posed a lesson of wider significance.

Imagine the challenge and hardship facing these colonial men, working so hard to support their families from one generation to the next. They eked out a living from this harsh soil, bent over in backbreaking labor to pile these stones one upon another. And, through years of toil, they succeeded. They fed and clothed and sheltered their families in the endless iron cycle of planting and harvesting.

In the end, the family moved on. It scattered wide, as families do in America, and lived on through different fates in distant parts of the country. The wooden farmhouse slowly sank back to the earth from which it came, leaving not a trace. The trees, by dropping seeds that sprouted into saplings, advanced year by year to reclaim the soil, leaving only this stone wall to course aimlessly through the forest—a poignant monument to the passing, perishing nature of a man's work.

But the far-flung family still lives on. And there is the lesson for any father: in the long run, only love endures.

Please remember these things if you ever have to choose between work or family. If you put your family first, no matter what the present sacrifice, your later years will be brightened by the deepest happiness. Your grown children and grandchildren gathered in honor around you will be your lasting reward.

HEART TO HEART

So often over my years in education, I would chat with a father who was clearly managing somehow to do an effective job with his children. To be sure, his kids were not perfect and neither was he, as he'd be the first to admit. But the children were of such high quality—so confident, competent, and responsible— that the father and mother deserved congratulations. This I extended them.

As I explained at the outset of this book, I also asked the dads how, despite so many obstacles today, including their own personal shortcomings, they managed to succeed. What they taught me in so many ways has comprised the lessons of this book.

Every now and then, especially after my prompting, they would sum up their overall approach to living and acting as a conscientious father. What kept them going? Where did they get the strength to persevere?

I want to leave you here with some of their remarks (as I remember their words) so that you can take heart and great encouragement, from their experience. This is what they told me:

"I love my wife more than I can say. We've been married for eighteen years now, and I still can't get over the fact that she, such an absolutely wonderful woman, agreed to marry me. . . . As I see it, my job with my kids is to make sure that they love and honor her, and

respect her wishes, every bit as much as I do. I won't settle for anything less from them. And that's the long and the short of it."

"Every now and then I remind myself that someday my son will be someone's husband—and my daughter someone's wife. My job is to work flat out, no matter what, to prepare each of them to build a great marriage and a great family."

"A few weeks after our oldest son was born, his eyes began to focus on mine when I held him in my arms. I'll never forget the first time he looked up with his large dark eyes straight into my face and gave a big smile of recognition. . . . It's hard to explain, but I felt within me a deeply moving surge of power and responsibility, a fierce conviction that I would do anything, endure absolutely anything, for this little guy's happiness. . . . The memory of that powerfully emotional moment has kept me going ever since."

"My children are as feisty and hot-tempered as I am, and it sometimes pains me inside when I have to correct them strongly, especially when they burst into tears. I remember the old cliché: 'This hurts me more than it does you.' Now I know what it means. What keeps me on track, though, is this: I'd rather they cry over minor things now than over some tragic situation twenty years from now. . . . Besides, I have the faith—and it really is a faith—that someday they'll understand and thank me."

"When both my children were small, it occurred to me one day how much I owed my own mom and dad. I recognized for the first time what they went through, how much they sacrificed for me and my brother and sister. One Sunday when I was visiting with them, I somehow summoned up the words to tell them this. I thanked them from the bottom of my heart. They were both moved, I could tell, and so very, very happy. . . . So, I would advise any parent: If your parents are still alive, go back and thank them. Thank them while you still can. You will make them deeply happy, and this expression of gratitude will change the way you deal with your own children. When you have to be firm with them, you can say to yourself, 'Someday, please God, they'll understand and thank me.'"

"In our family's Jewish heritage, the father plays a hugely important role with his children. He sees his children as a priceless gift from God, and his mission is to treat his children the way God treats all of us. This is what I saw in my father and grandfather, and this is what I

want my children to see in me. I will answer to God for the way my children grow up."

"I was never particularly religious until I became a father. Then my outlook changed. . . . Every now and then, I feel almost overwhelmed with things, at about the limits of my strength. At that point, I turn to my heavenly Father and ask Him to bridge the gap between what I can do and what needs to be done. I pray for His help, and this never fails to give me strength. . . . Besides, I notice that my prayers are followed by helpful 'coincidences' out of the blue. When you ask for miracles, you start noticing coincidences."

"I'll never forget when my little girl began to talk with me. I don't mean simply repeating words or stringing them together. I mean hearing her create completely rational ideas in original sentences, posing questions about things. I was struck with a sense of quiet awe—the startling realization that this little daughter of mine is a kind of living miracle. She's a completely separate person from me, a living human being with a destiny in life that's mysteriously entwined with my own. This sense of awe and vocational responsibility has never left me. Every now and then, she and the other children smile at me and hug me—and I feel a sense of mission in life, something sacred between me and each of them. This is what keeps me going."

And something I heard over and again from many great fathers:

"Whenever I feel at the end of my rope, when I've had a very tough week, whenever I'm tempted to discouragement, I do something that never fails to renew me. . . . I tiptoe into my kids' bedrooms at night and spend a few minutes looking down on them while they're sleeping. Just the sight of them lying there peacefully—so innocent and defenseless, so dependent on me—restores my peace of mind and strengthens my resolve. For the sake of their happiness in life and the welfare of their souls, I can do anything. . . . I will do anything. I'm their father."

You can see a thread running through all these men's thoughts and words. It is love.

It is the kind of love found within the hearts of strong men—conscientious, loyal, generous, quietly courageous, fiercely dedicated, steeled to manly heroic action.

This is the love that can move you to become a great father, a great husband, and a great man.

Postscript | A WORD TO THE WIFE

This final section, necessarily a postscript, I address to the wife of the man who's reading this book—that woman who, as dedicated wife and mother, supports her beloved husband in his efforts to live as a great father.

I earnestly hope that you, like your husband, will make the time to read through this book and learn from it. As you will see, a huge portion of what's in here applies as much to you as to him. Parenting is a partnership, and partners act in unity.

Moreover, you'll probably find that much of what I tell your husband reinforces what you've been trying to explain to him for some time now. Over the years, I've told countless men to listen carefully to their wives and to take their judgments seriously. Women have special insight and sensitivity to children's needs that men are mistaken to ignore. As you read through the book, I suspect you'll be tempted to underline certain parts and then tell your husband, "Whatever you do, read this. . . ."

But there's a more important reason for my addressing you directly, and it's this: *Your husband's success as a father depends enormously on you.*

If he follows what I explain in this handbook—drawn as it is on other men's experience—he can see his mission more clearly and act more effectively to carry it out. My point to you, his wife, is that you can hasten his progress and firm up his role if you keep some important matters in mind.

First, *don't expect him to be perfect.* No one is. What's described in this book about fatherhood is really an ideal. It's a composite of the best qualities in the finest fathers I've known. But no man can live up to an ideal altogether or all at once. Like every other human being, your husband has faults and shortcomings. Some he may never overcome, and so you must live with them as a fact of life. That's a huge part of what married love is all about—overlooking each other's unchangeable flaws.

Other faults he may work on conscientiously with fits and starts, ups and downs, making steady progress as your children grow up. Please be patient. And above all, give him credit for *trying.* Few things frustrate and anger men more than seeing their earnest best efforts go unappreciated. The very act of trying is itself a courageous step forward.

Second, *don't expect him to be like a woman.* That is, don't expect him to think and act and react to things as you do. He's a male, and males are different. Though at times his maleness may strike you as vexing and perplexing, it brings certain strengths to your children's upbringing. Your children do not need two mothers.

There are such things as gender differences, and in a healthy family these complement each other in subtle but important ways.

Here's an example. When siblings are acting nasty to each other (a normal occurrence even in the best of homes), each parent tends to treat the problem differently. The mother, dedicated as she is to family harmony and mutual love, tends to see the problem as a fault of charity: "It's *unkind* to rummage through your sister's belongings. Look how that offends her!" But her husband, with the male sensitivity to justice rather than charity, sees things in terms of fairness and rights: "You have no *right* to rummage through your sister's things. You're obligated to respect her rights to property and privacy!"

Obviously kids need to grow in both justice and thoughtfulness; so both parents team up to teach these lessons in complementary ways. Actually, in a healthy family both parents gradually learn from each other, appreciate each other's point of view, and come to share roughly the same viewpoint. By the time kids are adolescents, both parents have unconsciously learned from each other and think very much alike in important matters—without losing the strengths inherent in each gender.

Here's another gender difference: Men put high value on competence and on appearing competent. They're cautious in the face of tough-looking problems, especially unfamiliar situations. So, to avoid botching a new and untried challenge (and looking incompetent), they tend to hold back, look the situation over carefully and calculate how to act. Eventually they will act, but not before they study the problem so as to do it right the first time. This is a male trait; men are simply wired to behave this way. Unfortunately, many women, especially if they grew up without brothers or a strong father, view this caution as mere procrastination, unreasonable foot-dragging. They don't quite understand how their own feminine nature naturally gives them greater and more optimistic drive, stronger risk-taking ability, especially in interpersonal relations. Women are far more accustomed than men to mystery, to facing and handling out-of-control situations: the monthly cycle, the miracle of birth and nurturing, the rapid sensitivity to loved ones' needs, and so on.

So, bear all this in mind when your husband is trying to become a better father. Don't get on his case. If you seem to question his competence, you threaten his self-esteem as a man, and this will anger him. (Doesn't most anger derive from perceived threats to one's self-esteem?) What he needs from you is patience, understanding, and frequent encouragement.

Finally, *do all you can to lead your children to respect their father and his authority.* He simply cannot lead as a father without his children's respect. Your children's growth in character, their lifelong happiness, will rise or fall on how deeply they respect their dad.

This book gives your husband lots of counsel on how to win your children's respect. But you can speed up this dynamic, give it greater depth and power, by leading your children to honor their father. Lead them to view their dad as you do: a great man, a model of masculine strength and accomplishment, a self-sacrificing hero worthy of the whole family's gratitude and honor. Your children's respect for their dad will reflect your own esteem for him, and this is enormously important to his influence on their lives.

I vividly remember a story told me by a good friend of mine, an excellent husband and father. This is what he told me: "I was the youngest of five children in a single-parent home. My dad died when I was an infant, so I never knew him. My mother raised us as a widow, and she was a great woman. Every now and then, when I was rambunctious and getting out of hand as a boy, and even as a teenager, my mom would take me aside and say, 'Jimmy, your father would *never approve* of what you're doing right now! He would be very upset. So, stop it . . .' This never failed to touch me, not once. It always brought me to my senses and made me straighten out."

Do you see the point? The father of this home continued to influence his children for good, even after his death, because of his great wife's love and honor for him. He was still alive in her heart, so he was still the father of this family.

Remember, too, a more practical matter. It's in your own long-term interest that your children learn to respect their dad from infancy. Some day, when they're in their teens, they'll be too big and maybe too feisty for you to handle alone. This is especially true of your daughters. By that time, your sons and daughters should have—must have—a lifelong habit of respect for their dad's authority and judgment. They'll need a deeply ingrained habit of response to what he directs them to do in his deep male voice. When your children are adolescents, you'll need his firm control of the situation, his serious reminders to them—given in a no-nonsense way—that they must honor and obey you or else answer to him.

Every single time you support and encourage your husband, you also show your children what it means to be a great woman. Self-sacrifice, understanding, affection, encouragement, forgiveness, relentless generosity—all these make for great family love, and these strengths of family life come mostly from Mom.

Years from now, long after they've founded families of their own, your children will reunite as grown brothers and sisters. At that time they will look back and fondly enjoy the memories of your family's adventurous life together—so much fun and laughter, so many lessons learned, so much love implanted in their hearts for life. With deep affection and gratitude, they will all agree: "Mom and Dad were great people. . . ."